SPIRITUAL LIFE

EXPERIENCING GOD TOGETHER

HENRY T. BLACKABY

—— A N D ——

MELVIN D. BLACKABY

EXPERIENCING

G☩D

TOGETHER

GOD'S PLAN TO TOUCH YOUR WORLD

BROADMAN
&HOLMAN
PUBLISHERS

NASHVILLE, TENNESSEE

0–8054–2481–4

Published by Broadman & Holman Publishers, Nashville, Tennessee
The authors are represented by the literary agency
of Wolgemuth & Associates, Inc.

Category: CHRISTIAN LIVING/SPIRITUAL GROWTH/GENERAL

Unless otherwise noted, Old Testament Scripture quotations are from the
New American Standard Bible, © Copyright The Lockman Foundation,
1960, 1962, 1963, 1968, 1971, 1972, 1973, 1975, 1977, 1995. New
Testament Scripture quotations are from Holman Christian Standard Bible,
© Copyright 2000 by Holman Bible Publishers. Used by permission. Other
versions are identified as follows: Amplified, The Amplified Bible, Old
Testament copyright © 1962, 1964 by Zondervan Publishing House, used
by permission, and the New Testament
© The Lockman Foundation 1954, 1958, 1987, used by permission.
KJV, King James Version. NIV, the Holy Bible, New International
Version, © copyright 1973, 1978, 1984. Italic for emphasis in biblical
text is added by the authors.

1 2 3 4 5 6 7 8 9 10 07 06 05 04 03 02

"May they all be one, just as You, Father, are in Me and I am in You.
May they also be one in Us, so that the world may believe You sent Me.
I have given them the glory that You have given to Me.
May they be one just as We are one. I am in them and You are in Me.
May they be made completely one, so that the world may know You sent Me
and that You have loved them just as You have loved Me."

JOHN 17:21–23

Contents

SECTION TWO: GOD'S SALVATION IN THE CHURCH

SECTION THREE: GOD'S SALVATION THROUGH THE CHURCH

SECTION FOUR: GOD'S SALVATION AND THE KINGDOM

Introduction

I can't tell you how many times I hear Christians crying out for "something more" in their relationship with God. They have accepted Christ into their lives but don't seem to know what to do next. They hear others talking about abundant life in Christ, but abundant life seems to be just beyond their grasp. They become frustrated and depressed, even to the point of desperation. Their struggle tends to come from the fact that they never understood the nature of God's great salvation. More specifically, they never understood the corporate nature of salvation and their significant place within the people of God.

We often read together the simple record of the first church in Jerusalem described in Acts 2:46–47. "And every day they devoted themselves to meeting together in the temple complex, and broke bread from house to house. They ate their food with gladness and simplicity of heart, praising God and having favor with all the people. And every day the Lord added those being saved to them." Oh, how the early believers were overwhelmed with the grace of God and the power of the Holy Spirit in their midst. They were hungry to grow in their knowledge of God and experienced love for one another in a way they had never known before.

As a pastor, I earnestly sought for our church to experience fullness of life that I knew was available for them to know. I longed for the manifest presence of God in our midst and a quality of love that could only come from above. What we began to experience as a church was amazing, and it seemed to grow from year to year. We knew joy! Even in the midst of trials, we knew the joy of the Lord as we walked together as a church. I can recount much heartache that people endured, but they never endured them alone; we were a family.

I have fond memories of a church that was open seven days a week simply because people liked to be there. I can still see the cars that lined the street, students who were coming to our theological college, and the constant laughter in the foyer. I remember many visitors recount that when they first approached the building, they had a sense of God's presence. As they entered, they immediately saw joy and excitement on people's faces. Often at the close of a service, there would be people in earnest conversation, others weeping, still others praying. Nobody was in a hurry to go home; they would rather linger in the presence of God with their church family. People hesitated to take vacations over the weekend because they didn't want to miss what God would do on Sundays as we gathered for worship. And God added regularly those who were being saved.

Sound too good to be true? Sound like something you have longed for? I have known times when this wasn't true either. But once I tasted what God could do in and through a church, I didn't want to settle for anything less. I have come to realize that God's purpose for the church is much grander than many people have experienced or even knew was possible. God has provided everything we need in Christ, "who is the head over every ruler and authority" (Col. 2:10). What He has planned for His people is far beyond us; it is infinite in dimension.

We must remember that God's purposes and ways are from eternity to eternity. He seeks to bring salvation to humankind and expand the kingdom of God through His people. God, therefore, is creating for Himself a people through whom He can accomplish His purposes in our world. His eyes go "to and fro throughout the earth that He may strongly support those whose heart is completely His" (2 Chron. 16:9). Jesus established the church as a divine institution for the proclamation and extension of the kingdom. The church is not need-centered or people-centered but God-centered. When the church is God centered, they will know His awesome presence. When God grants His presence to a church, He expresses His wisdom, His power, and His activity to accomplish His purposes.

So how do we come to experience God in this way? Listen to what the Lord says in Proverbs 2:1–5:

> My son, if you will receive my sayings,
> And treasure my commandments within you,
> Make your ear attentive to wisdom,
> Incline your heart to understanding;
> For if you cry for discernment,
> Lift your voice for understanding;
> If you seek her as silver,
> And search for her as for hidden treasures;
> Then you will discern the fear of the LORD,
> And discover the knowledge of God.

According to the Scriptures, "the fear of the LORD is the beginning of knowledge" (Prov. 1:7). Have you studied, in order that you might fear the Lord? Almost everything in the evangelical community is against that. We have been told that we should have a good time, celebrate, praise, and shout to God, but not fear Him. But what we need more than any other time in human history is to fear the Lord our God.

To lose the fear of God is to lose the fear of sin. To lose the fear of sin is to lose the relationship with God. Don't let anybody tell you that "to fear the Lord" just means to have an "awe" of Him. It means far more than that. It will take much more than one little word to describe the fear of the Lord. We may choose to play games with God, but "the fear of the Lord" indicates that God is not playing games with us. He expects that we "fear the LORD your God, to walk in all His ways and love Him, and to serve the LORD your God with all your heart and with all your soul, and to keep the LORD's commandments" (Deut. 10:12–13). When we choose to take God seriously, when we begin to fear the Lord, He will then grant to us wisdom beyond human capacity to understand. He will show us the way of life, and life more abundantly. Let me finish the wonderful passage I started with by quoting Proverbs 2:6–11:

> For the LORD gives wisdom;
>> From His mouth come knowledge and understanding.
>> He stores up sound wisdom for the upright;
>> He is a shield to those who walk in integrity,
>> Guarding the paths of justice,
>> And He preserves the way of His godly ones.
>> Then you will discern righteousness and justice
>> And equity and every good course.
>> For wisdom will enter your heart,
>> And knowledge will be pleasant to your soul;
>> Discretion will guard you,
>> Understanding will watch over you.

It is clear that God desires to give you wisdom and show you His purpose for your life. Be prepared to receive all that God teaches you through the Holy Spirit. "The fear of the LORD is the beginning of wisdom," so we will seek to know God as He has made Himself known in the Scriptures. We will not try to impose our image of God on Him, but ask the Holy Spirit to reveal God's ideal for His people. We pray that God will reveal Himself, His purposes, and His ways to you in a much deeper way as you go through this book.

I was amazed to see how God has used my first major book, *Experiencing God,* to help people know and do His will. As important as this book has been to many people, *Experiencing God Together* is a necessary sequel. Christians must make the transition from knowing and doing the will of God as individuals to knowing and doing the will of God within a corporate body of believers. *Experiencing God* helped people get on track with God; this book will guide their journey within the family of God.

I asked my son Mel to coauthor this work with me on purpose. Not only does he have much practical experience as a pastor of an exciting church; he has earned his Ph.D., focusing a great deal of study on the nature of the church and its relationship to the kingdom of

God. Although I will guide you through this study, we have worked closely on this project. You will also enjoy several wonderful anecdotes out of Mel's ministry that we have inserted to illustrate the truths we are seeking to communicate.

This book will deal with many significant questions: What did God have in mind when He chose to save us? What is the corporate nature of God's great salvation?

We will also ask some reflective questions: What does it mean to be born into the family of God? How does God want us to relate to other Christians around the world? When people attend our churches, do they experience a well-run organization or the presence of God? Do our churches reveal the collective knowledge of people or the manifest wisdom of God? Does the world see our churches as places where good people do good things for God, or do they see the power of God working through His people to do what only He could accomplish? How can God use our lives to touch a world in need of God's great salvation?

Experiencing God Together is also divided into four distinct sections that both stand alone and build upon one another. Each section will unpack specific dimensions of God's great salvation and the purposes of God for our lives. When God's ideal is realized, the impact on an individual, a church, a community, or a nation will be enormous.

God's Great Salvation

What Is the Full Measure of Salvation?

Work out your own salvation with fear and trembling.
For it is God who is working among you
both the willing and the working among you for His good purpose.

PHILIPPIANS 2:12–13

By obedience to the truth, having purified yourselves for sincere love of the brothers, love one another earnestly from a pure heart, since you have been born again—through the living and enduring word of God.

1 PETER 1:22–23

ONE

The Family: God Has No Orphans

Experiencing God Together in Life

Our world is full of hurt and pain. As a pastor, I saw more than my share of heart-wrenching situations as people struggled through the pressures of life. I recall a certain couple who had joined our church, and it wasn't long before we had the opportunity to minister to their family. The husband had been an alcoholic most of his adult life. Although he had become a Christian, he still struggled to stay away from drinking. I was glad that he had chosen to join our church, for I knew he would benefit from the genuine love in our fellowship.

One day, however, the man got word that both of his parents had suddenly died. He was devastated. Sadly, he was alone when he heard the news and turned to alcohol to hide his pain. While driving home, he hit another car, but he continued to drive on without stopping. Fortunately nobody was hurt, but a citizen's arrest was made, and he was taken to jail. Some of the men in our church were made aware of the situation, and a small group of deacons drove to the jail to minister to him. They were able to secure his release and offer help through a difficult time. I drove to his wife's workplace to tell her what had happened, encouraging her that several of our men were with her husband. She wept on my shoulder and began to tremble. I reassured her of the church's love for her family and that her Savior's love was ever present in times of need. We took her home, and a group of us prayed together. The Lord was gracious to redeem fully a good man and his wife. As far as I know, he never drank again. In fact, he later found a place of service as an usher in our church.

Years later a young man approached me and told me that he was the son of this couple we had helped. He recalled the pain he endured as a young boy living in the home of an alcoholic. Then he said: "You will never know what the love of your church did for my dad and mom. You will never know what your love did for me as their son. Because of the love I saw in your church, I responded to God's call into the ministry and am serving the Lord in my own church. Thank you! I have always wanted to tell you what your church meant to my family."

God has no orphans—only family. He has provided for every child of His through the unlimited resources of heaven. No matter what mistakes we have made, God cares for those who have chosen to enter a love relationship with Him. Our world is full of hurting people who have no hope, but God made provision for their every need through Jesus Christ. He then made Christ the Head of the churches He has established, in order that He might bring healing through His people who have come to know His saving grace. That is the strategy of God's redemptive plan to touch a world.

Local churches, the gathered people of God, are crucial to God's eternal purpose in salvation and world redemption. If you are a member of a local church, by the direction and will of God, you are most fortunate. You are exactly where God wants you and where God will unfold to you the fullness of salvation. And it is here that God will cause you to reach out to a lost world for His glory.

Placed into a Love Relationship

The deepest longing in a person's heart is to have a relationship with God. When we open the Scriptures, we are surprised to discover how much God desires for His people to have a love relationship with Him. In fact, the more we study the Scriptures, the more we are overwhelmed at the greatness of God's salvation and the love relationship He seeks to develop with us. God's salvation set in motion everything He intended to accomplish in us. If we do not understand the extent of God's accomplished work on our behalf, we will never experience abundant life, nor will we fulfill God's purpose for our lives. God is not primarily interested in making us successful; instead, His heart desires for us to experience the full measure of His great salvation.

This is eternal life: that they may know You, the only true God, and the One You have sent — Jesus Christ.

JOHN 17:3

When God saved us, what was on His heart? What did He do to accomplish it? How does He implement His purposes in our lives? To answer these questions is to unfold the heart of God's message in the Bible, for the Scriptures reveal God, His purposes, and His ways so that we do not miss His activity in our lives. To experience God in our lives as He intended, we must have a thorough understanding of the greatness of salvation from God's perspective.

The writer of Hebrews urged the struggling believers of his day, "We must therefore pay even more attention to what we have heard, so that we will not drift away. For if the message spoken through angels was legally binding, and every transgression and disobedience received a just punishment, how will we escape if we neglect such a great salvation?" (Heb. 2:1–3). It behooves us to respond to this challenge today. It would be tragic for people to receive the riches of the gospel and then live as spiritual paupers, to accept such great love from Christ and then resent what He asks in return. Have we neglected God's great salvation and lived our lives far below what God purposed when He chose to save us?

The greatness of God's salvation is seen most dramatically in its far-reaching and comprehensive influence. Tragically, many Christians have never been taught the all-encompassing nature of their salvation. Consequently, they are neglecting major dimensions of the Christian life and are not experiencing the incredible relationship with God that is found in His salvation. It is like living one's life in black and white without seeing the full spectrum of colors in all their beauty. Many accept the gift of salvation because they want to go to heaven when they die, but they do not understand God's total plan and purpose in salvation and the unparalleled cost to God to grant it.

I was speaking in a conference in southern California when I encountered a man who stood before me in tears. He and his wife had driven almost six hundred miles simply to say, "Thank you." They had studied one of my previous books, *Experiencing God: Knowing and Doing the Will of God*, when suddenly they were overwhelmed at the greatness of God's salvation. The fullness of life that God promised to them was suddenly opened in a way they had never known. As tears ran down this man's face, he explained that he had taught theology in a well-known Bible college his entire career, but he had never understood what it meant to walk with God in real and practical ways. He also expressed the need to ask God's forgiveness for having taught many young students about God, without helping them to know how to walk with God. He and his wife now had meaning and purpose beyond anything they had dreamed. Now in their late sixties, they had a renewed joy and excitement concerning their relationship to God and an enthusiasm to serve Him with all their hearts. I have heard stories similar to this far too often—of individuals who were content to gather information about God and to feel secure in their eternal reward but who missed out on God's great salvation as He intended.

Salvation is always granted on God's terms, and it reflects the nature of God Himself. The most identifiable characteristic of salvation is the quality of our love, first toward God and then toward His people. Without a love relationship on both levels, vertically and horizontally, we have not experienced God's salvation. If we get this basic truth wrong, we are in desperate trouble. God's strategy to touch a world is vitally linked with these two basic relationships. When Jesus was asked about the greatest commandment, He said in Matthew 22:37–40 NASB, "'You shall love the Lord your God with all your heart, and with all your soul, and with all your mind.' This is the great and foremost commandment. The second is like it, 'You shall love your neighbor as yourself.' On these two commandments depend the whole Law and the Prophets."

This book will take us back into the heart of God and His purpose for our lives. I hear non-Christians say, "I feel as though there is something more to life than I am currently experiencing." What they are missing is God's great salvation. But I also hear Christians say, "I feel as though there is something more to the *Christian* life than I am currently experiencing." What they are missing is God's great salvation! They have not understood what God accomplished on their behalf. Their hearts have never been opened to understand what motivated God when He chose to save them from their sins and cause them to be born again into the family of God.

One of the first great truths concerning God's salvation is found in John 6:44. Jesus said, "No one can come to Me unless the Father who sent Me draws him." Jesus knew that God the Father must be active in drawing persons to Himself before they would ever know the joy of salvation. Have you understood how significant that statement is concerning your life? God has called you into a love relationship with Himself through Jesus Christ. In other words, you are special. You are the object of God's calling. You did not choose Him; He chose you. You can count on it; your salvation began in the heart of God, and the love relationship that He initiated is life-transforming and all-consuming.

I was in Tampa, Florida, when I received a call from my third son, Mel. He and his wife had just received news that their seven-month-old daughter had cerebral palsy. Mel is probably the most sensitive of my five children, and I knew he was hurting. The news had caught him by surprise. He sensed something was wrong, but he had no idea what the doctor would say, and he began to weep as we spoke.

After we had talked and I hung up the phone, I felt myself in an experience that I had not been in before. I turned to the only place I knew to go. I went into the presence of the One who created that little girl. Does God know my granddaughter? He does! Does God know my son? He does indeed! As I went through that experience, I came to know the tender love of God in a way I could have never known before.

My granddaughter will never know how I have prayed for her and how special she has become to the rest of the family and me. I remember being in their home about two years later. That child has sort of taken to her grandpa. She ran to me with a slight limp in her walk, put her arms around my leg, and hung on as though her life depended on it. Everywhere I went she wanted to follow me. She would look up with a big smile and say, "I love you, Grandpa!"

Do you know why I think she has taken to her grandpa? Because her grandpa has taken to her. Do you know why we love our Lord? Because He first loved us. In fact, while we were yet sinners, God loved us enough to send His only Son to die for our sin and set us free to know and experience Him. You can count on it; when we are born into the family of God, our heavenly Father loves us dearly. In fact, the more we experience the love of God, the more we are drawn into His presence.

Placed into a Spiritual Family

According to God's divine and eternal plan of salvation, those who enter a relationship with God through Jesus Christ are automatically born into the family of God. God has no orphans! Believers now enjoy an intimate love relationship with the heavenly Father and the rest of His children. Just as God designed for a baby to be born into a family to receive love and care, so He designed for those who are "born again" to enter a spiritual family that will love and care for them. There is a corporate dimension to the nature of God's great salvation that is at the heart of God's purpose for each individual Christian. Without a thorough understanding of our place in the family of God, we will experience a dysfunctional Christian life.

Unfortunately, when people are challenged to become involved with the family of God and walk with a particular church in serving the Lord, some refuse and keep their distance. I have talked with many people over the years about their relationship with God and occasionally hear the response, "My relationship with God is private." The only problem with that statement is that, though it may accurately reflect their experience, it is not biblical. Our relationship with God is personal, but it was never meant to be private. There is a clear difference between personal and private. Some, however, live as though they are the same. Salvation is intensely personal, but God never planned for our salvation to be private.

Everything in the Bible, Old Testament and New Testament, bears witness to the corporate life of God's children; this is by God's eternal design and purpose. "New birth" places a person automatically into a spiritual family with other believers. Here, in a local church, they are to be nourished, fed, protected, and guided toward spiritual maturity. Just as a child, when born into a physical family, has family, friends, and neighbors who rejoice in the birth, so it is the same when a person is "born again." He or she is born into a spiritual family who has prayed for this moment, and they celebrate their entrance into the family of God.

But to all who did receive Him, He gave them the right to be children of God, to those who believe in His name, who were born, not of blood, or of the will of the flesh, or of the will of man, but of God.

JOHN 1:12–13

We should not equate *spiritual* with *invisible* and *private*, for the Spirit-filled life is obvious to all who see it. The Bible describes Christians as the salt of the earth that makes a recognizable difference, a candle that gives light in a dark world, and a city set on a hill that all can see. Jesus did not say that we *have* salt or light. Jesus said that we *are* salt and light and will by our very nature impact everybody we encounter. The influence we exert is always the influence of what we are. Jesus challenges every believer to confess Him as Lord publicly and to live for Christ openly for all to see. Our faith is personal but never private. We cannot live our faith in isolation; that would run contrary to the purpose of God's salvation. This was true in Jesus' life and His relationship to the Father. No one in the Bible had a relationship to God in private. Rather, each had a significant involvement with God's people, for that is where God's heart is found.

Our relationship with God is personal,
but it is never meant to be private.

Today many people openly acknowledge their faith in Christ, but they have nothing to do with God's people and feel no connection to them. According to God's purpose, as revealed in the Scriptures, Christians are not orphans or in some way separated unto themselves. Salvation automatically makes God our Father and every other believer our brother or sister in the household of God. Together, we are "heirs of God, and joint-heirs with Christ" (Rom. 8:17 KJV). Christians cannot live unto themselves and still function as God purposed when He saved them. We are born into the family of God, and through Christ we have many "blood relatives."

Just as clearly as a child born into my family will automatically experience many things that happen only in our family, so this is true with God and His family. For example, only the Israelites experienced the joy and power of God during the time of the Exodus. Those who were in God's family were overwhelmed with the many miracles of God. But if you were not a part of His family, you did not receive the

> *So then you are no longer strangers and aliens, but you are fellow citizens with the saints, and are of God's household.*
>
> EPHESIANS 2:19 NASB

blessings of that relationship. To the family, however, God gave the Law with a great display of His power. To the family He provided manna, quail, and water. To the family He provided guidance through a cloud by day and a pillar of fire by night. As a result, the family experienced the care of the heavenly Father. The same is true today. God places His children in His family, for there they will experience Him and His salvation. He planned it this way. The local church is crucial to the life of every believer in his or her unfolding relationship with God.

How do you view those who are in the family of God? Perhaps the proper questions to consider are how does God view your relationship to those who are in the family of God, and how has He intended for you to relate to other Christians?

Let us start with a very basic Scripture: "And we have this command from Him: the one who loves God must also love his brother" (1 John 4:21). Anyone who calls Christ Lord is now our brother or sister, and God expects us to treat him as His family. He expects us to love other Christians just as much as He loves them. How much does He love them? First John 3:16 says, "This is how we have come to know love: He laid down His life for us. We should also lay down our lives for our brothers." That is a powerful statement of God's love and a penetrating statement about how much we should love the family of God.

The most convincing evidence that we have received the gift of salvation is that we demonstrate Christlike love to other believers. We can claim to love God all we want, but if we are not intimately connected to the people of God, we are deceiving ourselves. First John 3:14 states, "We know that we have passed from death to life because we love our brothers. The one who does not love remains in death." Do you recognize how seriously God takes your relationship with other believers? Have you made the connection? Would you pass God's test?

We can claim to love God all we want, but if we are not intimately connected to the people of God, we are deceiving ourselves.

Let me illustrate with my own family again. When our daughter was born, we already had four boys. She automatically had older brothers, whether she liked it or not. We had already been nourishing, teaching, and caring for the older boys. We loved them, invested a great deal of love in them, and were working hard to guide their lives. Our daughter, if she was going to grow and develop in our family, would have to learn to love her brothers. For if she loved her parents, she would love the other children whom her parents loved. Similarly, the rest of the family uniquely loved Carrie. Each brother would grow to love her precisely because of our love for her.

So it is with a church family. We love each member, and we are loved by each member. For God deeply loves each one and has made a significant investment in their lives. To love God, then, is to love each member in the family. Because of God's incredible love for each of His children, we now respond to God and His people in a new attitude.

And if you address as Father the One who judges impartially based on each one's work, you are to conduct yourselves in reverence during this time of temporary residence. For you know that you were redeemed from your empty way of life inherited from the fathers, not with perishable things, like silver or gold, but with the precious blood of Christ, like that of a lamb without defect or blemish. . . . By obedience to the truth, having purified yourselves for sincere love of the brothers, love one another earnestly from a pure heart, since you have been born again—not of perishable seed but of imperishable—through the living and enduring word of God.

1 PETER 1:17–19, 22–23

Those who have received God's great salvation and are now in the family of God must live their lives with an awesome fear of God. After all God has done on our behalf, we must respond with complete submission to His will. We will, and must, always see as God sees. For God's salvation came at a high price; it cost Him the precious blood of His Son, Jesus Christ. Through the death and Resurrection of Christ we now have faith and hope in God. Since we have received such love, we must now fervently love all people for whom Christ died. For a Christian consciously to refuse to love the children of God for whom Christ died is to dishonor His death and ridicule His love. But when we walk in a loving relationship with God's people, the testimony to the world is profound. John 13:35 says, "By this all people will know that you are My disciples, if you have love for one another."

God has called us to join the family gathering and enjoy the benefits of that relationship. There are things God does in, for, and through His family that He does nowhere else! We, therefore, are not living life alone. Just as biological families must interact and spend significant time together, so our spiritual family must walk together in love. In God's family we will receive strength, encouragement, and much-needed fellowship. We will grow in wisdom and maturity as we benefit from those who have walked with God for many years. We will find security in the family's watch care over our life and respond to its comfort and accountability. More than anything else, God our Father manifests His presence in special ways when two or three are gathered together (Matt. 18:20). When the family gathers, the Father is always present and active. He speaks to the family. He gives gifts in the family. He gives direction to the family. He gives His power to the family. Apart from God's family a Christian will never be pleasing to the Father. When Christians are joined with the family, the Father is free to pour out His blessing into our lives, even as He continually does to all who are related to Him.

Does your heart desire to gather with other believers in the family where God has placed you? Are you investing your life in the people of God and joining them in fulfilling God's purposes? God has no orphans! He desires for you to walk with the family. When you get close to the heart of your heavenly Father, His love for each member will be laid over your heart as well. Make no mistake—our spiritual family life is a vital part of God's great salvation.

> *But now God has placed the parts, each one of them, in the body just as He wanted.*
>
> 1 CORINTHIANS 12:18

Placed into a Living Body, the Church

The most dynamic expression of God's family activity is found in the local congregation. The church is God's primary means of redeeming the world. The call to salvation is a call to be on mission with Him, but we cannot be on mission with Him effectively unless we are vitally connected to the church. This is God's eternal strategy to touch the world.

There is a wonderful illustration of God's eternal purpose through each church in Ephesians 3:8–12:

> This grace was given to me—the least of all the saints!—to proclaim to the Gentiles the incalculable riches of the Messiah, and to shed light for all about the administration of the mystery hidden for ages in God who created all things. This is so that God's multi-faceted wisdom may now be made known through the church to the rulers and authorities in the heavens. This is according to the purpose of the ages, which He made in the Messiah, Jesus our Lord, in whom we have boldness, access, and confidence through faith in Him.

We have already seen how God the Father draws people into a love relationship with Christ the Savior. A critical Scripture that describes what Christ does upon receiving people whom the Father draws is

Matthew 16:15–18. Examine carefully what the Father was doing and how Christ responded to the Father's activity.

When Jesus asked the disciples who they thought He was, Peter answered, "You are the Messiah, the Son of the living God." When Jesus heard Peter's answer, His response was significant. He basically said, "Peter, you are very fortunate, because flesh and blood has not revealed this to you." Now remember, Jesus was flesh and blood. He had not made known His true nature to the disciples, but rather, the heavenly Father opened Peter's understanding and revealed to him that Jesus was the Messiah, the Son of the living God.

> *"But you," He asked them, "who do you say that I am?" Simon Peter answered, "You are the Messiah, the Son of the living God!" And Jesus responded, "Blessed are you, Simon son of Jonah, because flesh and blood did not reveal this to you, but My Father in heaven. And I also say to you that you are Peter, and on this rock I will build My church, and the forces of Hades will not overpower it."*
>
> MATTHEW 16:15–18

This pattern of God's activity is consistent with what we see in other passages of Scripture. In John 6:44, Jesus said, "No one can come to Me unless the Father who sent Me draws him." The apostle Paul describes the activity of God's Spirit to reveal spiritual truth. "Now we have not received the spirit of the world, but the Spirit who is from God, in order to know what has been freely given to us by God. . . . But the natural man does not welcome what comes from God's Spirit, because it is foolishness to him; he is not able to know it since it is evaluated spiritually" (1 Cor. 2:12, 14).

Peter had insight into the nature of Christ, because God's Spirit revealed it to him. He never could have known the truth if the Father had not taught him. But as soon as the Father revealed that Jesus was the Messiah, Jesus immediately made the statement, "On this rock I will build My church." What was the rock? What was the foundation upon which He would build His church?

Jesus was essentially saying, "On the basis of My heavenly Father's activity in the hearts of people, convincing them that I am the Messiah, the Son of the living God, I will build my church." Now when Jesus builds His church upon the Father's activity in the hearts of people, a dramatic event takes place. It is not our ability to convince people of truth; that is the job of the Holy Spirit. The gates of hell will not prevail against that group of people, for the Spirit of God is actively drawing them and guiding them to His Son, who has come to do His perfect will.

Is it true that when Jesus builds His church the gates of hell will not prevail against it? Whether we believe it is irrelevant; Jesus said it! Now what is the next logical step in the heart of God's people? We must ask ourselves: "Has Jesus built this church? Have we built this church? Or perhaps, has my denomination built this church?" How do we know if people built our church or if Jesus built it?

Our problem is that we are capable of running a religious organization, and we have learned to do it well. But too often our standard for evaluating the success of our church is to observe how large it has become. Church growth is not the biblical standard to evaluate the health of a church. A church can grow through effective marketing, but Christ may not have anything to do with it. Jesus said, "I will build My church." Yet we run around to church growth conferences to discover how *we* can build a successful church. Most conferences do not tell us how to recognize the activity of Jesus as He builds His church. Jesus, in this passage, gave two criteria: (1) the gates of hell will be coming down, and (2) we will be using the keys to the kingdom of heaven to free people from the bondage of sin and bring them into the presence of God.

Later we will discover what it means for Jesus to build His church, but I want to impress upon you at the outset that God's strategy to bring down the gates of hell and to touch a world *is found in the local church*. So, no matter what we say, if our life is not significantly related to the people of God in a local church, we are not effectively on mission with Him as He intended for us to be. His strategy of evangelism is the interdependence of each member related to the body and following Christ as the Head.

Those who resist gathering with God's people in a local congregation do not understand that they are neglecting a vital part of their salvation. In fact, one of the evidences of salvation is that Christians love other Christians (John 13:14, 34–35; John 15:12, 17; 1 John 2:9). Those who choose to stand aloof or refuse to be involved in a church have a serious heart problem. A Christian cannot stand outside the church, mock it, laugh at it, or call it a hypocrite; it runs against every fiber of faith. Christians *love* the church and would give their lives for it. In fact, 1 John 2:19 says that those who leave the church and never return were not really saved in the first place. For no one who has the Spirit of God can turn away from the people of God. To love God is to love God's people. To be on mission with God is to be involved in the church, God's strategy to touch the world.

Placed into a Loving Environment

Some of the best memories God has granted me come in the context of a loving church family. I constantly express my gratitude to God for placing me in various church families throughout my life; God worked in me through His family. They were there to witness my conversion and public profession of faith through baptism. They were there to teach me God's Word as a child and pray for me as I grew through the struggles of life. They affirmed my call into the ministry and encouraged me with opportunities to serve my Lord. They first placed the passion for missions in my heart and taught me to share my faith with the lost. They helped me care for the poor and the broken as we went together to the rescue mission of our city. They taught me to pray as we gathered together in prayer meetings. They helped me appreciate music as we sang our praises to the God Who saved us. They celebrated my marriage and cared for my children as God added

> *We who are many are one body in Christ and individually members of one another.*
>
> ROMANS 12:5

them to my life. They wept with me during personal crisis and family loss. In short, they loved me! Actually, God was loving me through them. I know that I would not be the person I am today without God's placing me into the care of His family in a local church.

Those who choose to stand aloof or refuse to be involved in a church have a serious heart problem.

The same testimony is true in the Scriptures. The fellowship in the early church was a constant source of joy for the believers. It is recorded clearly and simply in Acts 2 and 4. Every person who received the gospel and responded to Christ as the Lord of his life was immediately baptized, and God added each one to the church. Look carefully at Acts 2:41–47 and notice the activities of the first church family that was gathering in Jerusalem.

The natural and immediate response of the first believers on the day of Pentecost was to make a public profession of their faith through believer's baptism. Then the Spirit of God united their lives with other believers so they could grow in their newfound faith. We need to hear that carefully. This was not an accident or a decision from the hearts of believers; it was according to the divine purposes of God. Salvation brings believers into a relationship with God and His people, and both relationships are crucial. As a result, the new believers grew in their faith as they were taught by the apostles, as they prayed with the apostles, and as they fellowshiped with their new spiritual family. Because they were together, each one benefited from the presence of God as He performed miracles in their midst.

The fellowship and love in this early church grew exponentially. They began to care for one another's physical needs, even if it meant selling their possessions so that a brother in the Lord could be blessed. The striking characteristic of this moment was that they could not get enough fellowship. They loved to be together, for they experienced God together. Jesus knew this when He said, "I assure you: The one who receives whomever I send receives Me, and the one who receives Me receives Him who sent Me" (John 13:20). They met daily and grew to have one mind and heart. The fellowship went from the temple to the homes and into the streets. Their relationship with one another was an essential part of God's plan. As they gave God the glory, He continued to add to their number day after day. That was the result of an encounter with God; that was the result of God's great salvation.

This is a clear picture of the incredible transformation in a believer's life. Whereas sin leads to independence and self-centeredness, salvation leads to radical interdependence and Christ-centeredness. The sign of a healthy Christian, who has been set free from sin, is interdependence with other believers and commitment to function within the body of Christ. The apostle Paul wrote in Romans 12:5, "We who are many are one body in Christ and individually members of one another." That is a powerful statement of our interdependence and our corporate submission to the authority of Christ as the Head of the body. Life in the church family had become their very life.

A part of the nature of God's salvation is mutual interdependence among God's people. Sin had created isolation, separation, and independence, all of which lead to utter destruction. Sin magnifies self and cuts us off from relationships that God intended for us to experience. But in God's salvation, "He has rescued us from the domain of darkness and transferred us into the kingdom of the Son" (Col. 1:13). His Son reigns in the life of His people, and the particular expression of His reign is found in the local congregation of believers. In the church Christ is the Head, and each member is a vital part of His body. As

> *So those who accepted his message were baptized, and that day about three thousand people were added to them. And they devoted themselves to the apostles' teaching, to fellowship, to the breaking of bread, and to prayers. Then fear came over everyone, and many wonders and signs were being performed through the apostles. Now all the believers were together and had everything in common. So they sold their possessions and property and distributed the proceeds to all as everyone had a need. And every day they devoted themselves to meeting together in the template complex, and broke bread from house to house. They ate their food with gladness and simplicity of heart, praising God and having favor with all the people. And every day the Lord added those being saved to them.*
>
> ACTS 2:41–47

they follow Christ as their Lord, they are bound together for a common purpose.

In the eternal and predetermined plan of God, He designed that the local church would be the primary way Christians should walk together and carry out the work of Christ our Lord. The fact that there are many local churches does not divide Christians; it unites them around a common purpose under the lordship of Christ. Children are born into the human race yet belong to a specific human family. In the same way those who have been born into the kingdom of God are also entrusted into the care of a loving church family. This is not a human corruption of sinful humanity; it was by God's design. The family imagery is common in Paul's writing to the church. "Like newborn infants, desire the unadulterated spiritual milk, so that you may grow by it in your salvation, since you have tasted that the Lord is good" (1 Pet. 2:2–3). The church was intended to preach and teach the Word of God so new believers would grow into maturity.

The intimate relationships that are developed within a local church are significant. The more we grow in our relationship to the Lord, the more intimate and loving we grow in our relationships to one another.

A special relationship develops between members of a church family. Just as the helplessness of a baby creates a bond with the ones who give care, so the babe in Christ develops a special bond with the church family that provides nurture and love. This is not only a natural response, but God also designed it that way. He intended for church families to enjoy a deep bond of love for one another.

Jesus said, "I will build My church" (Matt. 16:18). Jesus calls people out of the world and gathers them together into a living body in which He lives and carries out His purpose. The Lord added to the church daily "those being saved" (Acts 2:47). This is still the pattern of how God works today. Those whom He saves, He immediately adds to a local church.

Placed into the People of God

God has a purpose for every person in His family. His purpose, however, is never for the individual; it has a corporate dimension. Unless the corporate dimension of salvation is understood, a person will never fulfill the purpose God had for his life when He chose to save him. From the beginning, God has chosen to work through His people. Even when God chose to go to Moses, He did not go simply to bless Moses. He went to free and bless the entire people of God. The heart of God is always turned toward all of His people, because as the people of God go, so goes the redemption of the rest of the world. Therefore, God's heart cry is always toward all of His people.

Over the last few decades, the focus has shifted away from God's people to evangelism and the lost. However, significant evangelism is a by-product of what God does with His people. If we bypass the people of God, we have shut down evangelism. But when we help the people of God know who they are in Christ and what God purposed for their lives through salvation, the world will be turned upside down. The most significant statement of the Great Commission is found in the third part: "Teaching them to observe everything I have commanded you. And remember, I am with you always, to the end of the age" (Matt. 28:20). If God's people are not practicing everything Christ has commanded, they will be ineffective in evangelism. But those who are walking in an obedient love relationship with their Lord will naturally share the good news of the gospel with convincing power.

Whereas sin leads to independence and self-centeredness, salvation leads to radical interdependence and Christ-centeredness.

When we examine how the early apostles implemented the Great Commission, we may be surprised. The apostles were not focused on evangelizing the lost. Rather, they turned their attention to teach the people of God to obey all that Christ commanded. Acts 6 gives us another clear picture of this strategy. The apostles' priority was to devote their efforts toward "prayer and to the preaching ministry" (Acts 6:4). As a result of their decision to walk with God and invest in God's people, "The preaching about God flourished, the number of the disciples in Jerusalem multiplied greatly" (Acts 6:7).

A Story from Mel

I had the privilege of pastoring a small country church in Texas while I attended seminary. I was a Canadian city boy trying to fit into small-town west Texas cowboy country. My wife and I had a wonderful time serving the Lord in that place.

As the time drew near for us to minister in Canada, the church began the process of putting together a pastor search committee. One of the members of that committee made an interesting comment. He said, "Mel, you were an evangelistic pastor; we need to pray about the kind of pastor we should have follow you."

My response was, "Tell me what we did that was evangelistic."

"Well," he said, "we have had an incredible number of people baptized this past year; you must have been evangelistic."

It was true that many people were responding to the Lord and were baptized into the church, but I pointed out that our focus was not on evangelism. I taught and preached on three major things: (1) what it means to have a growing relationship with Christ, (2) the nature of the church as God intended, and (3) the absolute necessity of prayer. When they became excited about their walk with Christ, the community began to see a difference in their lives. When they understood the incredible potential of a healthy church that followed Christ as the Head, they found confidence to do His will. When they understood the power of prayer to transform lives, they began to cry out to God to save their friends and neighbors. Evangelism was a by-product of a people in love with their Lord.

This has always been true among God's people. When the people of God were taught how to practice the truth of God's Word in their lives, evangelism was explosive. The key to this was the condition of God's people, not just a better church growth strategy. Who can forget the promise of God in 2 Chronicles 7:13–14, "If . . . My people who are called by My name humble themselves and pray and seek My face and turn from their wicked ways, then I will hear from heaven, will forgive their sin and will heal their land"? The key to touching our world is for the people of God to walk in a right relationship with Him and one another.

An exciting statement of this twofold relationship with God and His people is recorded in Jesus' high priestly prayer in John 17. Here is the heart of God for His people:

> I pray not only for these, but also for those who believe in Me through their message. May they all be one, just as You, Father, are in Me and I am in You. May they also be one in Us, so that the world may believe You sent Me. I have given them the glory that You have given to Me. May they be one just as We are one. I am in them and You are in Me. May they be made completely one, so that the world may know You sent Me and that You have loved them just as You have loved Me (John 17:20–23).

Jesus had an intimate relationship with His heavenly Father. Though the relationship was thoroughly and intensely personal, it was not private. The Father purposed that He would be deeply involved with each of the disciples because the Father was also involved in their lives. Jesus knew how deep His relationship with the Father was, and He brought the disciples to see and experience it (see John 14:7–11). Then He prayed that the disciples would have this same relationship with Him and His Father, so that their relationship with one another would be strengthened.

When this was true, Jesus said that the world would believe that the Father had sent Him. He knew this was God's eternal strategy, and He lived it out with His disciples. Life in God's family in the local church is vital to world redemption. True evangelism is a natural by-product of such relationships.

Placed into the Kingdom of God

There is one more dimension to salvation that we will develop through this study. Salvation automatically brings us into the kingdom of God. The gospel of the kingdom of God was at the heart of Jesus' preaching. Jesus urged people to *"seek first the kingdom of God"* (Matt. 6:33), not *the church*, but He established the church as a divine institution for the proclamation and extension of the kingdom.

It is amazing how many Christians need to be taught concerning the kingdom of God. We seek to follow the teachings of Christ, but we do not realize that the kingdom was the focus of His teaching. The New Testament does not exhort people to seek the church, but to "seek first the kingdom of God." Christ did not say, "Truly, truly, I say to you, unless one is born of water and the Spirit, he cannot enter the *church*." Instead He said, "He cannot enter into the *kingdom of God*" (John 3:5 NASB). Jesus traveled around the Sea of Galilee preaching, "Repent, for the kingdom of heaven is at hand!"

One of the reasons some peole struggle with understanding the kingdom of God is that it appears to be beyond them and in some way out of their control. Some find it hard enough to get a handle on the local church, let alone functioning with other churches within the kingdom. The kingdom, however, is what we are all about; we are kingdom citizens serving the King of kings and Lord of lords. If all we work at is building our church to the neglect of the kingdom, we are neglecting a major dimension of God's great salvation.

The basis for Christian unity among all believers is found in the kingdom of God. All who have been born again have entered the kingdom and are brothers and sisters in Christ, living together under the rule of their King. Everyone who responds to the gospel of the kingdom has a spiritual relationship that must be expressed through mutual love. Christ prayed for unity among God's people so that the world would see God's love in them.

Anyone doing the work of the kingdom is to be encouraged and supported. Although all churches do not structurally combine their efforts in kingdom work, all churches ought to applaud other groups and not compete with or fight against them. The key to cooperation between Christians is not whether they are "like us" but whether they are doing kingdom work. The kingdom provides the impetus for brotherly love and cooperation.

How should we treat other believers who are not following Jesus exactly the way we think they should? Jesus gave a clear answer to this question. John had problems with people who were not following

---

I pray not only for these, but also for those who believe in Me through their message. May they all be one, just as You, Father, are in Me and I am in You. May they also be one in Us, so that the world may believe You sent Me. I have given them the glory that You have given to Me. May they be one just as We are one. I am in them and You are in Me. May they be made completely one, so that the world may know You sent Me and that You have loved them just as You have loved Me.

JOHN 17:20–23

---

them but were doing miracles in Jesus' name. This incident is found in Mark 9:38–41:

John said to Him, "Teacher, we saw someone driving out demons in Your name, and we tried to stop him because he wasn't following us."

"Don't stop him," said Jesus, "because there is no one who will perform a miracle in My name who can soon afterward speak evil of Me. For whoever is not against us is for us. And whoever gives you a cup of water to drink because of My name, since you belong to the Messiah—I assure you: He will never lose his reward."

This forever settles the issue for every Christian about working together with others in God's kingdom. It takes all of us together to touch a hurting world. We must not waste our time fighting with other believers when we have a much greater battle before us. We will never make a difference in our world if we cannot love one another within the kingdom of God. But when love and cooperation are present, God pours His Holy Spirit upon His people and the gates of hell will come down all around us. We will see this more clearly later in the book.

Study Questions for Reflection and Response

1. What is the difference between being saved and living in God's great salvation?
2. How does God's great salvation relate to your involvement in a local church?
3. Can an individual experience the fullness of God's great salvation outside the fellowship of a church family?
4. How does the love between Christians impact the effectiveness of evangelism?
5. Have you been so focused on your church that you have neglected your responsibilities within the kingdom of God?

Father, the hour has come. Glorify Your Son so that the Son may glorify You, just as You gave Him authority over all flesh; so that He may give eternal life to all You have given Him. This is eternal life: that they may know You, the only true God, and the One You have sent—Jesus Christ.

JOHN 17:1–3

If we say, "We have fellowship with Him," and walk in darkness, we are lying and are not practicing the truth. But if we walk in the light as He Himself is in the light, we have fellowship with one another, and the blood of Jesus His Son cleanses us from all sin.

1 JOHN 1:6–7

TWO

Koinonia:
God's Love Expressed

Experiencing God Together in Life

An ordinary working couple came to our church. Nobody knew them until they joined, for the greater Los Angeles area had created many anonymous individuals. They joyfully entered into the church family and enjoyed the fellowship among the people. They often commented on the fact that they had never been loved in any church as they were experiencing in this one.

At Prayer Meeting many months later, the man began to weep. His brother had been injured in another part of the country and was left in a coma, not expected to live. His brother was not a Christian, and it broke his heart to think he was about to slip into eternity without any hope. If only he could get to his brother and share the gospel, but he did not have the finances to make the trip. Immediately people in the church began to respond and soon the plane fare was provided. One couple even cashed in some of their retirement funds to help pay his way!

As our church prayed, the man went to be with his brother and sought for an opportunity to share the gospel with him. Miraculously, his brother suddenly came out of the coma. He was able to share with him, and the brother prayed to receive Christ as his personal Lord and Savior. For the first time the two men rejoiced together as brothers in Christ. Then almost as suddenly as he awoke, the brother slipped back into a coma and never recovered.

Although sad at the loss of his brother, the man came home happy in the Lord. We rejoiced together as a church family, knowing that God had been gracious to one of our own. That moment was a powerful time in this man's life, forever grateful to the church for walking

> *This is how we have come to know love: He laid down His life for us. We should also lay down our lives for our brothers.*
>
> 1 JOHN 3:16

with him and praying for him during such a difficult time. But that is what God's people are supposed to do! We have a love that began in the heart of God and is expressed between members in the family of God. The greatest evidence that a person has been born again, is their love for one another within the family.

Koinonia: What Is It and How Do I Get Some?

People all over the world recognize that there is a God, but few have experienced a love relationship with Him. Many would tell us there probably is a god somewhere, but he is unknowable to human experience. If our relationship to God were based on our ability to know Him, their statement would be absolutely true; God would be unknowable. How can a finite creature know an infinite Creator? He can't unless, of course, the Creator makes Himself known to the creature.

The truth is that God has made Himself known, and He is active in the world today. He has revealed Himself to us through many different ways. The greatest revelation is found in the person of His Son, Jesus Christ. While talking to His disciples, "Jesus told him, 'I am the

> *Since what can be known about God is evident among them, because God has shown it to them. From the creation of the world His invisible attributes, that is, His eternal power and divine nature, have been clearly seen, being understood through what He has made. As a result, people are without excuse.*
>
> ROMANS 1:19–20

way, the truth, and the life. No one comes to the Father except through Me. If you know Me, you will also know My Father. From now on you do know Him and have seen Him'" (John 14:6–7). God loved us so much that He sent His Son to show us who He truly is and how we can know Him. We do not serve a God who watches from a distance. We serve a God who desires a love relationship with us that is real and personal. So how do we relate to God and experience a love relationship with Him in practical ways?

Koinonia is the practical expression of God's love toward His people. I want us to become well acquainted with this word, because it is where God's love is manifest in real life. *Koinonia* is agape love in action. It is how we experience the fullness of God's love *for* His people and *in* His people. In a real sense *koinonia* is the essence of God's great salvation.

If you are not familiar with it, the word *koinonia* is not a new and innovative word. *Koinonia* is a Greek word used in the New Testament;

it is rich with meaning and therefore not easily translated into English. Usually translated as "fellowship," it also can mean, "partnership," "sharing," or even "stewardship." When applied to God's relationship with His people, it takes on a much greater significance.

What an awesome realization to know that we have literally become *partners* with God—that is, a bonding of two lives for a common purpose. Nothing is withheld in a true partnership, but the resources of each one are shared with the other. Paul used the term as he talked to the other believers about their partnership with him in the gospel (Phil. 1:3–7). They shared his suffering, they shared his poverty, they shared his message, and they shared their very lives with him as partners in the gospel.

The term *sharing* also applies to the *koinonia* relationship with God. It is the release of everything there is in you to the one with whom you are sharing. God, therefore, has given us everything we need for life and godliness. Even more, we are told that we now share in the divine nature. In some way, we receive that which is divine into our lives. This is a thought too grand to comprehend, but true nonetheless.

> *For His divine power has given us everything required for life and godliness, through the knowledge of Him who called us by His own glory and goodness. By these He has given us very great and precious promises, so that through them you may share in the divine nature, escaping the corruption that is in the world because of evil desires.*
>
> 2 PETER 1:3–4

Koinonia also means *stewardship*. You have been entrusted with a relationship to God and now you are a good steward of all that God has brought to you. You are taking all the resources of God and letting these flow through you to the rest of the people of God. That stewardship is a powerful word to describe *koinonia*. A good steward receives not what is his but what is someone else's. And God has a purpose for what He has given to us. Let me use a phrase that the apostle Paul used regularly. "I do not receive the grace of God in vain." That is, I do not receive all the resources of God into my life and then do nothing with it. Paul put it this way in 1 Corinthians 15:10, "But by God's grace I am what I am, and His grace toward me was not ineffective. However, I worked more than any of them, yet not I, but God's grace that was with me." *Koinonia* receives the grace of God with a grateful heart and lets the resources of God flow through your life into the rest of God's family. Paul said, "Working together with Him, we also appeal to you: Don't receive God's grace in vain" (2 Cor. 6:1).

The essence of the church is found in the word *koinonia*. We fellowship with God intimately. We partner with God in His activity. We share in God's nature. We are given stewardship of that which is divine. We come to know God experientially! To describe an encounter with the living God defies human language, yet such an encounter is at the heart of what the New Testament writers were trying to convey through the word *koinonia*. The apostle John said, "We testify and declare to you the eternal life that was with the Father and was revealed to us—what we have seen and heard we also declare to you, so that you may have fellowship [*koinonia*] along with us; and indeed our fellowship [*koinonia*] is with the Father and with His Son Jesus Christ" (1 John 1:2–3).

True *koinonia*, in its fullest expression, can only be found in one place—the local church. Nowhere else is God's love displayed and experienced more deeply than in the midst of His people as they gather together. Oh how God loves the church. He delights to see His children gathering for worship. To watch believers walk with one another, helping each member to grow into Christlikeness. To observe people from different backgrounds and with different interests joining with one heart to serve their common Lord. God is honored when a church demonstrates to a watching world the love that comes from Him.

Koinonia with God

God's great salvation is nothing less than God's desire to fellowship with human beings. God's love, however, without practical expression is irrelevant. God's love must be experienced in real life in order for it to be of any value. Fortunately, God chooses to enter a love relationship with us that is real and personal. In fact, without a personal relationship with God, there is no salvation; there is no eternal life.

Many people have difficulty at this very point. Eternal life is not based on religion, but it is based on a relationship with God. Our relationship with God is not essentially about external acts of ritual; it is an internal response of the heart. God's great salvation frees us from sin in order that we might be free to know Him. Some think that we are freed from sin in order that we might *act* right, yet God's desire is that we *be* right. *Being* right speaks of the heart; it speaks of the core of our existence. What we need is to be in a right relationship with God. Jesus said in John 17:3, "This is eternal life: that they may know You, the only true God, and the One You have sent—Jesus Christ." Herein is the significance of *koinonia,* the personal interaction between God and His people. The first and greatest commandment is to love God with *all* our heart, soul, mind, and strength (Deut. 6:5; Matt. 22:37). The Amplified Bible may help us to see the extensiveness of salvation described in John 17:3. "And this is eternal life: [it means] to know (to perceive, recognize, become acquainted with and understand) You, the only true and real God, and [likewise] to know Him, Jesus [as the] Christ (the Anointed One, the Messiah), Whom You have sent." Indeed, salvation is nothing less than a personal love relationship with God, through His Son, Jesus Christ.

A Story from Mel

On January 25, 1985, my father was to fly to Hawaii to be the main speaker at a large conference. I know—tough job but somebody has to do it! What made this assignment especially inviting, was that we were having a bitterly cold winter that year. So my father decided to take my mother and make a vacation out of it.

On January 24, however, I was severely injured in a logging accident and was flown out of the back country to Edmonton, Alberta, for surgery. I was in bad shape; my femur had been shattered, some muscles had been torn, and I was hurting. As I lay in the hospital, I remember talking to my father on the phone. He said, "Your mother is already on her way to see you, and if you need me, I will call and cancel my trip to Hawaii." I thought to myself, *Hawaii versus Edmonton? Warm sun versus forty degrees below zero? Beautiful beaches versus a hospital room?* All that my father thought about was his son. He is my father! He loves me!

I know that my father loves me and would do anything he could to help me. But I also know that my father is limited. He can't always be there. He has limited resources. We live a long way from each other. But nobody can separate us from the love of our heavenly Father. Knowing how much our earthly fathers love us, how much more does our heavenly Father. That is *koinonia,* God's love expressed toward His children.

The apostle Paul had come to know the love of God in his life. He wrote one of the most impassioned statements about God's love toward His children in the Scriptures. Look at God's love toward your life as described in Romans 8:31, 35, 37–39:

> If God is for us, who is against us? . . . Who can separate us from the love of Christ? Can affliction or anguish or persecution or famine or nakedness or danger or sword? . . . No, in all these things we are more than victorious through Him who loved us. For I am persuaded that neither death nor life, nor angels nor rulers, nor things present, nor things to come, nor powers, nor height, nor depth, nor any other created thing will have the power to separate us from the love of God that is in Christ Jesus our Lord!

Koinonia with One Another

A Story from Mel

I pastored my first church while attending seminary in Texas. In a small town that boasted a population of 250, I quickly became involved in the community and was well-known by people in the area. At the same time, I knew what was going on in the town and sought to make a difference. One day I noticed a moving truck and furniture being unloaded. So I went to introduce myself to the newcomers with the intention of inviting them to church. The man was pleasant and quickly revealed that he was a Christian. Even more, the man was a Baptist! Being the pastor of the only Baptist church in the town, I was hot on the trail of a potential addition to our little congregation. So I pursued even further by asking where the man's church membership belonged.

"I belong to Bluff Dale Baptist Church," he proudly replied.

I was a little perplexed at this information and simply responded, "Well I am the pastor of Bluff Dale Baptist Church, and I have never seen you before!"

"Well I don't attend," he acknowledged, "but I was married in that church five years ago."

It was clear that this man had been brought up in a Christian culture but did not have the foggiest idea of what it meant to have a relationship with God and, therefore, a relationship with God's people.

I have found that many people are not sure what it means to be a Christian, not sure how to relate to God, and not sure how to relate to God's people. One of the most neglected aspects of God's great salvation is our fellowship with other believers. According to the Scriptures, it is spiritually impossible to have fellowship with God and, at the same time, be out of fellowship with God's people. "If we walk in the light as he himself is in the light, we have fellowship *[koinonia]* with one another, and the blood of Jesus His Son cleanses us from all sin" (1 John 1:7). Hear that Scripture carefully! Evidence that we truly have fellowship with God is demonstrated by our fellowship with one another. If we are not experiencing true *koinonia* with God's people—or any one of God's people—we are not having *koinonia* with God or walking in the light as He is in the light. It is impossible to have a relationship with God and not share it with the rest of God's people. The deeper the relationship to God, the deeper the relationship becomes with God's people. The two are eminently connected.

God expects us to love one another in exactly the same way that He has loved us. Some will undoubtedly cry, "Impossible!" Humanly speaking, it is impossible. But with God all things are possible. Fortunately for us, God placed His Spirit within us to enable us to love as He loves. This is a part of His great salvation too. When we are walking in fellowship with God, He gives us the ability to walk in fellowship with all of His people.

If a person claims to be in fellowship with God yet has broken relationships with other believers, what does the Bible call that person? A liar! Broken relationships with God's people are a symptom of a broken relationship with God. So if you see people at odds with one another, what is their problem? Their primary need is to be reconciled with God, and then God will help them to be reconciled with one another. How do you have fellowship in the church? Help people to have fellowship with God. Then the life of God in them will affect every relationship they have with other people.

If a husband and wife have a broken relationship, what is their problem? Do they need marriage counseling? Possibly, but if you did marriage counseling, you better talk with them about their relationship to God. It is spiritually impossible to walk in the light as He is in the light and not have fellowship with one another.

The same is true between parents and children. We had a son who gave us great difficulty during his teenage years. How do you help a family member come back to God? *You* come back to God! When our relationship with him was strained, we had to get *our* lives right with

God as the number one priority. But if your relationship to God is basically religious activity, you will drive your kids away. We confuse religious busyness with having fellowship with God, but they are not the same. In fact, our activity for God can often replace fellowship with God. And that will be reflected in the relationships we have with others.

I remember when my son was having trouble in school, when he ran with the wrong crowd of friends, when he slipped away from the Lord. I remember how broken I became. Late one night I slipped into the living room of our home and cried out to God to change the heart of my son. But God said, "No, I am going to change the heart of his father." That was a blow; it caught me off guard. I was at that time a director of missions. How much closer to God can you get? Oh, if only our ministry was an indication of our heart, but it is not. God needed to draw me closer to Him in order that I might be closer to my son. What God began to speak to me was exactly what the Scripture says. If I walk in the light as He is in the light, I will have *koinonia* with my son. That applies in every area of life.

First John 1:3–7 tells us that fellowship with God results in fellowship with God's people. John is careful to use the same word for both relationships, indicating that the fellowship we have with God is the same quality of fellowship we have with one another. We have said that a good working definition of *koinonia* is "agape love" or "God's love in action." So how has He expressed *koinonia* in your life? How has God loved you? What have you received from God because He loves you? He has forgiven you. He has been merciful to withhold what you, as a sinner, deserve. He has been gracious to give you what you don't deserve. He has given you protection. He has given you discipline in order that He might shape your character. He has given you direction. He has been your friend. He has expressed His love in a thousand different ways.

Now that we have a small sample of what God's love has done for you, look at John 13:34–35: "I give you a new commandment: that you love one another. Just as I have loved you, you should also love one another. By this all people will know that you are My disciples, if you have love for one another." Do you understand why we need to look at how God has loved us? It helps us understand how we should love one another.

Let me give a penetrating example of what the Scripture is saying. In the area of forgiveness, God expects that we will forgive others in exactly the same way He forgives us. Jesus said in the Lord's Prayer, "And forgive us our debts, as we also have forgiven our debtors." Look carefully at what Jesus said. If there was any doubt about what Jesus meant by that statement, He gave a commentary on it just two verses later. "For if you forgive people their wrongdoing, your heavenly Father will forgive you as well. But if you don't forgive people, your Father will not forgive your wrongdoing" (Matt. 6:14–15).

Can you see how important it is that we are forgiving in our relationships with others? Our relationships with other people directly influence our relationship with God. And it is certainly true that our relationship with God will affect our relationship with one another in the church. If we refuse to forgive a brother, the Lord will not forgive us. We can plead with God all we want, but He will not forgive our sin against Him unless we are also willing to forgive those who have sinned against us. God is seeking to reveal Himself through us, and for us not to forgive is to give a wrong picture of God to a watching world.

I am convinced that much of the trouble among God's people today is they are still carrying years of sin on their shoulders when they thought they had been forgiven. Their unwillingness to forgive another has left them unforgiven and under the weight of their own sin. Furthermore, their growing accumulation of sin has created a barrier between them and God. That barrier has left them feeling distant from God, and that distance from God has brought deadness to their Spirit. That spiritual deadness has left them without hope and void of any real joy in life. That void has left them in despair and in the depths of depression—all because they were out of fellowship (*koinonia*) with another person in the family of God. In the context of forgiveness, listen again to 1 John 1:7, "If we walk in the light as He Himself is in the light, we have fellowship with one another, and the blood of Jesus His Son cleanses us from all sin." Fellowship with one another and forgiveness of one another allows forgiveness of our sins and a right relationship with God.

> *We can plead with God all we want, but He will not forgive our sin against Him unless we are also willing to forgive those who have sinned against us.*

Let me drop forgiveness into the corporate arena. What happens when a church splits? I believe that if a church ever has a split, the members need to go back and reconcile with their brothers if they ever want to see the blessings of God again. But the tragedy is that a church will split and the very next Sunday both groups will pray, "Oh God, will you bless us today?" That is an affront to a holy God, for they have just broken fellowship with their brothers because they would not forgive. They treat relationships in the church like many are treating the marriage relationship, "irreconcilable differences." The world may say that, but there are no irreconcilable differences among God's people. If there were, that would mean there was a limit to God's ability to forgive you as well. And the cross would have been made void of its meaning. We must forgive as Christ has forgiven us.

Since God's salvation provided His Son to live His life in us, "the one who says he remains in Him should walk just as He walked. . . . The one who loves his brother remains in the light, and there is no cause for stumbling in him" (1 John 2:6, 10). That is what God's salvation looks like! Christ living His life in us and ministering to others through us. We are to treat others as Christ would treat them, for in reality that is what is happening.

God's desire for *koinonia* among His people is directly related to His strategy to touch a world. It is seen most clearly in the local congregation. Without getting overly technical, it is important to understand the basic meaning of the word translated *church* in the

English Bible. It is a rendering of the Greek word *ekklesia.* The word never denotes a building or a structure in which worshipers assemble; instead, it denotes the people themselves. The translation of this compound word is literally, "the called-out ones." The New Testament reveals that the first Christians were "called out" of the world and "gathered together" into religious assemblies; they acted as organized bodies. The word *church* is used for a congregation of believers who are committed to one another under the lordship of Jesus Christ and who are united through the bond of His Spirit. The fellowship [*koinonia*] among the people of God is a powerful force in the purposes of God.

Koinonia in the Church

I have never known a Christian to be walking in true fellowship with God who was not at the same time walking in true fellowship with God's people. Similarly, every time I have been involved with broken love relationships in a church, in a marriage, in a family, or in God's kingdom work, I have witnessed someone who was completely out of fellowship with God. Many have indicated that broken relationships among God's people result in a broken relationship with God. I have found it to be the other way around; broken relationships with one another are a symptom of a previous broken relationship with God. It is our relationship with God that determines all other relationships in our life.

The apostle Paul has given us a wonderful prayer that we need to pray for our church family. If you are a leader, this prayer should be on your lips regularly for the members of your church. It is found in Ephesians 3:16–19. Examine it carefully, for it lays the foundation for *koinonia* in the church.

> I pray that He may grant you, according to the riches of His glory, to be strengthened with power through His Spirit in the inner man, and that the Messiah may dwell in your hearts through faith. I pray that you, being rooted and firmly established in love, may

be able to comprehend with all the saints what is the breadth and width, height and depth, and to know the Messiah's love that surpasses knowledge, so you may be filled with all the fullness of God.

Paul prayed that each one would be strengthened by the power of the Holy Spirit and that we would be rooted and grounded in love. Love is the foundation of our relationships in the church. He prayed that all the saints, all the believers in the church, would come to know the love of Christ. What would happen if the church were filled with the love of Christ? They would then be filled with all the fullness of God! Do you see that? Can you imagine that? He is talking to the church!

When he talks about knowing the love of Christ, what does he mean? What does it look like when God brings His love through Jesus Christ into every member of the church? He then displays in that church the *breadth* of His love. How long does His love hold on to you? He displays the *width* of His love. How wide will His love reach, and how many people will it include? He displays the *height* of His love. How high does He lift and encourage every individual when He loves them? He displays the *depth* of His love. How far will His love go to reach the fallen sinner? Where sin abounds, grace does much

---

Just as you want others to do for you, do the same for them. . . . Be merciful, just as your Father also is merciful.

LUKE 6:31, 36

---

more abound. It doesn't matter how deep a person has gone in sin; God's love will go deeper.

To the extent that God loves us, we ought to love one another in the church. The one who experiences great mercy and forgiveness from God expresses mercy and forgiveness to others. To experience the patience of God in our lives causes us to have patience with others. To have a conscious awareness of God's faithfulness leads us instinctively to express faithfulness to God and His people. God expects that His children will love one another exactly the same way they have come to know the love of God. As we grow in our relationship with God, we automatically grow in our relationship with other believers.

What power is found in the church that is experiencing *koinonia* with God and one another! It is explosive! God's great salvation is best demonstrated when His love is being expressed among His people. Because the church family is a living body with Christ as the Head, it is vital that every member not only has a love relationship with Christ but also with every member of the body. If the "hand" is not listening to or speaking with the "eye," the entire activity of God through the body is hindered. God chose to make us mutually interdependent in our church family; we are spiritually connected in the body. When Christ has a mature body of believers that is in fellowship with Him and one another, He can effectively do the work of the Father to touch a lost world.

Koinonia, love in action, between the members is absolutely vital to the nature of the church and to the purposes God has for the church. This was God's strategy from the beginning when He made a covenant with His people, commanding them to love God and one another. These two commandments are dramatically tied together in the eternal strategy of God to touch a world. Jesus prayed that the fellowship He had with the Father would be replicated among His people. Their love for one another would then demonstrate to the world that Christ was the Son of God, and they would see His glory. Examine carefully Jesus' prayer in John 17 with a fresh understanding of *koinonia.*

> I pray not only for these, but also for those who believe in Me through their message. May they all be one, just as you, Father, are

in Me and I am in You. May they also be one in Us, so that the world may believe You sent Me. I have given them the glory that You have given to Me. May they be one just as We are one. I am in them and You are in Me. May they be made completely one, so that the world may know You sent Me and that You have loved them just as You have loved Me. Father, I desire those You have given Me to be with Me where I am. Then they may see My glory, which You have given Me because You loved Me before the world's foundation. Righteous Father! The world has not known You. However, I have known You, and these have known that You sent Me. I made Your name known to them and will make it known, so that the love with which You have loved Me may be in them and that I may be in them. (John 17:20–26)

Can you see it? Do you understand why Christ is so concerned about our relationships with one another? We are to experience the same love Christ had with His Father within our relationships in the family of God. His love is in us! And if His love is in every believer, how ought that to look in a church family? If it were present, would the world believe the gospel of reconciliation?

I tried my best as a pastor to teach our people to love God with all their hearts. We opened the Scriptures, especially the Gospels, and demonstrated how Jesus loved the Father and sought to do what was pleasing to Him. I then taught them what it meant to love one another as Christ has loved us. As people responded to God during our worship services, I helped the entire congregation to come alongside those who were struggling and love them through their brokenness.

One particular Sunday a woman came forward during the invitation weeping over her wayward son. I immediately guided the church family to gather around her, pray with her, share some Scriptures, and make arrangements to get involved with her (that is what love does!). The teenagers were enlisted to pursue her son. The men were encouraged to seek him out and be a father figure to him in this time of need. The ushers were alerted when he came to church. The entire body was alert and praying. Then we saw God drawing him, and we were ready to respond to God's activity in his life. He eventually did return with many tears, and the entire church was filled with tears of joy in God's activity through the body. This is *koinonia* at work. The body loving God and one another in real and practical ways.

A Story from Mel

We had a family that began to visit our church that was new to our town. They were a poor family that literally lived on the other side of the tracks in a run-down trailer in the field. They had five young children, and the father was out of work. I could tell they had a hard time trusting people and were therefore hesitant to get too involved. But they were welcomed into the church and eventually joined fellowship with us.

Almost the very next week, I heard that the man had run out of gas and was stuck on the highway. I called one of our older deacons, and the two of us went out to meet him. We picked him up and drove on into the next town to get some gas to take back to his van. While in town, Rob, the deacon, decided to take us out for lunch. The man was a little hesitant but didn't have much of a choice; he was riding with us! Then Rob pulled out his wallet and handed the man a one-hundred-dollar bill and said, "Whatever you have left over after filling your vehicle, get something nice for the kids." The man was taken back and couldn't believe his eyes. He didn't want to take it. The man finally asked, "Why are you doing this?" Rob answered, "You are part of the family, and we take care of our family." I will never forget the look of wonder on the man's face. He had never experienced that kind of love before.

Oh, I get excited thinking about it! God's great salvation lived out among His people is the most powerful force in the world. That is what is on the heart of God for our churches today. When the church is experiencing *koinonia* as God intended, there is no limit to what He can do through them to touch the world. We have just looked at Paul's prayer for the church. But notice the very next verses in Ephesians 3:20–21: "Now to Him who is able to do above and beyond all that we ask or think—according to the power that works in you—to Him be glory in the church and in Christ Jesus to all generations, forever and ever. Amen." When a church receives and distributes the love of God, they will experience above and beyond all that they could have imagined.

Keeping *Koinonia* in the Church

Koinonia, like love, cannot be taken for granted. Unfortunately, the neglect of our relationship to God will gradually affect our relationships in the church. When we are out of fellowship with God, fellowship [*koinonia*] within the church suffers dramatically. Busyness that leads to the neglect of relationships will affect a marriage, a business partnership, or a family, and it can ultimately be fatal. When we are busy doing things for God and yet we neglect time with God, the relationship falters. When our relationship with God falters, there is turbulence in the churches.

I am aware of a pastor who was troubled over two couples in his church that were going through the process of divorce because there was an adulterous relationship between the husband of one couple and the wife of another. The pastor essentially said, "These two couples were the most active people in the church. They were deacons, taught Sunday school, were involved in many areas of leadership, and were at the church whenever the doors were open. How could these people have marriages that were falling apart?" Yet in asking the question, he heard the answer. They were so busy doing things for God that they neglected the relationship to Him. They were so busy in their church activities that they never had time to spend with their own families. When relationships begin to falter, everything else will come crashing down all around us. We must learn to release our people from burdensome busyness in order that they might build healthy and strong relationships.

Proverbs warns us, "Watch over your heart with all diligence, for from it flow the springs of life" (Prov. 4:23). What is happening in our lives, whether in the church or in the home, is a reflection and expression of what is happening in our hearts. If our love for the Lord is neglected and we let the fire go out, it will soon be seen in our lives, especially our love relationships to others. This is true in every relationship in life. Three parables of Jesus express three ways we can lose that which is important to us in our church.

The parable of the lost sheep demonstrates how *distraction* may cause us to lose *koinonia.* People in the church can get distracted and unknowingly wander off into that which is dangerous. Leaders must be careful to keep watch care over those who seem to be straying.

The parable of the lost coin shows *carelessness.* Churches can simply be careless, not paying attention to what God has already given them. Each person sent by God is precious and ought to be protected as such.

The parable of the lost son illustrates how we can lose what we have by *choice.* There are times when we choose to disobey God or to overlook sin that has crept into the fellowship. As a result, we walk away from the blessings of God.

When we lose *koinonia* in the church, we have lost our very life. Jesus said to the church in Ephesus, "But I have this against you: you have abandoned [lost] the love you had at first. Remember then how far you have fallen; repent, and do the works you did at first. Otherwise, I will come to you and remove your lampstand from its place—unless you repent" (Rev. 2:4–5). When we lose our love for God and one another, we no longer have a message of good news to give the world. We cannot talk about reconciliation between God and man if we are not reconciled with one another. Without a vital relationship with God and His people, we have lost the essence of God's great salvation.

Is it important that we maintain *koinonia* in the church? It is our life! We must work hard at resting in Him in order that the love of Christ may fill our church. Do you recall what Jesus said in Revelation 3:20?

"I stand at the door and knock. If anyone hears My voice and opens the door, I will come in to him and have dinner with him, and he with Me." Who was He talking to? The church at Laodicea. He was saying, "If you want to have Me come into your church, just open the door." It is not that difficult; just let Him in! For those who may be thinking, *I need to go find a church that is enjoying true koinonia,* you may need to stay where you are and be the one to open the door for your church. God may have put you in your church so that He could work through you to express His love to the rest of the church. If one person recognizes it is Jesus who is knocking, and that one person opens the door, He will come in. Once He is in, He will begin to affect every part of the church through that one person's life. Don't leave the church; the church needs you. If you have fellowship with the Father, and you have fellowship with the Son, and you are filled with the Holy Spirit, and you are walking in the light as He is in the light, what do you think will happen? That *koinonia* love will begin to touch everybody in the life of the church. I have watched that happen. I have watched God do it. Could you be that one? Are you willing to be that one?

We must maintain *koinonia* with God in order to maintain *koinonia* in the church. The secret to building deeper relationships in the church is not more activities; it is not more potlucks; it is not more entertainment and fun. All of these may be a part of a strong church, but *koinonia* is a by-product of a vibrant and living relationship with God through Jesus Christ. *Koinonia* cannot be conjured up by human activity; the working of the Holy Spirit produces it.

Let me give one more word concerning *koinonia* in the church. The Scripture says in Luke 6:38, "Give, and it will be given to you; a good measure, pressed down, shaken together, and running over will be poured into your lap. For with the measure that you use, it will be measured back to you." This is a principle of the kingdom of God. The measure by which you measure to others will be measured back to you. It is an absolute with God. So if you have received much from God and give only a little to others, then God says He will give only a little to you. He will not respond to you in a way contrary to how you respond to others.

How then should you love one another? If God did not hold back His blessings to you, you should not hold back anything from others. In fact, the Scripture says: "Although He was rich, for your sake He became poor, so that by His poverty you might become rich" (2 Cor. 8:9). If you see a need in the church, you should do all you can to help meet it. That is what the early church in Jerusalem did, and the world did not understand that kind of love. What produced that kind of love in the early church? If we walk in the light as He is in the light, we have the same *koinonia* with our brother as we have with Him.

Let me finish with one more Scripture. First John 3:14 says, "We know that we have passed from death to life because we love our brothers. The one who does not love remains in death." According to that verse, if a person does not love his brother, he remains in death. That is an absolute with God. So what should you do when you see members of your church at odds with one another?

As a pastor, I always prayed and then went to talk with them. I had a responsibility to bring all members of our church into a deeper relationship with Christ. If I saw them not walking with Him, then I would risk everything to go and talk with them. And if they are Christians and they become offended, we will make up in heaven. But if I watched their lives and it seemed as though they "remained in death" because they had no capacity to love their brother, I had to help them. If they were grouchy old people who never showed evidence of love, I would go talk to them. And if they got offended, I knew that when they stood before God they would at least know that their pastor loved them enough to show them what the Scripture said: if a person does not love his brother, he or she may be abiding in death, and that is an eternal consequence. I can't say I love if I do not care whether a person spends eternity in hell. So I would go and share the truth in love.

I remember preaching in a large church that was pastored by a well-known pastor. I delivered a message on repentance, and when

I had finished, the pastor remained in his seat weeping. I turned the service over to him, but he just sat there for about five minutes. When he eventually got up, he said to the congregation, "In my life, I have heard many people preach on repentance, but this is the first time I have ever heard a message on repentance that was not spoken in anger." I couldn't believe my ears. How could a person preach on repentance with anger? I preach repentance with a broken heart because I know the consequences when a person doesn't repent. We must speak the truth in love, and God's love will break down the heart that is not walking with Him.

Let me illustrate what I am talking about. In the early days in Saskatoon, our congregation was small, around thirty people. One of the leaders decided that we were not functioning as he thought we should and said so in a business meeting. He stood up, his face got red, and said, "You are all going against the will of God, He will not bless you, and I am leaving." He summoned his wife and as he was walking out, he said, "As of today I am resigning all my positions in the church."

When he and his wife got out the door, I said to the group, "Will someone second that motion?" They said, "What motion?" I said, "He just resigned from his positions, and his attitude indicated that he should. A deacon should not act that way. But don't you vote on this unless you make a pledge to love him the way Christ loved you. I will not have you vote to remove him from all positions unless you at the same time vote to give your life to help redeem him." I don't have the right to criticize people unless I am willing to come alongside them and encourage them to become what God desires.

So the next week I went to this man and said, "I am the only pastor you have, and I want to help you." Guided by the Holy Spirit, I asked him, "Could you say that you love God with all your heart, mind, soul, and strength?" He said, "No. I fear Him, I worship Him, I serve Him, but I cannot say that I love Him." Then I asked if he would let me walk with him until he could truly say that he loved God with all of his heart, mind, soul, and strength. He put his head down and began to weep. He began to tell me that he grew up in a broken home where his dad never saw any good in him. He never heard his dad say that he loved him. He said, "I don't even know what love is, and I don't know how to love others."

About six months later, I will never forget the day he knelt with me and cried out in tears, "Lord, I love you." When he began to walk in fellowship with God, all the symptoms of bitterness and anger fell away. He became gentle and kind to everyone in the church. In fact, he no longer sought positions in the church; he just wanted to serve in the church. He has since died, but until the end of his days, he was a great encouragement to that church. What happened? He just needed help to walk in the light and He is in the light.

What will you do to help others know the love of Christ? What will you risk because you love your brother? Do you want to see the love of God flowing through your church? Then begin to love others as God has first loved you. Do you want God to be generous to your church? Then demonstrate a generous attitude to others in your church. You don't have to make *koinonia* happen; you need to walk with God and let Him produce *koinonia* in and through you.

Study Questions for Reflection and Response

1. From God's perspective, why is it important that the local church express *koinonia*?
2. Can a church truly *be* a church without *koinonia*?
3. How does unforgiveness affect *koinonia* in the church?
4. What effect does *koinonia* in the church have on the community in which it is located?
5. What are some practical ways you can express *koinonia* with your church family?
6. How do you maintain *koinonia* in the church?

Know therefore that the LORD your God, He is God, the faithful God, who
keeps His covenant and His lovingkindness to a thousandth generation
with those who love Him and keep His commandments.

DEUTERONOMY 7:9

In the same way He also took the cup, after supper, and said, "This cup is
the new covenant in My blood. Do this, as often as you drink it,
in remembrance of Me."

1 CORINTHIANS 11:25

But you are a chosen race, a royal priesthood, a holy nation,
a people for His possession, so that you may proclaim the praises of the One
who called you out of darkness into His marvelous light. Once you were not
a people, but now you are God's people; you had not received mercy,
but now you have received mercy.

1 PETER 2:9–10

THREE

The Cross: God's Covenant Relationship

Experiencing God Together in Life

I had a life-changing experience at Indian Falls Creek Assembly in Oklahoma a few years ago. It left an indelible mark on my heart with a fresh understanding of the cross and its impact upon the people of God.

I had been asked to speak twice a day for the entire week of meetings. On the final evening together, with a gathering of twenty-three hundred Native American Christians, a revered elderly man called me to the platform. I was taken by surprise, not knowing what was about to happen. As I moved toward the platform, a lifetime of prayers seemed to flood through my mind. For as a young boy, the Lord had given me an unusual love for these Native American people. I had made a covenant with God to release my life to Him and to be available to help bring a sweeping revival among native peoples across Canada and the United States. This covenant was a costly burden to me, but this covenant had now brought me to this moment in my life.

As I mounted the stage, several men were ceremonially folding a large wool blanket with many native artifacts on it. Another younger man was now standing at the podium as an older man held out his arms to me. He pronounced loudly, "Henry has been and is a spiritual warrior to the native peoples. We honor him tonight!" As the man carefully draped the folded blanket over my shoulders, he held me tight, looked deep into my eyes, and said, "This is the highest honor the native peoples can ever bestow on any man. Welcome into the native peoples of America!"

I began to weep uncontrollably, and the Holy Spirit caused me to remember the cross. For that is where God said, "I love you! This is the new covenant in my blood." I knew that the cross had set me free and had given me this opportunity to be a part of God's plan of salvation. As I stood there with the blanket over my shoulders, I sensed the devastating pain of the native peoples and knew that the cross was the only answer to bring healing to their community. I was convinced that the cross, once and for all time, demonstrated that God loved all people of the world.

A Covenant with God

God chooses to relate to His people through a covenant relationship. Did you know that? Were you aware of the expectations involved in your relationship to God? Entering into a relationship with God through Jesus Christ is not a legal contract, but it is a binding covenant with far-reaching implications. Blessed is the one who knows God and His covenant promises, for they will have confident expectation and security of heart in such a relationship, knowing that God will always act according to His promises within the covenant.

So what is a covenant? Simply stated, a covenant is a sacred pledge based on trust between two parties. The trusting relationship between the two parties becomes the most important factor, the basis from which everything else flows. The significance of this relationship cannot be understated when we talk about a covenant relationship with God. Let me explain.

God chose to create people in His own image and likeness in order that they might live as spiritual beings with the freedom to enjoy a loving relationship with Him. In that relationship they would be the fortunate recipients of all God's blessings. The one secret to their happiness was the trustful surrender of their lives to the will and purposes of God. As long as people would remain dependent on God in all things, they would enjoy an intimate relationship with Him and all the benefits of His presence. But sin entered the world through Adam's disobedience, and the intended relationship to God was

---

Now without faith it is impossible to please God, for the one who draws near to Him must believe that He exists and rewards those who seek Him.

HEBREWS 11:6

destroyed. His sin caused fear, and the trust relationship was broken. Adam lost so much!

Adam soon learned that people cannot save themselves from the power of sin. God must be the one to initiate and complete all that is necessary for salvation and a restored relationship, and if God is to do it in harmony with the nature of man, man must yield his willing consent as a free spiritual being and entrust himself to God. Herein is the heart of a covenant. God desires that people believe in Him. He desires that they trust in Him, for what a person believes will move and direct his entire life. Salvation, therefore, could only be by faith. God restoring the relationship that was lost by sin, and man in faith yielding to God's work in his life is now what had to take place.

When we examine God's dealings with individuals or groups of people, we understand that His primary desire is to get people to trust Him. When faith is found, God can do anything through those people. When unbelief is present, God chooses to do nothing through His people. For unbelief always leads to disobedience and sin. The writer of Hebrews said it this way, "Now without faith it is impossible to please God, for the one who draws near to Him must believe that He exists and rewards those who seek Him" (Heb. 11:6). The emphasis of a covenant relationship is our faith in God and our subsequent obedience to Him and His will.

Because our covenant is with the holy God of the universe, it is a serious agreement that we choose to establish. I have found that the deeper we enter the covenant relationship with God, the more significant eternity becomes; and as eternity begins to affect our heart, the closer we are to revival. Understanding what it means to have a covenant with God is crucial for a church, as well as every individual.

God's covenant with His people is always a revelation of His purposes, describing a definite promise that God desires to accomplish in and through His people. But more than a revelation of His purposes, the covenant also serves as a security, and it guarantees that God will care for His people. The covenant becomes an anchor whereby Christians can hold on to God's faithfulness even in the midst of confusing circumstances. What confidence we can have in a covenant-keeping God! He is unchanging and faithful to do all that He has promised, and we must never forget that the covenant was God-centered. God chose to initiate the covenant, and He willingly entered into the relationship with Israel so that He might accomplish His purposes through them and demonstrate to the world what He is like.

> *"For the mountains may be removed and the hills may shake, but My lovingkindness will not be removed from you, and My covenant of peace will not be shaken," says the LORD who has compassion on you.*
>
> ISAIAH 54:10

Through His people God would reveal Himself and His purposes to the rest of world. The purpose of the covenant was to draw all people to Himself, that He might be their God. He would be the One in whom they put their complete trust, and the One in whom they would find abundant life.

This covenant built on God's covenant with Abraham; God promised that from him He would build a great nation, and this nation would bless all nations of the world. Exodus chapters 19–20 describe this first covenant relationship between God and the Israelites. This covenant began at God's initiative when He encountered His people on Mount Sinai. At the center of the agreement were the Ten Commandments, the guiding requirements of the relationship. The commandments were not for the world in general, but for God's people in particular. They were for the people who had chosen to enter into a covenant with Him. This covenant determined how God would relate to the people from that day forward. If they kept the covenant, they would be blessed. If they broke the covenant, they would be cursed. This is clearly seen in passages such as Deuteronomy 30:15–20 (see also Deut. 28; Lev. 26) where God said, "I call heaven and earth to witness against you today, that I have set before you life and death, the blessing and the curse. So choose life in order that you may live, you and your descendants" (v. 19).

The people of God were given the standard by which they must relate to God. He was holy, and therefore, they were to be holy. It was a covenant they had chosen to enter; if they remained true to the covenant, God would bless everything they did. He would bless them when they went in and when they went out. He would bless their children, their cattle, their crops, and anything they put their hands to accomplish. He would go with them in battle and defeat the enemy, demonstrating to the entire world that they belonged to God. When the world saw the people of God, they would know what God was like. God would, therefore, reveal Himself to the world through His people who were in covenant with Him.

But the opposite was also true. If the people of God broke the covenant, they would experience the cursing of God. He would curse them when they went in and when they went out. He would curse their children, their cattle, their crops, and anything they put their hands to accomplish. Their enemies would defeat them in battle, and all the people of the world would see how God deals with people who break the covenant. Whether they were true to the covenant or whether they violated it, God would show the world how He deals with people in a covenant relationship with Himself.

A Story from Mel

One of the amazing inventions of our time is the airplane. We take it for granted today, but consider its ability to do that which at one time seemed impossible. It is parked on the tarmac, anchored firmly to the ground by the laws of gravity. But then the engine begins to rumble, and the plane starts toward the runway. The jet engines kick in, and it starts to race down the airstrip. The natural laws of gravity pull hard to keep the plane down, but soon another law begins to take effect. The laws of aerodynamics state that under certain conditions a heavy object can rise against the force of gravity and be lifted high into the air.

Although air travel means sending an enormous metal object into the sky against the laws of gravity, air travel is considered one of the safest modes of transportation we know. The laws of aerodynamics work with great efficiency! A 150-ton metal object can soar through the sky, high above the earth with relative ease. To be honest, I don't understand the laws of aerodynamics; they are still a mystery to me. But I don't have to; I simply have to get on the plane, sit down, drink a Coke, eat peanuts . . . and relax. I can sit by the window and look down on the earth and enjoy the ride. I believe that the plane will fly, and I commit myself to that plane and get on board! In an amazing way I enjoy the benefits of the plane's victory over gravity. Because the plane overcame gravity, so do I—as long as I remain on the plane.

One day I was driving to the airport with my daughter, who at that time was about five years old. We looked up and saw two men floating down to earth with parachutes. My daughter asked me where they came from. So we looked more fervently and spotted a small plane flying overhead. I began to explain that the plane took the two men into the air, and then they jumped out. Then in a way only a five-year-old could ask, she said, "Dad, did they want to get out?" She knew there was safety in the plane, and to step outside also meant stepping outside of its safety.

In a similar way Christians enjoy the benefits of a covenant relationship with God, whether we understand how it works or not. Jesus carries the repentant sinner right to the throne room of God, having overcome the law of sin and death. We enjoy the fruit of Christ's work

---

What a wretched man I am! Who will rescue me from this body of death? I thank God through Jesus Christ our Lord! . . . Therefore, no condemnation now exists for those in Christ Jesus, because the Spirit's law of life in Christ Jesus has set you free from the law of sin and of death.

ROMANS 7:24–25A, 8:1–2

on our behalf, when He died on the cross for our sin and rose again. The key to that relationship is to believe in Christ and commit our lives to Him as Lord and Savior. But we must remain in Christ, to enjoy life in Christ. If we ever "step out of the plane" and try to live without Him, we immediately begin a rapid decent away from His blessings. The covenant is still in place, but we have stepped outside of it and miss out on life as God intended.

The covenant had tremendous benefits when kept and enormous consequences when broken. The conditions were clearly established and known to the people of God, and they were expected to live according to the relationship that was established. Because God was the initiator of the covenant, no obedience was too demanding, no dependence too absolute, no submission too complete, and no confidence too certain. To be in a covenant with Almighty God was a privilege beyond imagination. Of all the peoples of the earth, God chose to enter a covenant with the Israelites, His chosen people.

Yet God's people continually struggled to fulfill their part of the covenant. In fact, the covenant exposed the futility of mankind to live according to God's law. Listen to the terms of the covenant: "If you will indeed obey My voice and keep My covenant, then you shall be My own possession" (Exod. 19:5). "Obey My voice, and I will be your God, and you will be My people" (Jer. 7:23). Obedience was the condition of blessing, but sinful mankind was bent toward disobedience. The old covenant was faithful to set a clear standard that would always expose sin in God's people and reveal His holiness. The result was that God's people became convinced of their sin and were humbled to confess their inability to live according to the standard of God's law. Mankind was awakened to the need for a new covenant, the fullness of God's grace that would be completed in the work of Christ. Everything in the Old Testament covenant pointed to the coming of Christ.

A New Covenant in Christ

What mankind could not achieve according to the law in the old covenant, Jesus Christ came to fulfill in the new covenant. In the New Testament Jesus introduced us to a new covenant in His blood. In this new covenant, Jesus would accomplish all the requirements of God's law on our behalf. "In Christ" we have everything necessary for life and godliness, and we literally become partakers of the divine nature.

The difference between the old covenant and the new covenant is enormous. In the old, man failed to fulfill his part of the covenant. In the new, God is to do everything in him. The old gave laws written on tablets of stone; the new writes the laws of God on our hearts. The old brought conviction of sin; the new forgives sin and cleanses us from all unrighteousness. The old reveals a corrupt heart that resists the will of God; the new provides a new heart that is responsive to the heart of God. The old gave laws to follow but no power to follow them; the new covenant gives Christians the Holy Spirit who will empower us to know and do God's will. Look carefully at the new covenant described by Ezekiel, "I will give you a new heart and put a new spirit within you; and I will remove the heart of stone from your flesh and give you a heart of flesh. And I will put My Spirit within you and cause you to walk in My statues, and you will be careful to observe My ordinances" (Ezek. 36:26–27). Can you see the difference? In the old

---

Therefore, no condemnation now exists for those in Christ Jesus, because the Spirit's law of life in Christ Jesus has set you free from the law of sin and of death. What the law could not do since it was limited by the flesh, God did. He condemned sin in the flesh by sending His own Son in flesh like ours under sin's domain, and as a sin offering, in order that the law's requirement would be accomplished in us who do not walk according to the flesh but according to the Spirit.

ROMANS 8:1–4

covenant God said, "*If you obey* . . . you will be blessed." In the new covenant God said, "*I* will put My Spirit within you and *cause you to walk* in obedience." Both covenants deal with the heart, but the new covenant includes the power of God working in our hearts, which causes us to obey His commands. Incredible!

The old covenant, established on Mount Sinai, was clearly understood, though not always followed. The result was that the people of God experienced the blessing or the cursing of God according to how they lived within the covenant established. The question comes today, "What are the conditions of the new covenant?" "Are blessing and cursing involved in the new covenant as in the old covenant?" More fundamentally, we might ask, "Did you even know that your decision to become a Christian was at the same time a decision to enter a covenant with God through the blood of Christ?" Truly, the terms of the covenant are the title deeds of our inheritance, the promises of God for His people to enjoy. This may be why many have never understood or enjoyed the greatness of God's salvation.

> *For His divine power has given us everything required for life and godliness, through the knowledge of Him who called us by His own glory and goodness. By these He has given us very great and precious promises, so that through them you may share in the divine nature, escaping the corruption that is in the world because of evil desires.*
> 2 PETER 1:3–4

To lack knowledge of the covenant relationship will cause the Christian to be unsure or unstable in his life. We are warned about the consequences of living the Christian life without confidence in God's promises. James said, "Let him ask in faith without doubting. For the doubter is like the surging sea, driven and tossed by the wind. That person should not expect to receive anything from the Lord. An indecisive man is unstable in all his ways" (James 1:6–8). I have found that when people understand the covenant relationship with God, they live in confidence and assurance that God will be faithful to keep His promises. These people are not doubters or unstable people; they are standing firm on the promises of God and are receiving answers to their prayers. Their strength is not in self-confidence but in absolute confidence that God will be true to fulfill the promises of the covenant.

This new covenant in Christ was not established with a nation. It was established with anyone who would enter a relationship with God through the atoning sacrifice of Christ on the cross. The blessing of this covenant is described in 1 Peter 2:9–10. Christians enter into a relationship with God that transforms every part of their lives. They now belong to God, for they have put their faith in Him and have chosen to follow Christ as their Lord.

> *But you are a chosen race, a royal priesthood, a holy nation, a people for His possession, so that you may proclaim the praises of the One who called you out of darkness into His marvelous light. Once you were not a people, but now you are God's people; you had not received mercy, but now you have received mercy.*
>
> 1 PETER 2:9–10

Though this initial covenant with God is extremely personal, it is never private. The context of God's salvation is always in the larger purposes He has for His people. So the individual was aware that his personal relationship with God always affected all the people of God among whom He had now placed him. The entire nation of Israel would be affected by each individual's personal covenant relationship with God. God had made them personally and collectively interdependent.

The law that followed to guide them included how each individual was to keep himself in a love relationship with God, but it also included many commands to the entire nation to keep the covenant together. The nation affected every individual, and every individual affected the nation.

In the New Testament this relationship between Christians in the early church also demonstrates the interdependent relationship between God's people. Individuals who entered a saving relationship with Christ also entered into a vital relationship to God's people in a local church. God added them to the church as it pleased Him (Acts 2:47; 1 Cor. 12:18).

I have found that when people understand the covenant relationship with God, they live in confidence and assurance that God will be faithful to keep His promises.

Christ has become the mediator of the new covenant between God and man (1 Tim. 2:5). The apostle Paul understood this when he said, "For every one of God's promises is 'Yes' in Him [Christ]. Therefore the 'Amen' is also through Him for God's glory through us" (2 Cor. 1:20). The new covenant with God is through Christ. In Him all the promises of God are fulfilled. In Christ our redemption was secured. At the cross Jesus paid for our sin and set us free from its consequences.

The cross is the pivotal center of the new covenant, the epicenter from which its authority advances. Jesus talked of the new covenant in His blood that grants to us the forgiveness of sin and a relationship with God. The cross, therefore, is the heart of the covenant, forever symbolizing the love relationship God offers to people who put their faith in Him. I love Peter's tender yet forceful exhortation: "You are to conduct yourselves in reverence during this time of temporary residence. For you know that you were redeemed from your empty way of life inherited from the fathers, not with perishable things, like silver or gold, but with the precious blood of Christ, like that of a lamb without defect or blemish" (1 Pet. 1:17–19). How awesome are God's great salvation and the covenant He extends! The blood of the new covenant flowed from the body of God's only begotten Son, Jesus Christ, to those who believe Him and who enter into a covenant relationship with Him.

Jesus set His focus on going to the cross, for it was there that the new covenant would begin. He continually told His disciples that He must go to Jerusalem and be crucified. He knew that He must go in order that the power of the cross might be exerted over all people. Much to the disciples' dismay, it was better for Him to go to the cross than to stay with them; the power of the cross, resurrection, ascension, and Pentecost could not come on all men without Jesus going to the cross.

Even so today, personally and as a church, to resist the cross is to lose its power in us and through us. Jesus said we must deny self, take up our cross, and follow Him. If we try to avoid the cross, as did the disciples, we cannot go with the Lord or experience the blessings of the new covenant. But if we take up our cross, we must also realize that the cross is not something for us to suffer on; it is something to die on! The cross in our lives means that the covenant is not to be taken lightly. Jesus gave everything, even His own life, in order that we might walk in the covenant. We, too, must be willing to give our all, even our own lives, in order to walk in the covenant with God.

Entering the Covenant

In keeping with the nature of mankind at creation, people are given the privilege to enter a covenant with God according to their own free will. Because of God's mercy and grace, He has chosen to offer this tremendous gift, the gift of a relationship with Himself. Yet we must respond to His offer and enter into a covenant relationship with Him. He has never and will never force spiritual possessions upon us; He relies upon us to receive them. So how do we do it? How do we enter a covenant relationship with God and receive the purpose of our creation?

Wholeheartedness is the secret of entering the covenant with God. It is all or nothing. Either you trust Him completely, or you do not trust Him at all. The first and greatest commandment is, "You shall love the Lord your God with all your heart, with all your soul, and with all your mind" (Matt. 22:37). The covenant requires wholehearted love; nothing is held back. This decision to enter a relationship with Almighty God is one that demands a complete surrender of all that we are to all that He is and has promised to be in our lives and in our churches. It cannot be any other way; the way in which we respond to God is a reflection of our belief in God. And without faith it is impossible to please Him.

> *Give, and it will be given to you; a good measure, pressed down, shaken together, and running over will be poured into your lap. For with the measure that you use, it will be measured back to you.*
>
> LUKE 6:38

Within the covenant the one who gives less than his whole heart will receive much less than what he could have experienced in his relationship with God. He promises and gives in the same measure that we are ready to receive by faith. The more we depend on Him, the more we will experience His care. To hold back will severely hinder our relationship with God, for He, too, will hold back His blessing in our lives. His giving depends on our taking; it is a principle of the kingdom! The only way to experience abundant life as God intended is to surrender completely to His will and to love Him with our whole heart.

The blessings that Jesus bestowed in the days of His flesh on earth appear to be directly related to the faith of those who received them. He said to the centurion, "Go. As you have believed, let it be done for you" (Matt. 8:13). He said to the woman who had suffered with a hemorrhage for twelve years, "Have courage, daughter. . . . Your faith has made you well" (Matt. 9:22). He said to the two blind men who sought healing, "Let it be done for you according to your faith" (Matt. 9:29). He said to the mother who sought healing for her demon-possessed daughter, "Woman, your faith is great. Let it be done for you as you want" (Matt. 15:28). The measure of one's faith has a direct correlation to the measure of God's response. Great faith equals great blessing; little faith equals little blessing; and no faith equals no blessing. One of the most tragic statements in the Bible is this, "And He did not do many miracles there because of their unbelief" (Matt. 13:58). This is true not only for every believer but also for every church.

Wholeheartedness is the secret of entering
the covenant with God.

I was in a group of leaders who were discussing foreign missions and the task the Lord had given them. We were dealing with some challenging Scriptures when a man, who was overseeing the financial side of the organization, suddenly blurted out, "Well, you just need to know I'm the doubting Thomas in this group." It was clear what he meant by that statement. He was skeptical of anything that required faith. So I responded, "Before, or after you met the living Christ? Because after Thomas met the living Christ, he was not the same again. After that encounter with Christ, there is no evidence that he ever doubted again. In fact, tradition tells us that he traveled to India, shared the gospel, and was martyred for the sake of Christ. But you never find Thomas doubting after he had an encounter with the living Lord."

It is amazing to me that Christians who have met the living Christ are unwilling to walk by faith. Let me suggest that if you are by nature a doubting person, God does not necessarily criticize you. But prolonged doubt becomes unbelief, and He does deal with that. If you have doubt, you need to move that doubt into the presence of God until He resolves it. If you choose not to believe every time you encounter Him, that is a much more grievous situation to God. He does not overlook unbelief, and your persistent doubt can have a devastating effect on the life of the people of God if you continue.

I wonder if the reason many Christians experience "little blessing" is that they entered into a relationship with God with "little faith." Their walk with God is halfhearted, and they wonder why they are not experiencing the promises of God in all their fullness. Could it be that we are reaping what we have sown? The tendency of some churches is to lower the standard in order to attract more people and build bigger churches. Yet in lowering the standard we have many in our churches who do not have a wholehearted walk with God. They were simply told how to get to heaven when they die and were not instructed in the covenant relationship with God and its inherent expectations. A love relationship with God is not merely an accessory to our life; it *is* our life.

The measure of one's faith has a direct correlation to the measure of God's response.

When we enter a covenant with God and receive His great salvation, we must come prepared to give our lives to Him. All that we are and all that we ever hope to be is laid down at the foot of the cross. We can do nothing less if we desire to know God in His fullness. We deny self, take up our cross, and follow Him. And Paul assures us that in knowing Him fully, we are "filled with all the fullness of God" (Eph. 3:19).

A Covenant to Remember

The Lord desires that we remember the covenant. In fact, He has commanded that we regularly acknowledge our covenant with Him in our lives and in our churches. So when does a person remember and acknowledge the covenant he has entered with God? First, it is acknowledged when he observes Communion (or the Lord's Supper). Christians are in a new covenant, sealed in the blood of Christ, and the Communion service is remembering, or renewing, that covenant.

> *The Lord Jesus took bread, gave thanks, broke it, and said, "This is My body, which is for you. Do this in remembrance of Me." In the same way He also took the cup, after supper, and said, "This cup is the new covenant in My blood. Do this, as often as you drink it, in remembrance of Me."*
>
> 1 CORINTHIANS 11:23–25

This is why the apostle Paul urges us to examine ourselves (1 Cor. 11:28) before taking Communion. For a broken relationship with Christ is paramount to a broken covenant with God. A holy God will not bless a people who have broken the new covenant, and Communion is our opportunity to examine our relationship to Christ and to be restored to the blessings of a covenant relationship.

As a pastor, I always helped our people to understand that Communion was a reminder of the incredible cost to God for us to enter the new covenant. People needed to examine themselves, because if one member of the body was out of fellowship with God, it affected the whole body. That is the nature of the covenant. In the Old Testament the sin of Achan and his family caused the Israelites to be defeated when they went to battle against the city of Ai (see Josh. 7–9). In the New Testament the sin of Ananias and Sapphira was jeopardizing the entire work of God in the early church, so God dealt with them severely (see Acts 5:1–11). Knowing that God's Word shows us the ways of God and how He deals with His people when they are out of fellowship with Him, I was determined to lead our people to renew the covenant and confess their sin regularly. The Communion service was established for such an occasion.

Some of the greatest revivals in history came as a result of God's people participating in Communion. To remember the cross and the new covenant in Christ's blood will make a deep impact on those who take it seriously. In 1727, the Moravian Brethren were so impacted by the sacrificial death of Christ that every member of the church was drawn back to God and His purposes for their lives. They saw their relationship to one another and to Christ in such a way that they felt the need for repentance and cleansing. Immediately, God heard their cry and brought revival to the congregation, and through a revived people, God made an impact that literally reached every corner of the earth. In England churches used to take a whole week for Communion; they thought it took a significant amount of time to examine themselves thoroughly and get right before God. Why? Because they were a covenant people.

A second place that the covenant is established is in the ordinance of baptism. Baptism helps us remember the new covenant, as we observe the symbolic reenactment of the death, burial, and resurrection to new life in Christ. The cross is the central picture in this powerful act of obedience in a believer's life. Just as Jesus died for our sin and rose again, so the new believer dies to sin and rises to live a new life with Christ as Lord.

The act of baptism will not save a person; it is an outward expression of what God has done on the inside of a person to transform one's heart and cause one to be born again. It is symbolic, but it is much more than just a symbol. It is an act of obedience to the commands of our Lord. Jesus commissioned His disciples to "go, therefore, and make disciples of all nations, baptizing them in the name of the Father and of the Son and of the Holy Spirit, teaching them to observe everything I have commanded you" (Matt. 28:19–20). Baptism was a part of God's plan, causing all believers to acknowledge

---

Therefore we were buried with Him by baptism into death, in order that, just as Christ was raised from the the dead by the glory of the Father, so we too may walk in a new way of life. For if we have been joined with Him in the likeness of His death, we will certainly also be in the likeness of His resurrection.

ROMANS 6:4–5

publicly what Christ has done for them. Just as Christ identified with sinful humanity through baptism, so we now identify with Christ, the Holy One, through the same ordinance. And in that moment we are acknowledging before a watching world that we willingly enter the new covenant in Christ.

Receiving members into the church family is another moment when individuals are challenged to live in covenant with God and His people. Whenever a person feels God is leading him to join fellowship with a local congregation, he is at the same time entering a covenant. I would always ask those who came to our church three questions. First, "Have you personally repented of your sin and surrendered your life to Jesus Christ as Lord?" Second, "Have you followed the Lord in believer's baptism by immersion, picturing death to the old life and resurrection to the new life in Christ?" And third, "Do you believe that God is clearly adding you to this body?" If they responded positively to those questions, I would then ask, "Would you then enter into a covenant with God and His people, allowing Him to work through you to strengthen and build up this body?" Next, I would turn to the church and ask them to enter a covenant with new persons, committing themselves to pray for them, walk with them, and help them to become all that God wanted for their lives. Those were special times; we would renew our covenant together as a church that we might walk in harmony with God and one another, ready to fulfill God's purpose for our church. We reminded ourselves that we were a covenant people.

Many churches also have an invitation time at the close of their worship service. This allows individuals to respond to the work of the Holy Spirit as He draws them either to enter or restore the covenant relationship with God. People may need the opportunity simply to come and pray, restoring the relationship that has been broken by sin. People may realize for the first time their need for a Savior and respond to God's invitation for salvation. Others may sense God's leading them to serve Him in a new direction, and during the invitation they respond to God and publicly commit their lives to obey. Whatever the case, the invitation given in the corporate worship experience affords the opportunity for people to respond to the covenant relationship for their life and for their church.

The Covenant Includes God's People

We cannot understand the covenant relationship with God without also understanding that the essential nature of the covenant relationship includes God's people. When God established a covenant with His people in the Old Testament, it was corporate. All the people stood together and willingly entered the covenant, accepting all of its conditions and resultant consequences.

I want to take you to the life of Daniel to illustrate how our lives are linked with one another as the covenant people of God. Early in Daniel's life he made a commitment to God that he never broke. Daniel 1:8 says, "Daniel made up his mind that he would not defile himself." Even though people all around him were compromising, he would not compromise. Even when others were turning away from God, he remained true to the Lord God. Because of his faithfulness, God granted him favor in the eyes of the ruling officials in Babylon. King Nebuchadnezzar himself was taken with Daniel, promoting him to be ruler over the whole province of Babylon and the chief prefect over all the wise men. As much as Daniel found favor in man's eyes, he was much more concerned with finding favor in God's eyes. Throughout his life this was true, even if it meant being thrown into the lions' den.

The people of God as a whole, however, did not follow the ways of God. In fact, they had turned away from God. But Daniel did not separate himself from them. Quite the opposite, he identified with them and pleaded to God on their behalf. Because they were all in the covenant relationship together, Daniel became the instrument through whom God would bring restoration to all of His people.

Daniel 9 contains one of the greatest prayers in the Bible. It is Daniel's prayer to God, pleading for mercy on behalf of the Israelites.

I will not quote the entire prayer, but look at a portion of it and notice how Daniel prays.

> "Alas, O Lord, the great and awesome God, who keeps His covenant and lovingkindness for those who love Him and keep His commandments, *we* have sinned, committed iniquity, acted wickedly, and rebelled, even turning aside from Your commandments and ordinances. "Moreover, *we* have not listened to Your servants the prophets. . . ."
>
> "And now, O Lord our God, who have brought Your people out of the land of Egypt with a mighty hand and have made a name for Yourself, as it is this day—*we* have sinned, *we* have been wicked. O Lord, in accordance with all Your righteous acts, let now Your anger and wrath turn away from Your city Jerusalem, Your holy mountain; for because of *our* sins and the iniquities of *our* fathers, Jerusalem and Your people have become a reproach to all those around *us*. So now, *our* God, listen to the prayer of Your servant and to his supplications, and for Your sake, O Lord, let Your face shine on Your desolate sanctuary. O my God, incline Your ear and hear! Open Your eyes and see *our* desolation and the city which is called by Your name; for *we* are not presenting *our* supplications before You on account of any merits of *our* own, but on account of Your great compassion.
>
> "O Lord, hear! O Lord, forgive! O Lord, listen and take action! For Your own sake, O my God, do not delay, because Your city and Your people are called by Your name" (Dan. 9:4–6, 15–19).

What an amazing prayer! Had Daniel sinned? Had he committed iniquity, acted wickedly, rebelled, and turned away from the commandments of God? No! Yet you would never know it if you had only read this prayer without knowing the details of his life. Daniel completely identified with the rest of the people of God. Their sin became his sin. And his righteousness became their prayer. And because he stood with God's people in their time of need, they were all spared from the wrath of God. Listen to the answer to Daniel's prayer:

While I was still speaking in prayer, then the man Gabriel, whom I had seen in the vision previously, came to me in my extreme weariness about the time of the evening offering. He gave me instruction and talked with me, and said, "O Daniel, I have now come forth to give you insight with understanding. At the beginning of your supplications the command was issued, and I have come to tell you, for you are highly esteemed" (Dan. 9:21–23).

Incredible! Because of Daniel's upright character, as soon as he began to pray, the issue was given to send Gabriel from the throne room of God to go and meet with him. Now what would have happened if Daniel had left the people on their own? What would have happened if he had not interceded on their behalf? Fortunately, we won't know the answers to those questions, for Daniel understood what it meant to be in a covenant relationship with God and His people.

Let me ask another question. When your church is in a time of trouble, what should you do? Go to a more healthy church? Criticize them and stand aloof? Because you are in a covenant relationship, you will stand with them and intercede on their behalf. For what happens to them, happens to you. Romans 12:5 says, "We who are many are one body in Christ and individually members of one another." We are connected to one another in the body of Christ. Whether we find ourselves in good times or in times of trials, we must walk together before God. How we live our lives affects all the rest of the body. How the body responds to God also affects our lives. How then ought we to encourage one another in the Lord? How then should we pray for one another?

The New Testament views Christians who have entered into the new covenant as a "chosen race, a royal priesthood, a holy nation, a people for His possession." Why? "So that you may proclaim the praises of the One who called you out of darkness into His marvelous light" (1 Pet. 2:9). Can you see how God views Christians today? We are the people of God! We are chosen by God and belong to God. We therefore are all under the new covenant together and must walk together as His people.

I mentioned earlier in this chapter how we would enter into a covenant with each person whom God led to join fellowship with our church. We recognized that God had taken the initiative to move within a person's heart to obey Him in all things. We, therefore, made a pledge before God to be a good steward of every life God added to the body. We were to help each person to become God's best, whatever that might require. Knowing that God had added him to the body and knowing that He saw what lay before him in the days ahead, we were committed to helping him through life's journey. If he started to wander and fall away, we pledged to remain faithful to him and not let him go. This covenant we had with God and with one another allowed us to keep those who came to the church; we were determined not to let them slip through the cracks. If a person's attendance began to slip, we knew something was wrong. To us nonattendance was a symptom of a deeper problem, and we were committed to care for one another's needs.

I see a trend happening in churches today that is alarming. That is, when a person is not walking in line with the vision of the church, the church cuts him off and sends him elsewhere. Or, if a person has fallen away from God and is living in sin, she is quickly criticized and put outside of the church body. We have become so driven by evangelism that we have forgotten to take care of the people of God. One of the Scriptures that is constantly used for evangelism is where Jesus said, "[I have] come to seek and to save the lost" (Luke 19:10). That was a direct quote from Ezekiel 34, referring to the people of God. And it is a condemnation of the shepherds who have let the flock be scattered into the mountains, being exposed to the elements and in danger from wild beasts. The Lord chastised those who would not go after the sheep, bring them back, feed them, and care for them. And in that chapter God said that He would raise up a shepherd that would seek out and save that which was lost. That shepherd is Jesus. The sheep are the people of God. We are in trouble if we have more concern for the unbeliever than we do the believer. God's heart always looks to

His own first, for as go the people of God, so goes His purpose to redeem the rest of the world.

There are a thousand different ways to walk with the people in your church. You don't always have to wait until there is a crisis or until someone has completely fallen away from God. You take time along the way to encourage people at any stage in their Christian lives. For what God is doing in their lives touches you as a part of the body.

My wife and I are currently members at a large church. A significant part of our service is a time of prayer, where people can come from their seat to pray at the altar. One Sunday I watched a young man go forward to pray, and I could tell that he was shaking. So I got up from my seat, went down to the front, and knelt beside him. I waited for a moment, then I proceeded to pray for this young man. His head turned around, and he interrupted my prayer: "Dr. Blackaby, you have come to pray with me! You don't know what that means to me and the decision I am wrestling with today." I discovered that he was a college student studying law, and he sensed God was calling him into the ministry. He has responded to God's call on his life and is now preparing to serve the Lord.

That is called encouragement. Is that hard to do? No, you just have to do it. When we are walking in a covenant relationship with other people, we must find ways to help them become God's best. Whether it is a college student seeking direction for his life, a young girl who feels the call to missions, an older man who has wasted many years but now wants to make his remaining days count, or other people who need someone to come alongside them, encourage them.

You may be aware that my wife and I have five children. When our children were young, not many people were brave enough to invite our family of seven over for a meal. But gathering around the table with other believers is a wonderful way to keep connected, and it encourages others in the Lord. If you know some single parents who are struggling with their children, ask them to come for a meal in your home. You have no idea what that will do to encourage that parent and those children. Don't let other believers in your fellowship struggle alone;

intercept their life before they get discouraged and fall away. Why? You have made a covenant with God and them to walk together.

We are in trouble if we have more concern
for the unbeliever than we do the believer.

Jesus said in Matthew 12:30, "Anyone who is not with Me is against Me, and anyone who does not gather with Me scatters." In other words, if we are not actively trying to gather together with Him, we are scattering. There is no neutrality. When you are in the body, you are either positively building up the body, or you are negatively tearing it down. Be careful that you do not let a divisive spirit remain in your life or in your church. We must examine our lives to see how we have positively contributed to the work of God by encouraging one another in the Lord.

Let me leave you with a wonderful verse of Scripture that is found in Hebrews 10:24–25: "Let us be concerned about one another in order to promote love and good works, not staying away from our meetings, as some habitually do, but encouraging each other, and all the more as you see the day drawing near."

Study Questions for Reflection and Response

1. How significant is the cross in God's new covenant with us today?
2. What is the most important difference between the Old Testament covenant and the New Testament covenant?
3. How does a violation of the covenant with God affect the church?
4. How can a local church help its members to walk in the covenant relationship? What are some practical things you can do to build up the body?
5. Because we are in a covenant relationship with God and His people, how should we see ourselves in light of Daniel's example?
6. How does the new covenant affect the "back door" of the church and become a greater incentive to care for God's people?

God's Salvation in the Church

How does a church function in the greatness of God's salvation?

Christ loved the church and gave Himself for her, to make her holy, cleansing her in the washing of water by the word. He did this to present the church to Himself in splendor, without spot or wrinkle or any such thing; but holy and blameless.

EPHESIANS 5:25B–27

Introductory Comments

It is important to understand how the word *church* will be used throughout the remainder of this book. When I talk of the church, I mean "the local congregation of believers who have united together under the lordship of Christ." When I talk about the *kingdom of God,* I mean "the reign and rule of God worldwide in the hearts of His people." When we think of all believers, it is best to refer to them as being a part of the kingdom. When we refer to a specific group of believers who have gathered together in order to worship and serve the Lord in a specific place, it is most accurate to refer to them as a church.

Today many have confused the church and the kingdom, leaving the impression that they are the same thing. This is simply not true. We will go into more detail later in the book, but a few comments are appropriate before we launch into what it means to experience God together in a local congregation.

The New Testament does not exhort people to seek the *church,* but to "seek first the *kingdom* of God." Christ did not say, "Truly, truly, I say to you, unless one is born of water and the Spirit, he cannot enter the *church*"; but "he cannot enter the *kingdom* of heaven." Jesus traveled around the Sea of Galilee preaching, "Repent, for the *kingdom* of heaven is at hand!" We are not born into or commanded to seek the *church,* but the *kingdom*! Yet Christ established the church as a divine institution for the proclamation and extension of the kingdom. As God gathers His people together into an organized body, He can then effectively do His work through them. Through the local church God planned to reveal the good news of Christ, to care for new believers who respond to Christ, to build up all believers into maturity in Christ, and to take that group of believers into the world to do His will.

I often hear people talk about "the church" as if it were some mystical mirage that nobody can find, yet everyone belongs to. I want to ask, "Where is this church, and when can I go to it?" You see, according to Scripture, a true church has some identifiable marks. It has the capacity to assemble. It has leadership to teach its members the Word of God. It has authority to discipline and correct its members when they are in error. It has an organization to minister effectively to the needs of its members as well as those in the world. Its visible structure produces an influential presence in the community. It observes the ordinances of baptism and the Lord's Supper as given by Christ. It has unity in doctrine. It has *koinonia,* or fellowship, among the members. As an autonomous body, it has direct and immediate access to God through His Word and prayer. It has the capacity to respond quickly to the will of Christ, the Head of the church. It has the power of the Holy Spirit resident in its midst. It has the tools to fulfill the Great Commission: to make disciples; to baptize in the name of the Father, Son, and Holy Spirit; and to teach new Christians to practice all that Christ has commanded. In summary, the local congregation embodies all the marks of the New Testament church. There we discover the Lord's strategy to touch the world.

Whenever I hear the term *invisible church,* I cringe. Nowhere in the Scriptures will you find that the church is invisible. That would

---

"The One who holds the seven stars in His right hand and who walks among the seven gold lampstands says: I know your works, your labor, and your endurance . . . . But I have this against you: you have abandoned the love you had at first. Remember then how far you have fallen; repent, and do the works you did at first. Otherwise, I will come to you and remove your lampstand from its place — unless you repent."
REVELATION 2:1–2, 4–5

contradict its very nature! Christians, who constitute the members of the church, are made analogous to the salt of the earth that makes a recognizable difference; a candle which gives light in a dark world, and a city set on a hill that all can see. The visibility of the church consists in the visibility of its members. Those who do not live under the lordship of Christ, making a difference in the world, ought not to assume that Christ is their Savior. The church that is not visible in the world ought not to assume that it is a church belonging to Christ. Jesus did not intend for the church to be hidden from the world but that it be sent into the world as a visible entity proclaiming the kingdom of God.

One should not equate spiritual with invisible, for the Spirit-filled life is obvious to all who see it. One cannot attempt to unite all believers into one invisible church, for that would destroy the church's very nature. To call the church "invisible" is to give it a characteristic that it does not want. To call the church "invisible" is an admission of its failure to be the true church in the world. Jesus walks through the golden lampstands, the churches, to see if they are true to God's standard, not the standard of human reasoning. If they are not functioning as salt and light in the world, he will remove their lampstands. Biblically, the church is visible in the world, making a dramatic influence wherever God gathers His people together and charges them with a kingdom assignment.

The Bible also uses the image of "the body" to describe the church. It is used most often in Paul's writing, and he uses the image in two perceivable manners. He primarily used the image to promote functional unity in the local congregation, where individual members work together to fulfill the commands of Christ, who is Head of the church. Paul identifies the church with the living Christ (1 Cor. 12:27), and the unified church is an instrument of His redemptive work on earth as a continuing incarnation of Christ. The church is not just an organization but a living organism. Christ, however, is the head of the body, guiding His people through the work of the Holy Spirit.

A second way that Paul applies the image of "the body" is in a general way to encourage unity of the Spirit and brotherly love toward all believers. Where this is true, the emphasis is upon the character of the believers and their duty to the whole family of God. Indeed, Christians have a responsibility to treat all believers as brothers and sisters in Christ. This will be discussed in detail later in this book.

With these brief comments on how the word *church* will be used, let us see how the church functions in the greatness of God's salvation.

We know that all things work together for the good of those who love God: those who are called according to His purpose. For those He foreknew He also predestined to be conformed to the image of His Son, so that He would be the firstborn among many brothers. And those He predestined, He also called; and those He called, He also justified; and those He justified, He also glorified.

ROMANS 8:28–30

FOUR

God Purposes

Experiencing God Together in Life

The church's prayer meeting can be a significant time in the life of God's people. I have come to know about God and His love for the church in those tender moments of prayer. In our church, the prayer meeting was informal, allowing the body to interact and share what God was doing in their lives. It became a time of teaching, sharing, praying, and suffering together. We tried to situate ourselves in a circle or in some pattern so that we could look into one another's eyes and unite our lives together.

I recall one meeting when a new believer, recently baptized, began to weep as she spoke. "I asked you to pray for me as I told my

> *Surely the Lord GOD does nothing unless He reveals His secret counsel to His servants the prophets.*
>
> AMOS 3:7

83

parents about the joy of my salvation and my baptism. But they did not take the news well. At first they were furious; then they became fearful. They are going to drive five hundred miles to speak personally with their bishop because they believe they may lose *their* eternal salvation because *I* was baptized. They had stood at the altar of their church when I was born and vowed to God they would raise their baby girl to be faithful to their church." As we listened to this new believer, the church began to feel her pain and to minister to her. We shared from Scripture, we prayed with her, and we wept with her. I recall the pain in the hearts of the church family as we felt her suffering for the sake of Christ. Her Lord was real, and His encouragement through the church sustained her. She continued to be faithful to the Lord, her church, and her family. As a result, the entire church was inspired.

> *For He chose us in Him, before the foundatsion of the world.*
>
> Ephesians 1:4

This situation was not uncommon among our young adults. I recall the first prayer meeting after Christmas one year, when two brothers had gone home during the break to tell their parents they had been baptized into our church. When their parents heard, they refused to let them come home, even though it was Christmas. They said, "You have rejected us, your grandparents, and your entire family by doing this. You are no longer our sons!" They were broken, and the church wept with them too. They became even more loving toward their parents and tried to show them that their new faith was real. When they both married women in our church, it caused further disruption, but they were determined to reach out to their family anyway. They have since "outloved" their parents, who now see that they did not lose their sons after all. As a result, other family members have responded to Christ. The church became the most significant and stabilizing factor in their Christian lives.

As I look back on some of those difficult moments in the lives of our church members, I understand how important it was that we prayed together and loved one another. Those young believers needed the church to keep them on track and encourage them to remain faithful to the Lord and to their family. God had a purpose for their lives, and Satan was trying his best to destroy them. We cried together, we laughed together, and we stood in the presence of God together. To this day God is fulfilling His purposes through those people in ways they never could have imagined. Just as He has an eternal purpose for each person, He has a purpose for each church that is beyond what we could ask or imagine.

The Eternal Purpose of God

We are a generation of goal setters. How often I have heard said, "If you don't set a goal, you are bound to reach it every time." Or, "If you set a goal and don't reach it, you will still accomplish more than you would have without setting one." All this, and much more, comes straight from the world and the culture around us. But the world around us does not believe in God. Their only option is to set goals for themselves.

As Christians, however, we do not function like the world around us. As servants of the most high God, we don't have the right to determine the direction of our lives or our church. God alone sets the purposes, objectives, and goals for His people. In the matter of setting goals, Proverbs 29:18 is often quoted from the King James Version: "Where there is no vision [goals?], the people perish!" The best translations, however, translate this passage in the following way: "Where there is no revelation, the people cast off restraint" (NIV). We are not to be people of *vision,* as the world uses the term, but a people of *revelation.* We don't dream our dreams for what we want to do for God; He sets the directions that He is going and reveals them to us. My own interpretation of what this passage is saying is this: "When God's people don't have a clear word from Him, they do what is right in their own eyes!" The result of having each person cast a vision and "going for it" is usually spiritual anarchy.

God never asks His servants, "What do you want to do for me?" God is the Master, and He knows what He is doing. He, therefore, sets the vision or directions for His people. His people simply obey Him when He speaks to them. From before the foundation of the world, God knew what He was doing and what He purposed to accomplish through our lives. He then, generation after generation, let His people know what He was doing, so they could join Him and let Him work through them to accomplish His eternal purposes.

When Jesus called His disciples, the Father had planned that moment in history before the world was ever created (Eph. 1:4). Now, after centuries of planned and purposeful activity, He had sent His Son "in the fullness of time"—His time. And He gave twelve disciples to His Son and told Him what to tell them and how to walk with them. The Father knew precisely what He was about to do. "In Christ, God was reconciling the world to Himself" (2 Cor. 5:19). The disciples were chosen and called to join Jesus as the Father brought His great salvation to the world through the death of His Son on the cross. The disciples, in the plan of God, would be taught by the Son of God, and then they would be entrusted to take the message of salvation to every creature, to every nation, even to the uttermost parts of the earth. And their risen Lord would be with them to the end of the age. The Father has continued through two thousand years to carry out this plan of salvation in every age, including ours.

What an awesome truth! We have also been entrusted with His message of good news in Jesus Christ. The keys of the kingdom of heaven have been given to us. Our Lord's promise to be with us to the end of the age includes us! Every church must not only study this truth; it must also respond personally to Christ as the Head of the church, who will guide the members to obey the Father's commands.

I have been the pastor and interim pastor of many churches. I have earnestly sought to gather God's people together, to look to see what the Lord was doing, and to join Him as He is on mission in our world. I have sought to live this out personally; I have sought to guide our family in the final command of the Lord found in Matthew 28:19–20, "Go, therefore, and make disciples of all nations, baptizing them in the name of the Father and of the Son and of the Holy Spirit, teaching them to observe everything I have commanded you." It has led us on many exciting adventures with Him.

As each child of God seeks to follow and obey his or her Lord, it is important that we ask the right questions. For if we ask the wrong questions, we will get the wrong answer every time! Instead of asking, "What should we do this year?" we need to ask: "What is God doing this year, and how can we join Him? What adjustments do we need to make in our lives in order to fulfill God's purpose for us? What does God want to accomplish in and through our lives this year? What has He been saying to us as a church that we must carefully obey?"

Listen to Paul's understanding of God's activity and His goal for His people:

> Blessed be the God and Father of our Lord Jesus Christ, who has blessed us with every spiritual blessing . . . before the foundation of the world, to be holy and blameless in His sight. In love He predestined us to be adopted through Jesus Christ for Himself, according to His favor and will, to the praise of His glorious grace that He favored us with in the Beloved (Eph. 1:3–6).

Paul let God's people know that God's activity in their lives was purposed before the foundation of the world. The work in their lives was "according to His good pleasure that He planned in Him" (Eph. 1:9). God's goals, not ours, are crucial for God's people. When we know what God has eternally purposed, we can more carefully respond to His activity in us and through us. Paul stated this in another way in Colossians 1:27, "God wanted to make known to those among the Gentiles the glorious wealth of this mystery, which is Christ in you, the hope of glory." God's goal for the body is Christlikeness—individually and corporately as a church. When He accomplishes this in our lives, He is glorified, and His purposes are fulfilled.

God has commanded us to reach out to every person. So we watched to see how He would direct us. It took us to children, to senior adults in rest homes, to police officers and firefighters, to city hall, to the public school system, to college campuses, to prisons, to various ethnic groups. We began to reach out to refugees as they arrived in the country. We went to skid row and reached out to alcoholics and people with every imaginable problem. We determined to touch every person with the gospel—not because we wanted to make a name for ourselves but because God commanded us to do it.

Conformed to the Image of Christ

Our relationship to Christ is central to seeing the purposes of God fulfilled in us. Christ knew the heart of God. He knew the purposes of God. And He knew the ways of God. Knowing all this, He ordered His life so the Father could accomplish His purposes through Him. That is exactly what the Father desires from our lives and especially in His churches. For in God's great salvation, we now have a personal relationship with Christ who will guide our lives and our church. We no longer have to live according to our own limited wisdom or set future goals when we don't know what the future holds. We can live according to the plans and purposes of God one day at a time, as Jesus did.

> Now we have not received the spirit of the world, but the Spirit who is from God, in order to know what has been freely given to us by God. We also speak these things, not in words taught by human wisdom, but in those taught by the Spirit, explaining spiritual things to spiritual people. But the natural man does not welcome what comes from God's Spirit, because it is foolishness to him; he is not able to know it since it is evaluated spiritually. The spiritual person, however, can evaluate everything, yet he himself cannot be evaluated by anyone. For: who has known the Lord's

mind, that he may instruct Him? But we have the mind of Christ (1 Cor. 2:12–16).

What a powerful truth is found in this passage! We have been given the mind of Christ! Just as Christ knew what the Father wanted for His life, so He knows what the Father wants for our lives. To those who develop their relationship with Christ, He will clearly guide us to do the Father's will, as He did in the days of His flesh.

God's goal for the body is Christlikeness — individually and corporately as a church.

In Jesus' day the religious community would not touch a leper; they would leave lepers to die in isolation. The Father, however, loved them and sent His Son to touch them, heal them, and tell them of God's great love. There are people in every church community whom others may not reach out to and touch. Christ, as the Head of your church, desires to do through you what He did in His own ministry. Who do many avoid, resist, and even resent among your church? A man called me and said, "I've called four pastors, and they said they don't reach out to men like me. But three of them said you did! Will you help me?" I found out he was a hard alcoholic. Now alcoholics can be demanding to reach, falling back into their alcohol—until Christ sets them free. I found out later that he was standing on the third floor window ledge of a downtown hotel, and if I refused to help him, he had planned to jump to his death. He was the only child of a Christian family that lived in another state, and nobody was reaching out to him. But our church took him under our wing. It took several months, but he was saved and transformed by the power of God. I still recall meeting his gray-haired mother on the day he was baptized into our church. His mother was so grateful that our church would not turn anyone away who was seeking the Lord.

The heart and mind of Christ were given to us, and we responded to him as Christ would have responded. Listen to Jesus' heart at the beginning of His ministry as He read the scroll of the prophet Isaiah: "The Spirit of the Lord is upon Me, because He has anointed Me to preach good news to the poor. He has sent Me to proclaim freedom to the captives and recovery of sight to the blind, and to set free the oppressed, to proclaim the year of the Lord's favor" (Luke 4:18–19). Is the heart of the Lord obvious in you, especially among a lost world that is watching? Are there any around you who do not feel welcome, maybe because they really aren't welcome? Repent and return to Him!

God purposed that we would live our lives under the guidance and influence of Christ. We are to allow His presence to make a profound impact upon the daily and practical situations in our lives. When Paul said in Galatians 2:19–20, "I have been crucified with Christ; and I no longer live, but Christ lives in me," it was more than just a figure of speech. He literally allowed Christ to live in him and through him. Paul talked about having the mind of Christ in another passage:

> Make your own attitude [mind] that of Christ Jesus, who, existing in the form of God, did not consider equality with God as something to be used for His own advantage. Instead He emptied Himself by assuming the form of a slave, taking on the likeness of men. And when He had come as a man in His external form, He humbled Himself by becoming obedient to the point of death— even to death on a cross. For this reason God also highly exalted Him (Phil. 2:5–9a).

This was the mind and heart of Christ, lived out in His life. This is the mind and heart of Christ being lived out now in the life of His body, the church. Is your church aware of this? Are they (and you) responding to the Head, even Christ, as He expresses Himself in and through your church? What evidence is there to you and the world around you that your church, a living body of Christ, has His mind guiding you? From this passage ask:

1. Do you cling to your rights as a church and protect yourselves from those on the outside?

2. Are you seeking to have a reputation or are you making yourselves of "no reputation"? Are you willing to take upon yourselves the form of a servant like Jesus Christ as a church in your community?

3. Are you absolutely obedient to the Father's goals for His church, even at ultimate costs? Are you as a church willing to pay the price of obedience to Christ?

4. Is God, therefore, highly exalting and using your lives together as a church?

Prayer and the Word of God

Since each church is a living body of Christ, prayer and the Word of God will be preeminent in the life of the church as it was in the life of Jesus in the days of His flesh. One of the most obvious disciplines of Jesus' life was His prayer life. He constantly turned aside to pray. The writer of Hebrews described His prayer life as offering up "prayers and appeals, with loud cries and tears, to the One who was able to save Him from death, and He was heard because of His reverence" (Heb. 5:7). His entire life was a life of prayer—early in the morning, during the day, late in the evenings, and even at times all night long. Through prayer He would know the will and purpose of the Father in and through His life. He lived this way and urged His disciples "to pray always and not become discouraged [not quit]" (Luke 18:1). They, too, must know the Father's will for their lives. He also said, in very strong terms, "My [Father's] house will be a house of prayer" (Luke 19:46).

Since Christ is the Head of every church, every church ought to be known as a house of prayer. Every member of His body will marshal themselves to be a person of prayer, even as Jesus, the head of the body, was a person of deep prayer. Then their life together as a body will be a life of prayer, and their church will be known as a house of prayer. He will not be any different in us as a church than He was in the days of His flesh—a man of prayer. Through His prayer life He always knew the goals, purposes, plans, and activity of the Father. Out of His prayer life He knew the Father's will and obeyed. It will be the same in every church; the church that prays together as a body of Christ will both know and do the will of God.

You cannot read about the life of Christ and not be overwhelmed at the place of Scripture in His life. From the beginning to the end, you see Him quoting Scripture in doing the Father's will. The Gospels constantly read, "This He did that the Scriptures might be fulfilled." With Scripture He faced Satan's temptations, and with Scripture He faced the cross and knew the Father's eternal purposes in His life. Since this was true in His life, it will be true in the life of His people. Before He ascended to the Father, Jesus "interpreted for them [disciples] in all the Scriptures" (Luke 24:27). Then the life of the disciples in the early church in Jerusalem and their preaching was immersed in the Scripture concerning the purposes of God. This is seen throughout the Book of Acts and the rest of the New Testament. Peter used Scripture at Pentecost; Stephen used Scripture in his defense before the religious leaders; and Philip used Scripture in Samaria. This must be true of every church, especially in seeking to know God's goals for each church.

Jesus did not specifically address many things about church life, but if you want to know what He desired for the church, take a close look at the apostles. Jesus invested three and a half years teaching them to function within the kingdom of God. After the Resurrection, He stayed another forty days with the apostles in order to give them instructions concerning what they should do once He ascended back to the Father. We are not told everything He taught them in those days, but look at what they did after He left.

Let me show you at least one passage that highlights the spontaneous priorities of the apostles. In Acts 6, the church was feeling growing pains. They had begun with a large influx of new believers on the day of Pentecost, but it didn't stop. If we trace the growth through the early chapters of Acts, we find that by the time we reach Acts 4:4, the number of men came to be about five thousand. If each man had a wife and just two children, the church was running about twenty thousand people. Acts 6 begins with the phrase, "As the number of the disciples was multiplying, there arose a complaint." There was a problem with the Hellenistic widows being overlooked in the daily distribution of food. A legitimate problem arose, and it needed to be taken care of immediately. But notice the wisdom of the apostles. They led the church to appoint seven men to meet the need, and they continued to care for the most important things in the church. "We will devote ourselves to prayer and to the preaching ministry" (Acts 6:4).

What they were saying is simply this, "We must not neglect the place of prayer and the Word of God; it is our very life." In the terminology of today's churches, "We have a great church growth program going, and we don't want to get sidetracked!" If they were going to do anything, they were going to spend adequate time in prayer and God's Word. It was in both of these that they would know God's will for His people in the church. Peter and the other apostles were not the leaders of this church; Christ was the leader. They must maintain a relationship with Him in order to guide the people who were being added to the body.

If prayer and the Word of God were paramount in the life of Christ, if it was the priority of the apostles in the early church, it must be the focus of our churches today. We are not merely talking about Sunday school and Bible studies. We are suggesting that every decision in the life of the church must be immersed in prayer and the Word of God. The church staff, the deacons, and all the leaders must set the example before the church of the importance of seeking the face of God through prayer and the Word of God. All must come from the immediacy of God's direction in the life of the church. This is how Jesus lived in the center of the Father's will, and this is how He will direct His body, the church.

As in the church in Jerusalem, prayer and the ministry of the Word *must* characterize the pastor and the staff of every church. First, they themselves must develop an authentic and healthy time alone with God in His Word and in prayer. This should be a daily and disciplined time with God. At times it will lead to time away in personal and leadership

team retreats. These times need to be put on the calendar and protected. It is life to the church, as it was for Jesus and the apostles.

But just as important, the church itself must accept this pattern for
their leaders, encourage it, and protect it for their own health as a
church. It may be that they would provide an opportunity for their
pastor to take a trip to the Holy Land for personal enrichment. The
church needs to invest in helping their leaders be all that God wants
them to be. The church will greatly benefit from an investment in their
pastor and staff.

If Jesus was so careful in His time of prayer and the study of the
Scriptures, His presence in every believer will begin to draw us into
that same set of priorities. If God desires to "conform us" into the
image of His Son, be ready for every member of the church to take
seriously the role of prayer and the ministry of the Word for their lives
as well.

Love and Obedience

To become like Jesus, love and obedience must characterize our
lives and our churches. He not only lived out the example of such a
life; He also taught His disciples that love. If we don't obey Him, this
is an indication that we don't love Him. Jesus said in John 14:15, 21,
23, "If you love Me, you will keep My commandments. . . . The one
who has My commandments and keeps them is the one who loves Me.
And the one who loves Me will be loved by My Father. I also will love
him and will reveal Myself to him. . . . If anyone loves Me, he will
keep My word. My Father will love him, and We will come to him and
make Our home with him." Do you see the connection? Jesus certainly did. No matter what you claim about your love for Him, if you
truly love Christ, you *will* obey Him.

Loving and obeying God produce the blessings of an intimate relationship with Him. One of the most thought-provoking chapters on
the intimate relationship between believers and their Lord is John 15.
In that great passage on the vine and the branches, He brought love
and obedience together again. He said, "If you keep My command-

ments you will remain in My love, just as I have kept My Father's commandments and remain in His love. I have spoken these things to you so that My joy may be in you and your joy may be complete" (John 15:10–11).

> *From then on Jesus began to point out to His disciples that He must go to Jerusalem and suffer many things from the elders, chief priests, and scribes, be killed, and be raised the third day.*
>
> MATTHEW 16:21

Nothing in the life of a church will bring greater joy than love and obedience. In pure love to our Lord and in clear and simple obedience, we saw God not only add new believers to our church, but we also saw God add a greater dimension of joy. I was surprised to see so many college and university students being saved, added to our church, and reaching out to their friends. Soon our church had the largest and best-known ministry on the university campus. As a steady stream of new students came, joy filled the church. These students were full of life, and their newfound love for God was contagious. I am convinced that every church that walks in obedience to Him will soon find the joy of their salvation in abundance.

Thus the life and teaching of Jesus in the days of His flesh will be lived out in the life of each church today. The greatest challenge of a pastor and a church is faithfully and thoroughly to develop and sustain the intimate love relationship with Christ. Out of that love relationship will flow all the other relationships in our lives. This is far more than the initial call to salvation; it is a daily, lifelong pursuit. Each member who walks with the Lord in this way will be encouraging, teaching, and being "concerned about one another in order to promote love and good works" (Heb. 10:24).

I so often hear pastors and other leaders say, "But how do we do this?" Unfortunately, we constantly look for a program or a method, something successful that we can use in our situation. My answer is usually, "Just learn to love! Love God, and love His people." This ought to be the most natural instinct of a Christian—to love God and His people with all one's heart.

Yesterday I encountered this simple response as I was riding with a religious leader. He said, "As you spoke and I watched you, I came under severe conviction of my sin." I inquired further about what God was doing in his life. He said, "You mentioned in your teaching about an Old Testament (New Testament too!) way of life: 'elders at the gate!' You said mature believers would sit at the gate of a city and be available to counsel and assist those in need. You urged us in our church not to hurry out after the worship service but to linger and become available for any who were hurting and in need of counsel and prayer. Then I watched you after you had spoken. You did not leave or even give the slightest impression you were in a hurry. People lined up to talk with you. You took time with each one who came. You looked into their eyes and showed them pure love. And with most you put your hand on them and prayed. I could also tell you were sharing Scriptures with them, and they responded with grateful hearts. I had to confess to the Lord that I always am in a hurry to leave after the service. And I was grieved that I did not linger at the gate to be of help to God's people. I will never hurry away again!"

Isn't it interesting that the natural response of a Christian has become unnatural? We have been so conditioned by the world that we hurry away to our own home and don't want to get involved in the lives of God's people. Love cannot hurry away; it is expressed in the time and energy we invest in one another. The greatest testimony of a loving church is how fast the building empties after the service has concluded.

The Suffering Servant

Since the life of Jesus, revealed in God's Word, is to be our example and our goal, then we must receive *all* of its instruction. A church that is walking in fellowship with one another and with their Lord, seeking to obey the head of the body, will never be *out of character* with the Christ revealed in Scripture. No aspect of the life of Christ is resisted, even resented, any more than that of His suffering. God's people need a new theology of suffering if they want to represent Christ effectively in our day and follow Him fully.

The greatest testimony of a loving church is how fast the building empties after the service has concluded.

The Suffering Servant is a powerful image of Christ in both Old and New Testaments. We are familiar with the Old Testament passage of Isaiah 53:3 that describes Jesus as a "man of sorrows and [thoroughly] acquainted with grief." The entire chapter of Isaiah 53 ought to be studied by every Christian and by every church. Our suffering Savior is the same Savior who is now the Head of our churches. He will now guide us into a complete understanding of what it will cost us to do the will of the Father in redeeming our world. "This is how we have come to know love: He laid down His life for us. We should also lay down our lives for our brothers" (1 John 3:16).

Pop theology today refuses to acknowledge suffering as a key ingredient in God's salvation. But hear Jesus when He said, "If anyone wants to come with Me, he must deny himself, take up his cross, and follow Me. For whoever wants to save his life will lose it, but whoever loses his life because of Me will find it" (Matt. 16:24–25). If we are unwilling to deny self and pick up a cross, we cannot follow Jesus. The decision to make Christ Lord is also a decision to be His servant and to obey Him in all things. Before we ever chose to follow, He warned us that discipleship involved a cross—His cross to bring us salvation and our cross to share salvation with others.

Through suffering on a cross Jesus would set us free from sin and redeem all who would believe in Him. Through suffering our Lord brings salvation to a lost world, but now His suffering is through His people in the local church. The early church was hounded, put in prison, threatened, driven from place to place, and even killed as the

Lord took God's good news of salvation for all people through them. In so suffering God turned their world upside down. Our world will never come to Christ in our day unless the life of Christ is freely lived out through His people in the churches, and this will involve a measure of suffering and pain.

Sometimes, especially in the Western world today, God's people show great resentment when they are persecuted. It should be a mark of great pride that their Lord counted them worthy to suffer with Him. The Scripture says, "It is a clear evidence of God's righteous judgment that you will be counted worthy of God's kingdom, for which you also are suffering" (2 Thess. 1:5). Listen, God's goal for His people and His churches is Christlikeness, and this includes suffering, followed by the exaltation of God, who is honored through them.

This past century, I am told, has had more Christian martyrs than all the previous centuries from Jesus' day combined. Almost worldwide, Christians are suffering. So extensive is this suffering today that great appeals have been made to the governments of the free world to intervene. But we must remember that suffering is a part of what it means to be a Christian.

How may this be expressed in our day, and how should this affect our churches? First, new believers, especially children and youth, may receive great pain and rejection at home. A church must know how to prepare one another for the suffering and have a plan to care for them. I deliberately gave special care to a ten-year-old girl and her twelve-year-old brother who were being cared for by their grandmother. Their mother and father had been on drugs and could not care for them. Over the months the grandmother was grieved for her daughter and fearful for her grandchildren. Not only did Marilynn and I care, but we also tried to prepare all of them for what could happen if the two children were saved and baptized. This came to both of them, and we rejoiced together, but soon the mother demanded they be returned to her. We have not seen them since, but we have strongly ministered to and loved the grandmother. We continue to pray with her for the future of the children.

Opposition, pain, and even rejection can come into the workplace. Some may be bypassed for a promotion, even released in a sudden downsizing of the company. The church must not only watch this but also prepare the members for it and walk with them when it comes. People in our churches are going through a great deal of pain and suffering, but that is why God brought them to the church. In the presence of God and His people, there is peace.

A Story from Mel

I have had the opportunity to walk with many young adults as they were making major life decisions. As college students began to respond to God, it rearranged everything in their lives. One young man was gloriously saved but immediately put to the test. He had been in love with a girl for many years, hoping that someday he would marry her. They had known each other from school but were never more than friends. Wouldn't you know it, as soon as he became a Christian, the girl suddenly wanted to date him.

They began to date, but it immediately became apparent that he had a decision to make. He had chosen to follow Christ, but she did not want anything to do with it. They could not talk about God without getting into a big argument. She had grown up in a non-Christian religion, a cult that had deeply influenced her family. Although she had turned away from it, she could not think of a single relative who was not a member of the group.

The young man came into my office one day weeping his heart out. I have rarely seen a man so troubled. "I love her deeply, but I know I must put God first in my life," he said. As we talked through the decision, he knew he had no option but to end the relationship. The Scripture is clear, "Do not be mismatched with unbelievers. For what partnership is there between righteousness and lawlessness? Or what fellowship does light have with darkness?" (2 Cor. 6:14). So I encouraged him, "If God wants you to marry her, she will become a Christian. If He does not want you to marry her, His will is best, and

He has somebody even better for you." He agreed. He broke up with her.

The girl could not believe it. She was angry. She was more than angry, even thinking about burning down our church for influencing him in this way. But what she didn't realize is that God's Word was guiding him in the decision. The Holy Spirit was leading him to break up with her, and we were walking with him in the decision. After a couple of days, she began to ask, "What could cause him to make such a decision?" She knew how much he loved her, but now she realized that there was something more significant in his life. So she began to look into "this Christian thing." She started to read the Bible. She attended an occasional church service. She even came to talk with me in the pastor's office. And it wasn't long before she was saved, baptized, and the two were married in our church.

There are difficult times when people begin to follow Christ and obey His commands. Jesus said:

> Look, I'm sending you out like sheep among wolves. Therefore be as shrewd as serpents and harmless as doves. Because people will hand you over to sanhedrins and flog you in their synagogues, beware of them. You will even be brought before governors and kings because of Me, to bear witness to them and to the nations. . . . You will be hated by everybody because of My name. And the one who endures to the end will be delivered. . . . A disciple is not above his teacher, or a slave above his master (Matt. 10:16–18, 22, 24).

When we live like Christ, we may be treated like Christ. The darkness does not like the light, for it exposes evil deeds. And often the Christian who lives a life of righteousness will be accused of judging others for the way they live. We don't judge, but our lifestyle becomes so different to those around us that their sin appears magnified. The world will want us to be like them, in order to justify the lifestyle they have chosen. So it is no wonder that the world will persecute the Christian, for they did the same thing to our Lord.

The church is fighting a spiritual battle, and the battle will be fought in real-life situations. Can you see how much we need one another in times of suffering? Can you understand how vital the church is for every believer? How much we need to pray for one another? The apostle Paul, whom we consider a bold and courageous witness for the Lord, made this request of the church in Ephesus: "Pray also for me, that the message may be given to me when I open my mouth to make known with boldness the mystery of the gospel. For this I am an ambassador in chains. Pray that I might be bold enough in Him to speak as I should" (Eph. 6:19–20). I believe the reason Paul stood strong and bold had something to do with the churches that were praying for him. He needed the church!

When we live like Christ, we may be treated like Christ.

A church is not just a place where you can go to be comforted but also a place where you can give comfort and support for others who are hurting. Some have told me, "I don't need others' support." But let me ask you this, "Do others need your support?"

Study Questions for Reflection and Response

1. What is more important: what God desires to do through your church or what your church plans to do for God?
2. How can a church have the "mind of Christ"?
3. How important is it for the church to be a "house of prayer"?
4. Can an individual or a church truly love God without obedience?
5. What role does suffering have in God's great salvation?

By obedience to the truth, having purified yourselves for sincere love of the brothers, love one another earnestly from a pure heart, since you have been born again—not of perishable seed but of imperishable—through the living and enduring word of God.

1 PETER 1:22–23

FIVE

The Son Accomplishes

Experiencing God Together in Life

God places His people in a church in the most strategic areas to demonstrate His presence and power to a watching world. The first church I pastored in California was in a rough city in the greater San Francisco area. It seemed as though I knew someone involved with almost every major crime, before or after the incident. I was in and out of almost every prison, including San Quentin and death row. God had strategically placed His people in that area to say to a hurting community, "I love you."

We had heard that a new youth gang had been formed called The Untouchables. Many were from a low-rent district where some of our church members lived. They soon gained an awful reputation and began to terrorize that area. One Sunday evening twenty-five of the gang members walked noisily into our service, folded their arms, and leaned their metal chairs back against the rear wall of the auditorium. Little did they know that I grew up familiar with gang warfare, and their grand entrance did not bother me a bit. Not only was I not afraid of them, but I cried out inside, "Got you! You will now hear from God!" God began to work in their lives, and within six months twenty-three of the twenty-five had been saved. Our church rejoiced that God was doing a great work through our lives to touch the community in which we lived.

Later I was invited to a law enforcement banquet. During the program that evening, an officer who worked with young offenders had me stand. He said, "An area of our city used to have the highest calls of crime. Now it has the lowest. This young man (I was twenty-six at the time) and his church have made the difference." In reality, it wasn't the church or me; it was Christ working through our church to impact the community.

God desires to build a church and shape it for His purposes in order that Christ might have a body through whom He can make a difference in communities across our land. The saving presence of Christ will then be manifest through the church that is willing to be used of God. The key is Christ in us, for He will always fulfill the purposes of His Father. And the Father desires to touch the world and bring them into a relationship with Himself.

Christ Is the Head

The greatest truth a church must understand, if it wants to be of any use to God, is that Christ is the Head of the church. It is one thing to believe it theologically; it is quite another to live it practically. What does it mean, and how does a church function under His headship? I pray, as did the apostle Paul, "that the eyes of your heart may be enlightened, so you may know what is the hope of His calling" (Eph. 1:18) toward the church. For when we follow Christ as the Head of our churches, we will be overwhelmed at what He will accomplish through us.

A Story from Mel

While serving in my first church, I had many unusual experiences. Being a small west Texas town, it seemed as though everybody was involved in everything, doing their parts to help in the community. I didn't realize, however, that being called as the pastor of the only Baptist church in town meant that you were automatically drafted into the volunteer fire department. Apparently all the men in town had real jobs to attend to during the day, and the pastor and the retired men had plenty of time to fight fires. I did my part to chase grass fires and help in any way I was needed.

The other part to living in a small town that I found interesting was how intense the rivalry was between the towns in the area. I had one deacon who was seventy-five years old and still lived on the same property on which he was born. In other words, the rivalries had a long-standing history and ran deep. I was drawn into the rivalry because the volunteer fire departments often competed against one another—not just in sporting events but also in getting better equipment, doing better training, and having a reputation for effectively doing their job.

One day it just so happened that the guys in the town down the road were having an elaborate training exercise. They were to go out into the country to an abandoned home and practice putting out a house fire. The house was set on fire, and the blaze was spectacular. They followed procedure to the letter and put the fire out with great efficiency. Everything went great! Except for one minor detail; it was the wrong house! As you could well imagine, we tried our best not to harass them in their hour of great humiliation, but we failed!

Somehow they misunderstood the details of the assignment. They had the wrong directions. The people in charge of the training exercise had failed to communicate clearly the job to be done. They did a great job, just the wrong job.

Churches are in danger of doing a great job but the wrong job. We may be enthusiastic, creative, and effective in what we do, but we had better know what the heavenly Father wants us to do. Jesus has told us that the Father is not impressed with doing good things well; He is only looking for obedience to His will (Matt. 7:21–23). The only way we will know what the Father wants us to do as a church is consistently listen to His Son, who is the Head of our church. In fact, unless Christ directs us, we will never know the will of the Father. Consequently, we may be burning down the neighbor's house!

The fullest description of what God did in making the local church a living body of Christ, is found in 1 Corinthians 12; Romans 12:3–21; and Ephesians 4:1–16. Christ is described as the head of the body. The head controls, directs, instructs, guides, motivates, and keeps the body functioning according to His purposes. Listen to how Paul describes the body to the Ephesian church.

> But speaking the truth in love, let us grow in every way into Him who is the Head—Christ. From Him the whole body, fitted and knit together by every supporting ligament, promotes the growth of the body for building up itself in love by the proper working of each individual part (Eph. 4:15–16).

Paul instructs the Corinthian Christians with the following description of the church: "But . . . God has put the body together, . . . that there would be no division in the body, but that the members would have the same concern for each other" (1 Cor. 12:24–25).

When members are faithfully related to Christ, the Head, His life flows to them and through them to the rest of the body. When members function where God placed them in the body (1 Cor. 12:18), the body edifies itself in love. But the key to a healthy body is Christ and our relationship to Him. For Christ, the Head, determines everything in the body. When every member is responsive to the Head, Christ has a new body through whom He can obediently carry out the will of the Father in our day.

He is also the head of the body, the church.

COLOSSIANS 1:18

While Jesus was in the flesh, He always knew the will of His Father. He never misunderstood the Father, for the Holy Spirit was directing His life. And once He knew the will of the Father, He was always quick to obey His Father (John 4:24; 5:30; 6:38; 8:29). We need to have a firm grasp on how Jesus functioned while on earth in the first century, for He will function in the same way in the church today.

The key is Christ in us, for He will always fulfill the purposes of His Father.

Now look carefully at Mark 16:19–20: "The Lord Jesus was taken up into heaven and sat down at the right hand of God. And they went out and preached everywhere, the Lord working with them and confirming the word by the accompanying signs." This Scripture says that the Lord was taken up, the disciples went out, and the Lord worked with them. How could that be? How could Jesus be with them after He had gone back to the Father? Jesus came back in a whole new way. He was never going to leave them or forsake them.

The same Jesus who always knew the will of the Father and always obeyed the Father now has a new body through which to work. The Father fashions together a church with Christ as the Head and each believer as a part of the body. Now the living Christ will lead the rest of the body to fulfill completely the purposes of God. When a church is completely yielded to Christ, there will be no limit to what God will do through that church. Paul said it this way, "'He [God] put everything under His [Christ's] feet' and appointed Him as head over everything for the church, which is His body, the fullness of the One who fills all things in every way" (Eph. 1:22–23).

Christ is the Head of each congregation, present and actively working to do the will of His Father. Everything the Father accomplished in His great salvation has been given to Christ. Everything that sin has done, God fully defeated and placed under Jesus' feet. All things are fully under Jesus' sovereign control. In His letter to the church in

Colossae, Paul affirmed this: "He erased the certificate of debt [caused by sin], with its obligations, that was against us and opposed to us, and has taken it out of the way by nailing it to the cross. He disarmed the rulers and authorities and disgraced them publicly" (Col. 2:14–15).

The same Jesus who always knew the will of the Father and always obeyed the Father now has a new body through which to work.

God's absolute victory in the cross was given to Jesus, and God "'put everything under His feet' and appointed Him as head over everything for the church, which is His body, the fullness of the One who fills all things in every way" (Eph. 1:22–23). Christ is the Head, and we are the body. The Head now directs the body, instructs the body, and motivates the body according to the sovereign will of the Father. Let me clearly say it again; while Jesus ministered on earth:

1. He never failed to hear the will of the Father.
2. He never failed to understand the will of the Father.
3. He never failed to do the will of the Father.

As a result, the Father could perfectly accomplish His will through Jesus during His life on earth. Now Jesus again is doing the will of His Father through the local churches. Do you believe this? Would you learn to respond personally as the Head instructs you in your place in the body and learn to respond together as a corporate body in the life of your church? As you know that the Head will always be faithful to the Father, will you then be faithful to the Head?

The Body Is Connected to the Head

A Story from Mel

I pastored a church in British Columbia, Canada, a place filled with beautiful mountain ranges, trees, and rivers. A member of our church worked for the federal government in the area of water conservation and flood control. One day George asked me if I wanted to go with him to check the readings at one of their remote stations. This was the middle of winter, and heavy snow had already arrived. So we loaded up the gear, drove as far as we could go in the truck, and unloaded the two snowmobiles to go the rest of the distance, another forty-five-minute ride.

It was a cold January day, but we were prepared. George took off on his machine, and I followed on mine. Now George is not your average man. He had spent most of his career working in harsh, Canadian weather. He had numerous stories of hunting expeditions, and he spent a great deal of time in the backwoods of the mountains. On the drive out there, he laughed as he told me of a dangerous encounter he had with a bear and many other stories that caused me to question whether I ought to be there. Remember, I am a preacher! Whereas he may have animal heads on his wall, I have educational diplomas hanging on mine.

We were ready. George hit the gas and aggressively raced off into the woods. Still getting used to the snowmobile, I launched out with caution, trying to get the feel of the machine I was riding. I quickly realized that George was leaving me. That, however, was not what caused me the most concern. I saw that some other snowmobiles had been in the area, and there seemed to be a thousand trails going every direction through the woods. The thought crossed my mind, If I lose George, I will never be seen again! I will never find my way back to civilization! So I hit the gas, lowered my head to get more streamlined, leaned into every corner, and kept my eyes firmly fixed on the man I needed to follow. If I were going to die on that day, it would not be from getting lost—though hitting a tree was a very real possibility.

Do you see the lesson God taught me? Many roads lead through life. Others have left trails that lead away from the destination God has for me. As a pastor, I must keep my eyes firmly fixed on Jesus, or I will be hopelessly lost. I must help others see Him and encourage the church to follow Jesus with their whole heart. Unless our church sees the Lord and is determined to follow Him, we will neither reach the destination He has for us nor fulfill His purpose for our lives.

Jesus turned to His disciples and said to them, "If anyone wants to come with Me, he must deny himself, take up his cross, and follow Me" (Matt. 16:24). Being a Christian is to be a follower of Christ. Being a church is nothing less than being a follower of Christ. So how does that look? How do we follow Christ as the Head of our church without getting sidetracked by distractions?

One of the most beautiful and practical Scriptures describing how the body (members in a church) relates to the Head is Ephesians 4:7, 11–13.

> Now grace was given to each one of us according to the measure of the Messiah's gift. . . . And He personally gave some to be apostles, some prophets, some evangelists, some pastors and teachers, for the training of the saints in the work of ministry, to build up the body of Christ, until we all reach unity in the faith and in the knowledge of God's Son, growing into a mature man with a stature measured by Christ's fullness.

The body is composed of people who have been called out of the world and gathered together by God Himself. Through the body the Son of God works to complete everything the Father asks Him to do. As in the days of His flesh, so now through each local church, God's will is done. It is crucial, therefore, that the members of the body are connected to and following Christ as Lord of their lives and Head of their church.

Let us lay aside every weight and the sin that so easily ensnares us, and run with endurance the race that lies before us, keeping our eyes on Jesus, the source and perfecter of our faith.

HEBREWS 12:1–2

Each member is directly related to the Head by God's great salvation. They are disciples of Christ. He is their Master. He teaches them about their new relationship with the heavenly Father and His eternal purposes that are being worked out in the world around them. Their Lord instructs them about their life in the body and how they fit into those greater purposes of the Father. He fills them with His love in order that they might share His love with every other member in the body. He gives them everything they need to edify and build up the body. He is the life of each believer and the life of the body.

Individual Christians, therefore, cannot participate effectively in the life of the church unless they are participating in a deeply personal relationship with Christ. There are no substitutes for our own walk with Him. As important as it is to be fed by good biblical preaching and teaching, they are not adequate by themselves if you want to "do your part" in the body (Eph. 4:15–16). We cannot be satisfied with others telling us about a relationship with God; we must have a relationship with Him on our own. For our relationship to God does not come through the church; it comes directly from a personal encounter with Him. The writer of Hebrews said, "Since we have boldness to enter the sanctuary [holy place] through the blood of Jesus, . . . let us draw near with a true heart in full assurance of faith" (Heb. 10:19, 22). As Christians, we have the ability to draw near to God and enter into the holy place. We have access to God's presence and fellowship with Him. We can make His presence our dwelling place, enjoying all the benefits of such a relationship and learning directly from Him.

To enter the holy place is a call to come out from the world and into the presence of God. It is a call to stop wandering around and to enter into the promised land of God's blessing. It is a call to all lukewarm, halfhearted Christians to stop lingering in the outer court of the temple, the fringes of religious life, and enter into the heart of the Christian faith. It is a call to all doubting and thirsting believers who long for a better life to cast aside their doubts and to believe that Christ will bring abundant life. To enter the holy place is a call to dwell in the full light of God's countenance. And when you do, God pours into your life the blessings of heaven, filling you with His Spirit and allowing you to walk with Him.

The relationship to God is for more than just enjoying life with Him. God has a much greater purpose in mind. His work in your life enables you to build up other believers and equips you to function in the body where He placed you. To come *out of* the world is to be *into* the people of God. To stop wandering around is to find purpose within the will of God. To come from the fringes of religious life into the heart of the Christian faith is to be in the middle of God's activity. To live in the full light of His countenance is to live your life with meaning and significance. God designed the church for such a life.

It is, therefore, of the utmost importance that each member function in the body where God has placed him or her. Then, relating to one another in love, the entire body responds to Christ, the Head, with one heart and one mind. When the early church in Jerusalem functioned this way, the Word of God was spread with boldness and "believers were added to the Lord in increasing numbers—crowds of both men and women" (Acts 5:14; see also Acts 6:7 and ultimately Acts 9:31).

Every member is responsible for every other member. The deepest desire of every member should be first his or her relationship with Christ and second the maturity of every other member of the body where God has placed the believer. You ought to seek to know how Christ will bring others to maturity through you. It may be by encouraging, teaching, helping, exhorting, giving, or ministering. God's goal through you is for every member of the church to be greatly blessed through His life in you.

The Body Is Shaped for His Mission

Paul assured the church in Corinth that "God has placed the parts, each one of them, in the body just as He wanted" (1 Cor. 12:18). He was describing how God shaped each local church according to His purposes for them. Each church in the New Testament was unique in its makeup and its purpose, for God put each of them together as it pleased Him. This is seen as we read Revelation 2–3, where the churches are described with their uniqueness of makeup, location, and assignment. The Lord knew them better than they knew themselves and was present to guide them according to His purposes.

I have often thought of each church being unique, according to God's assignment, in the light of sports. A person trains his body to match his assignment. A sprinter trains his body differently than does a power lifter. Their bodies look and function differently because their bodies are asked to perform two completely different tasks. Even in football an offensive lineman trains differently from a wide receiver. Although they are working together to win the game, one trains for power and strength while the other trains for speed and agility. Each trains his body for maximum efficiency in his assignment. The goal for all the team is to win the game. But each must be equipped and function in his position assigned to him by the coach. Even so God has the assignment for each church. So He adds members who help the body fulfill its assignment and places each member in the body by His design for maximum efficiency. Each member is vital to the body. There are no unnecessary members. Each one has a special place in the body to help the entire body function at its greatest ability.

As you see that God is adding to the body where you are a member, it gives added significance to your life. You begin to see a new assignment being given by God, simply because He chose to add another to your body. The new members may give an indicator to the rest of the body of what God is seeking to do through them. When God began to add college students to our church, we realized several things:

1. God does not add members accidentally but as it pleases Him.
2. God was alerting us to His intentions, so we watched carefully to see what He was doing.
3. The church immediately noticed that God was calling many of the young adults that He had added into the ministry.

4. The church adjusted its activities to help them fulfill their call from God.

5. The church soon realized that God wanted them to establish a training center to equip those whom God was calling.

6. As the church made the adjustments and provided training, God began to bring people from many other places to come there to study.

7. We rejoiced as God's purpose for our church was accomplished, as the Head led us to do the will of the Father.

God had developed the body of believers to match His assignment for them. We saw our assignment taking on new dimensions by those whom He was adding to the church family. The ones being added were not only to help us fulfill our assignment already given, but they were to add to and clarify our assignment in greater detail. Many of those who were trained are now serving faithfully across the nation, fulfilling the purposes of God through their lives.

Paul instructed the church in Corinth that the whole body is not an "eye," for the body also needs the "ear" for hearing. It needs the "nose" to smell. It needs the "hand" to touch. One member of the body is not the whole body. Each part is important, but only as it is functioning along with the rest of the body parts. We are, in the church, interdependent. We need one another and are needed by one another. God shaped the church to function as a living organism that must work together in order to realize each member's potential.

A Story from Mel

I love sports, and when I was younger, I had the privilege of playing on some championship teams. Among the many sports I played, soccer was one of my favorites. Our team had a great coach and many talented players who worked together as a unit. Because of our success we had the opportunity to travel and play in some international tournaments.

On one occasion we played in an invitational tournament that brought many teams from across North America. The competition was fierce, and the athletes gave their all in order to win. We were doing well, and the competitive spirit in me was driving me to do anything to win. Unfortunately, as I stretched to make a play, another player kicked me in the back of the leg with all of his force. Immediately I felt my calf muscle tighten and pain surge through my body. My initial reaction was to crumble and attend the injury, but my desire to win would not let me stop. I reasoned that I needed to keep the muscle stretched and not let it cramp up on me. So I limped on into battle, unwilling to take myself out of the game.

The injury became apparent to everybody, especially my coach. I was not making plays I would normally make. I did not have the speed that I once had. I did not have the concentration I needed, for my mind was distracted by the pain. And even though I was determined to play through the injury, my coach, who was determined to win, decided that I was more of a detriment than a benefit to the cause. I was pulled off the field.

When one part of the body is not functioning as it should, the rest of the body cannot perform to its potential. As much as the rest of the body wanted to play, it was hindered because of one part that was injured. The same is true in a church. The church body may be determined to limp forward, but it will be ineffective in doing the will of the Father unless it helps all the members to function where God has placed them. No matter how badly a church wants to go forward and

---

Now we who are strong have an obligation to bear the weaknesses of those without strength, and not to please ourselves.

ROMANS 15:1

do the purposes of God, if it doesn't take care of all its members, it will be severely hindered. We must also be aware that the Father has the right to remove us from our position in the spiritual battles we are fighting, if we are not doing what He called us to do. Can you see the Lord as he walks through the churches in the Book of Revelation? He is looking to see if we are doing what He asked us to do. If we are not able to fulfill our purpose, He calls us to repent and return to Him. Unless He brings healing and wholeness to our lives, we are of little use to Him. That is why we must take special care of one another. That is why the health of the body is so crucial. The purposes of God are at stake.

God shaped the church to function as a living organism that must work together in order to realize each member's potential.

Not only does God fashion the body, but He also equips all members of the body to function effectively where He placed them. This He does by the Holy Spirit, which "is given to each person to produce what is beneficial" (1 Cor. 12:7). This role of the Holy Spirit is the power of each member and the life of each church. We will see this more clearly in the next chapter.

The Body Must Respond to the Head

As God begins to work through His Son to accomplish His purposes, the church and its response to their Lord is vital. Each church must respond immediately to what He is doing. He knows what He is doing! He has a plan to fulfill His purposes. He has the power to complete His purposes. He just needs people who love Him and who will respond to His leading and let Him carry out His purposes through them.

Since God adds to the body as it pleases Him, the first thing the church must respond to is the people whom He sends and adds to them. They must receive people with utmost care and sensitivity, knowing that they are a part of God's purposes for the church. Jesus said, "The one who receives whomever I send receives Me, and the one who receives Me receives Him who sent Me" (John 13:20). A church's response is most significant, therefore, to God. As a pastor, I always watched carefully to see who united with our church. God was often alerting us to a particular assignment He had for us. He was literally fashioning our church for His assignment.

He added a wonderful couple to one of the churches I pastored, who had a teenage son in prison. This was a first for us. But I alerted the church to God's activity when the couple joined fellowship with us. Sure enough, it wasn't long before we as a church saw one of our ministries was to the youth prison in our city and later to the adult prisons. Further, God began to add university students. We saw this as God fashioning our church to reach out to college students. Over the next few years we baptized scores of young adults into our fellowship. Over the twelve years of ministry in this church, God "added to the church" many people. For each one who came, we continued to look to the Father and ask what He had in mind when He sent them to us. As best we knew, we tried to be good stewards of each person God sent. Why? Because God sent them and was fashioning our church for His purposes. We didn't have an option! As the body of Christ, we must respond to the Head.

A second part of our response to God's adding a member was the way we received those He sent. We tried to receive new members by a solemn, covenanting process that publicly acknowledged we had responded to what God had just done to us and to them. We spent time teaching the church what it meant to respond to God in this manner. We taught them the meaning of a covenant in the heart of God and how that effected our relationship with one another. We gave careful exposition of Scripture (especially Matt. 16:13–27) and traced how the early church in Jerusalem lived out its relationship with Christ in the Book of Acts. We helped them see how a church responded to Christ by studying Romans 12, 1 Corinthians 12, and Ephesians 4. We helped them see how Christ was present and personal in His relationship with us as described in Revelation 1–3.

The church had to see the heart and purposes of God as revealed in Scripture. That allowed us to respond adequately as God worked in our church. So much was at stake for us and for the kingdom of God. Those who joined were also challenged to let God work through them to help the body become all that God desired for it to be. The rest of the church pledged to walk alongside the new person whom God had added, helping him or her to fulfill all that God desired for their lives, and challenging them to minister to the body to which God had just added them. This had a significant effect on them and on our church family.

This watch care of the members included the children and the youth as well. To neglect them was to leave them disoriented to God's great salvation offered to their lives. Again, love is the key. Since we loved our Lord, we loved each one He gave to us. A church will be entrusted with more if we are faithful to care for the ones He has already given us. In fact, church growth is in the hands of Christ, and He bases it on the response of the members to the Father's activity in their midst. After all, each one who comes is choosing to become a disciple of Christ.

Could we boldly ask you, How do you personally receive those God adds to your church? How does your church receive those God adds to you? Do you make adjustments in how you respond to God's "assignments" through those He adds as He shapes your church? Are you seeking to see that each one is bonded to Christ and following Him as a faithful disciple?

Too often all we do is encourage them to be faithful in attendance to all the church's activities. We push them to give faithfully and be a soul winner. This may be a natural by-product of being a disciple of

> *"His master said to him, 'Well done, good and faithful slave! You were faithful over a few things; I will put you in charge of many things. Enter your master's joy!'"*
>
> MATTHEW 25:21

Jesus, but it is *not* what Jesus meant by "make disciples." The heart of making disciples is really seen in the final part of the Great Commission, "Teaching them to observe everything I have commanded you" (Matt. 28:20). That is, help believers to practice the commands of Christ until it has become a spontaneous and authentic lifestyle. This is exactly what the apostles did in the early church. Read carefully what they did with the new believers that God added to their number in Acts 2:4–47. But notice carefully, it was the apostles, the leaders, who ensured that every believer knew and lived out what it meant to be a disciple of Jesus.

Leaders in the Body

Since Christ is the Head of every church, what place does the pastor have? He is not the Head; that position is already occupied. And Christ is not just a "figurehead." He is present and active in His body as the people live together and function as a church. He is present and active in His body as He seeks to guide His people to do the Father's will. Believe it or not, He really does desire to direct and guide His body. He really does speak to His people to guide them into His ways.

The pastor, then, is an undershepherd who obeys Christ as the Shepherd and Head of His own people. The pastor ensures that every member is not only fully connected to the Head but that each one is growing toward Christlikeness. He will enlist every member to function in the body where the Father has placed them. He will then encourage members to live their lives to their maximum potential in Christ. He will be a spiritual catalyst in the body for Christlikeness. What a joyful assignment the pastor has been given! His role is not to get everyone to follow him; his role is to help the members of the church to follow Christ as their Lord.

He is also the head of the body, the church.

COLOSSIANS 1:18

So how would the church follow Christ and know when He is speaking to them and guiding them to do the Father's will? How would they recognize His leadership among them? How does Christ, the Head, communicate with each member of His body, and how does He unite them into one heart and mind to follow His leadership? These are not only proper questions; they are practical questions. When pursued, they can guide a church to live together under Christ their Lord.

The answers to these questions begin with the leaders. When God adds a particular pastor to a church, does He specifically place him in that body? If we take our answers and guidance from the culture around us, we may see the pastor as a "religious chief executive officer," leading a religious organization. But a church is not merely a religious organization (though it is highly organized as a body). It is a living body of Christ—a living organism. God adds a pastor to help His people be all *He* has purposed for them to be! Knowing the condition of His people, He will add a pastor uniquely qualified in his relationship to Christ to take His people from where they are to where God wants them to be.

If God's people are greatly discouraged and brokenhearted, He may bring a Barnabas to encourage and strengthen them. If they are spiritually sick, He may bring a spiritual physician to bring healing into their midst and to deal with the sin that has caused such trouble. If His people are mature and ready to go on mission with Him, He may bring a pastor with a great missionary heart. If a church is greatly broken and divided, He may bring a pastor with a shepherd's heart— who is patient, kind, long-suffering, gentle, and has a strong gift of reconciliation. If a church has been thoroughly discipled and is growing in Christ, God may bring a pastor with a heart for evangelism to help the people bear witness to the Christ they have come to know. If the church has been immersed in evangelism for many years and has many people hungering to be fed the Word of God and discipled to grow toward Christlikeness, He may bring a pastor with a great heart for teaching and discipling.

The pastor must be a servant of God and submissive to the Head. The church is not his church; it is Christ's church. God Himself has been shaping the church for His purposes before he got there to be the pastor. The pastor, therefore, must be preeminently a man given to prayer and the ministry of the Word (Acts 6:4). He must take the people to Christ through prayer and the ministry of the Word. God's people must not only know about Christ; they must also be experientially connected to Him. Like a branch and the vine, the people must be attached to Christ. Like the sheep to their shepherd, the people must know and follow their Lord. Like the body to the head, they must function together. This is the great task of the pastor, helping the people walk in a vital union with the Lord.

The apostle Paul talked about the mystery of "Christ in you." Pastors must then say as Paul did: "We proclaim Him, warning and teaching everyone with all wisdom, so that we may present everyone mature in Christ. I labor for this, striving with His strength that works powerfully in me" (Col. 1:28–29).

To do this, every pastor must himself be passionately striving toward this goal for his own life—to be mature in Christ. This does not come through college courses or a seminary degree but by a constant personal relationship with his Lord. To this end the pastor must have developed a shepherd's heart for God's people. He is not merely to have an administrator's mind for a large organization. The command given to him by the Lord is still "make disciples . . . baptizing them . . . teaching them to observe everything I have commanded you" (Matt. 28:19–20). And the Lord's promise is that He will be with them to help carry out the command, even to the end of the age.

One of the gravest dangers in God's churches today is the real danger of a pastor's becoming merely an administrator of an organization. This is not his primary role as defined and given by Jesus. Even if he is greatly gifted in this area, he must strenuously resist this temptation or even the demands of the people. Usually a pastor, or shepherd, is the only one the people have to lead them. Others can do the administration, but only the pastor can be the pastor. Most people want, and certainly need, a genuine pastor. And there is no substitute if God has assigned you to this special place of service. I talked with a pastor who had just moved from a smaller church to a church that runs over twenty-five hundred in attendance. In making the adjustment, the Lord gave Him some clear directions in the priorities of His ministry. He said, "I have had to ask myself, what are the things that only the pastor can do? I must do them well. What are the things I am doing that others could do? I must let others do them." He was right! Pastor, you must be the pastor!

Likewise, the other leaders in a church (staff, deacons or elders, teachers, administrators, musicians, etc.) are primarily to help God's people grow to Christlikeness. Or as Paul said, God gifted the leaders "for the training of the saints in the work of ministry, to build up the body of Christ, until we all reach unity in the faith and in the knowledge of God's Son, growing into a mature man with a stature measured by Christ's fullness" (Eph. 4:12–13).

This is every leader's first and primary responsibility. It is not merely setting goals and efficiently organizing and running activities for church growth. God will "add to the body" (i.e., take care of church growth). That is what Christ promised to His disciples from the beginning: "I will build My church" (Matt. 16:18).

Because I knew that every leader, in whatever place of responsibility, was first assigned to edify, I would have an instruction time at the beginning of each church year for our church leaders. I would remind them *not* to put their work or ministry assignment first. Their primary assignment was to assist each member under their care toward Christlikeness. As leaders, they were to work together to make sure this was accomplished. For example, though the finance committee handled the financial matters of the church, or the missions committee

Whenever you come together . . . all things must be done for edification.
1 CORINTHIANS 14:26

was to guide the church to be on mission with God, it was still the primary task of each leader to help each member of their committee to grow toward Christlikeness as disciples of Him. It was in the context of their ministry assignment that their primary assignment of building up the body could happen. If they were faithful to the primary assignment, they would get their work done.

Every leader is to use everything God has placed within him or her to edify the members of the body. He is to take his place in the body for the purposes of building up the body. This is clearly established in Romans 12:8–21 and 1 Corinthians 12–14. These passages should be studied regularly among the leaders of God's people. In many ways these passages are a spiritual plumb line and a standard by which the leaders in a church must function.

Study Questions for Reflection and Response

1. Is Christ truly the Head in every church, or is He merely a figurehead?

2. If Christ is the Head of the church, would anybody know by the way we make decisions?

3. How important is unity in the body as it follows Christ the Head?

4. What role do leaders play in ensuring unity in the church family?

5. How important is it that the members are healthy in order for the whole body to respond to Christ as the Head?

6. How does God shape your church for His purpose?

While He [Jesus] was together with them, He commanded them not to leave Jerusalem, but to wait for the Father's promise. "This," He said, "is what you heard from Me; for John baptized with water, but you will be baptized with the Holy Spirit not many days from now. . . . But you will receive power when the Holy Spirit has come upon you, and you will be My witnesses in Jerusalem, in all Judea and Samaria, and to the ends of the earth."

ACTS 1:4–5, 8

SIX

The Spirit Empowers

Experiencing God Together in Life

A Story from Mel

I pastored in a small town in west Texas. While leading a group in my home through a Bible study, I had the men and women break into two groups to pray. My wife led the women, and I led the men. During the prayer time we began to pray for several young couples in the community that needed to respond to Christ. Many of their parents were leaders in the church, but the children had strayed and were a great burden upon the hearts of our people.

As we cried out to God on their behalf, the Holy Spirit guided me in a way He had never done before. I sensed that He wanted us to drive to where we could see their homes and pray for God to bless their families. I told the guys what I sensed we needed to do, not knowing what they would think of such a strange idea. They agreed that it sounded strange, but I was their pastor, and they decided to go with me. All of the couples lived outside of town on either a large ranch or on acreage off by themselves. By the time we had been to three houses, it was after 10:30 at night, and we had two more to go.

As we approached the next house, we did so with much caution. The man who lived there was as tough as they come. He loved to fight. He would go to bars and fight just for the fun of it. He also was an avid hunter, killing almost anything that moved. This guy even hunted rattlesnakes, a sport this poor Canadian city boy thought was a bit over the edge. I had been in his home and was amazed at the arsenal of weapons that I saw. He had crossbows, knives, handguns, rifles, sawed-off shotguns, and hunting dogs to track down the game. But what he was known for around town was that he was a self-appointed vigilante. If there was trouble in town, he was glad to take care of it and run any troublemakers out of town. Needless to say, we parked the car a long way away and turned off the lights. As we looked toward his house across the railroad tracks, beyond a large field, and in the midst of some trees, we saw a single porch light in the darkness. Our hearts went out to the family as we prayed for God to work in their lives.

We finished praying and headed off to the last house. As we drove down the country road, I saw headlights in my rearview mirror approaching fast. Before long a big truck was tailgating us with its high beams on. We figured the person either wanted to pass us, or it was the man we had just prayed for trying to hunt us down and kill us! Either way we decided to pull over. Sure enough, the truck pulled in behind us.

I told the guys to pray for me, and I stepped out of the car. As I did, I heard the chamber of a gun load, saw the barrel of a shotgun protrude out of the truck window, and then noticed the low-pitched growl of a well-trained hunting dog. I had heard about spiritual warfare, but I was not prepared for this! So I quickly identified myself, and fortunately he recognized who I was. As I approached the truck,

I had the strange realization that I was in the hand of God, sent to be there by the Holy Spirit. When the man asked what I was doing, the Holy Spirit simply said, "Tell him!" So I did. I said, "We were not trying to cause trouble; we wanted to pray that God would bless you and your family." He didn't know what to say. He quickly changed the subject and told me of a man he ran out of town the week before.

We chatted for a minute, and the Holy Spirit said, "Tell him again!"

So I did. I said, "It is late, and I don't want to keep you. I hope you understand that we did not want to cause any trouble. We wanted to pray that God would bless you and your family." Again he didn't know what to say, so he said good-bye and sped off in a cloud of dust.

As I went back to the car, I noticed that all of the men were slouched down, trying to stay out of sight. But it didn't matter; I had already told the man who was in the car. So we decided that the Lord knew we would be caught, and we made a commitment to keep this night a secret and continue praying for God's will to be done. The next day everyone in town knew that some men from the church were out praying. But they knew we did not plan on being seen and were therefore sincerely concerned.

It wasn't long before God did do a tremendous work. The first family to respond belonged to the man who had caught us that night on the road. Within a month his wife was knocking at my door. As I opened it, she began to cry and say, "I need to get saved. Can you help me?" In the next few weeks, I would not only baptize her but also her husband and all three of their children.

God wanted to do a work in that family's life. So He prompted the Holy Spirit to get the attention of His people and invite them to be a part of His plan to reach them. God had it all worked out, and we had the privilege of being used by Him. Without the Holy Spirit working in our lives, speaking to us and guiding us to do the Father's will, we would have never seen that family respond to God. What a difference the Holy Spirit makes in the life of a church!

The Church as a Living Body

The Holy Spirit is God's essential gift to the church. He has been given to implement the Father's purposes in the church and empower the members to obey Christ, as He leads them on mission in the world. Jesus made two awesome statements to His disciples. Both reveal the fullest provisions God has made for His people when He saves them.

First Jesus announced: "I will ask the Father, and He will give you another Counselor to be with you forever. He is the Spirit of truth, whom the world is unable to receive because it doesn't see Him or know Him. But you do know Him, because He remains with you and will be in you. I will not leave you as orphans; I am coming to you" (John 14:16–18). In other words the Holy Spirit, who had been present in the life of Jesus during His ministry, would now be in them too! Jesus was not going to leave them helpless but would provide for them through the sending of the Holy Spirit.

The disciples heard John the Baptist bear witness of Jesus saying: "He whom God sent speaks God's words, since He gives the Spirit without measure. The Father loves the Son and has given all things into His hands" (John 3:34–35). More than the verbal testimony, they beheld the mighty acts of the Holy Spirit through Jesus' life. They had come to know the awesome power that accompanied Jesus as He did the will of His Father.

Peter expressed his witness to the place and work of the Holy Spirit in Jesus' life. He said to Cornelius and his household, "You know the events that took place throughout all Judea, beginning from Galilee after the baptism that John preached: how God anointed Jesus of Nazareth with the Holy Spirit and with power, and how He went about doing good and curing all who were under the tyranny of the Devil, because God was with Him" (Acts 10:37–38). Peter was not talking about something he heard; he walked with Jesus and saw the mighty power of the Holy Spirit in the many miracles that were performed.

The Holy Spirit, who was with Jesus, was now to be the life of God in the churches. Each church would have Christ as their Head and the Holy Spirit giving power to know and carry out the commands of Christ in our world. God's great salvation for His people includes these two major truths. Each church has the presence of His Son, Jesus Christ, as Head of the church. And each church has the presence of the Holy Spirit as His enabling power to work in and through the church.

Jesus assured each of His disciples:

"Don't you believe that I am in the Father and the Father is in Me? The words I speak to you I do not speak on My own. The Father who lives in Me does His works. Believe Me that I am in the Father and the Father is in Me. Otherwise, believe because of the works themselves.

"I assure you: The one who believes in Me will also do the works that I do. And he will do even greater works than these, because I am going to the Father. Whatever you ask in My name, I will do it, so that the Father may be glorified in the Son. If you ask Me anything in My name, I will do it" (John 14:10–14).

Further in this same passage Jesus then begins to describe the awesome presence of the Holy Spirit who is available to them. The Holy Spirit would be God's life in His people, the churches. He would teach them all things, bring to their remembrance all that He had said to them, guide them into all truth, and glorify Him in them. "But the Counselor, the Holy Spirit, whom the Father will send in My name, will teach you all things and remind you of everything I have told you" (John 14:26). "When the Spirit of truth comes, He will guide you into all truth. For He will not speak on His own, but He will speak whatever He hears. He will also declare to you what is to come. He will glorify Me, because He will take from what is Mine and declare it to you. Everything the Father has is Mine. This is why I told you that He takes from what is Mine and will declare it to you" (John 16:13–15).

The church, therefore, experiences a dynamic relationship between God and His people. God has a purpose for His people. This is why He has gathered them together into a congregation. He then places His Son as the Head of that church to accomplish His purposes through them. The Holy Spirit then empowers the people to fulfill all that the Lord leads them to do. The church is not just another organization, but it is a functioning body that is active and alive.

Life in the Body

With Christ as the Head of the body, the Holy Spirit is His life in the body. The best picture of the Holy Spirit as the Lord's life in the body is found in 1 Corinthians 12. The Scripture says that "no one can say, 'Jesus is Lord,' except by the Holy Spirit" (v. 3). We are told that "a manifestation of the Spirit is given to each person to produce what is beneficial [to the body]" (v. 7). "For we were all baptized by one Spirit into one body" (v. 13). "And we were all made to drink of one Spirit" (v. 13).

God composes the body as it pleases Him, and the Spirit enables every member to function where God has placed them to assist every other member of the body. God's provision, as a vital part of His salvation, is the Holy Spirit working in every member for the good of all. This is the key to a healthy body; everyone must understand that the Spirit was given for the building up of the entire body.

The life that is essential to each church is literally the life of the Spirit. Paul assured the church at Corinth that "a manifestation of the Spirit is given to each person to produce what is beneficial" (1 Cor. 12:7). He then gave one of the most thorough descriptions of church life given anywhere in the Scriptures. God places each member in the body; God gives the Holy Spirit to work in each member; God places Christ as the Head of the body to live through them to accomplish His Father's will; and Christ, as the Head, instructs each member to function in the body, seeking the well-being of every other member. Significantly, Paul makes clear that there are *no* unimportant members in a church (vv. 14ff). "God has put the body together, giving greater honor to the less honorable [in the eyes of others]" (v. 24). "So," said Paul, "the eye cannot say to the hand, 'I don't need you!' nor again the head to the feet, 'I don't need you!'" (v. 21). He adds, "On the contrary, all the more, those parts of the body that seem to be weaker are necessary" (v. 22).

This truth has tremendous implications for life in our churches today. No one, including the pastor or any other leader can, directly or indirectly, say in word or deed, "I don't need you!" Paul said emphatically, "The members would have the same concern for each other" (v. 25). To "lose" one member means that the entire body suffers, and life in the body (local church) is deeply affected. You can never say, "Our church is better off because they left," and then wash your hands of any responsibility to redeem them.

Life in the body is indispensable for Christ to fulfill the Father's purpose. If the Father adds a member, He has something in mind for him or her, and the new member is therefore important. If, however, a church merely becomes a "religious organization," using the methods and attitudes of the business world, individuals can be fired or let go in order for the church to be more efficient and to be able to reach its goals. This should never happen in a church, which is a living body of our Lord Jesus Christ! Paul, in Ephesians 5:25–27, 32 says, "Christ loved the church and gave Himself for her, to make her holy, cleansing her in the washing of water by the word. He did this to present the church to Himself in splendor, without spot or wrinkle or any such thing, but holy and blameless. . . . This mystery is profound, but I am talking about Christ and the church." What a statement! Each member is deeply loved by Christ, the Head. The Word of God is being used to bring members to health and life as they function with one another in the life of the body. This is so Christ can "present to Himself" a glorious church! This is indeed what Christ is now doing with your church. Do you treat church members as Christ is treating them? Or are you letting some go and feeling good about it?

Again, Paul insists that "God has put the body together, giving greater honor to the less honorable" (1 Cor. 12:24). If God is doing this, how then should we treat the "lesser" members? Let them go? Drive them off? God forbid that this would ever happen in the sight of God! Paul adds that God does this "that there would be no division in the body" (v. 25). Life in the body is precious to God. Life in the body is significant to Christ, the Head. Life in the body is given and maintained by the Holy Spirit. We are the recipients of this incredible life that can only be found in the local church. I have lived this out for thirty years as the pastor of several churches, and Mel has now pastored three churches. We both have experienced this to be true, and it is wonderful. When we sought to live as the Scripture has told us, every member was challenged to grow toward Christlikeness. God then did wonderful works through each of these churches, and we believe God was honored as a result. This can, and must, be true of every church in our day. Revival would come quickly if each church and each member in the churches lived out their lives as God designed and purposed.

Unity in the Body

Unity in the body is paramount in God's strategy to touch a world. God cannot use a church that is not unified, for unity allows the body to function together as God intended. It ensures that people are functioning where God has placed them. It is the visible evidence that the members of the body are all following Christ as the Head of the body. And only the Holy Spirit working in each member can bring such unity. It is impossible otherwise. Paul urged the Ephesian church:

> I, therefore, the prisoner in the Lord, urge you to walk worthy of the calling you have received, with all humility and gentleness, with patience, accepting one another in love, diligently keeping the unity of the Spirit with the peace that binds us. There is one body and one Spirit, just as you were called to one hope at your calling; one Lord, one faith, one baptism, one God and Father of all, who is above all and through all and in all. Now grace was given to

each one of us according to the measure of the Messiah's gift (Eph. 4:1–7).

Members of the church are to walk in a manner worthy of their calling. With all lowliness and gentleness, with long-suffering, they were to bear "with one another in love" (NIV). Each member of the body is significant as we strive together to keep the unity with the Spirit. This is God's great provision for every member, causing a dynamic interaction for the good of the body. For each one was enabled through the active working of the Holy Spirit in their lives.

> *Now the works of the flesh are obvious: sexual immorality, moral impurity, promiscuity, idolatry, sorcery, hatreds, strife, jealousy, outbursts of anger, selfish ambitions, dissentions, factions, envy, drunkenness, carousing, and anything similar . . . those who practice such things will not inherit the kingdom of God.*
>
> GALATIANS 5:19–21

And if all members were to walk in union and harmony with the Holy Spirit, they would not fulfill the lusts and work of the flesh, which will always destroy a church. When a person causes dissention in the church and has a divisive spirit, you can count on it, he or she is not walking in the power of the Holy Spirit. The Spirit, therefore, is the only way to achieve unity in the body, as God desires. Every member must be filled with the Spirit, as was Jesus. When that happens, the Holy Spirit will maintain the unity in the body. But they will need help to know what this means and how to experience what God has commanded. Each member is to help the other members, so that Christ is honored in their midst. Paul said, "Be filled with the Spirit: speaking to one another in psalms, hymns, and spiritual songs, singing and making music to the Lord in your heart, giving thanks always for everything to God the Father in the name of our Lord Jesus Christ, submitting to one another in the fear of Christ" (Eph. 5:18–21).

Being filled with the Spirit is the key to a unified body. Look at the contrast between the *works of the flesh* and the *fruit of the Spirit:* "But the fruit of the Spirit is love, joy, peace, patience, kindness, goodness, faith, gentleness, self-control. . . . Now those who belong to Christ Jesus have crucified the flesh with its passions and desires. If we live by the Spirit, we must also follow the Spirit" (Gal. 5:22–25). Here is the true source of unity in the body! When Christ is the Head, giving to each member *His life* through the presence of the Holy Spirit, there will be unity in the life of the church. Every member in every church must be careful to maintain this "unity" which the Holy Spirit creates (Eph. 4:3).

Let me share an opportunity to practice and strengthen such unity. Many times one of the members of a body has a burden too heavy for him or her to carry alone, and it is affecting the life of the church in an ever-increasing way. Or perhaps a member is "overtaken" or "caught" in sin. Galatians 6:1 says, "You who are spiritual should restore such a person with a gentle spirit, watching out for yourselves so you won't be tempted also." Burden bearing is a "law of Christ!" It is therefore not an option; it is a necessity in maintaining the unity in a body.

Think about your own physical body. If the leg is broken or the arm is severely bruised, then (1) the entire body feels the pain; (2) the rest of the body is hindered and limited in its activity; (3) the entire body must wait until that part of the body is healed and can resume its function in the body; (4) patience is required until the body is whole again. Other factors are involved, but can you see how this applies to a church family as a living body of our Lord? You cannot merely discard a member of the body because it is sick, wounded, or even broken! This is unthinkable! Rather, those who are strong or healthy in the Lord must come alongside the one who is struggling and share their health, until the weaker member is made whole. Then the unity of the body is restored, and the body can maintain its life again.

How sad it is to see churches hobbling along with members cut off and no one pursuing them with a heart of restoration. A body cannot lose a hand or foot and still function with maximum effectiveness.

When one of the members experiences a great loss because of a death or some other crisis, the life in the body is affected. If the body is healthy, the other members ought to come alongside this one, sharing faith, comfort, inner strength, finances, or other help until the member is through his or her pain. This show of love and care not only maintains the unity in the church, but it actually strengthens and enlarges it. The body is stronger after the crisis than before it occurred. This demonstration of love always has a tremendous effect on the watching world, and it can be used of God to draw them to Christ. For it is Christ Himself who has orchestrated such love.

Many times our church helped a member who was hurting during a death in his or her family, and we were given the opportunity to lead several other members of the family to Christ. The lost family members had never experienced such oneness and caring before; they were open now to hear the gospel. The "good news of God" now made sense to them as they saw it lived out in the church.

When a couple in the church was struggling in their marriage and it appeared they could be headed toward divorce, I would begin to marshal the entire church family to help. The women would walk carefully and thoughtfully with the wife; the men would gather around with counsel and strengthen the husband. If needed, the Sunday school teachers would walk carefully with the children or youth involved until healing came to this marriage, and health was restored. In thirty years of pastoring, I only saw one divorce in my ministry where I pastored and helped the church members to care for one another.

Unity was thus maintained in the churches, health came to the members, and Christ was honored. I knew that the essence of the church's message was reconciliation (2 Cor. 5:14–21). All the work of God and the resources of God were present in our church for reconciliation. He had committed to us this "ministry of reconciliation"

(vv. 18–19). Our message to a watching world hung in the balance. Our testimony to the grace of God, the mercy of God, and the love of God were all in the balance. Our message to a lost world had to be lived out in our lives, especially as a church. Unfortunately some feel we can neglect the saving of marriages and homes *in* our churches and still have a message of integrity to a lost world. As a matter of fact, we still feel we can "ask God to bless us" when we dishonor Him by refusing to draw upon His presence and power to bring healing in our families. Further, we feel we can continue to function as a religious organization in spite of such utter brokenness in the body. When marriages are not healed, the church family is deeply affected, especially in its *unity*.

I have found that if the church family and I did not actively pursue healing for struggling marriages, it made all the rest of the members nervous. They knew that if their lives or homes became threatened in any way, we probably would not pursue them either! One marriage that is saved strengthens the unity of the body and gives great confidence in witnessing to a lost world. The presence and power of our living Lord is experienced, and joy becomes the order of the day.

But the members have to be taught! A strong, relentless teaching of what a church is and what God can do through His church is crucial to having unity in a church. We taught and practiced faithfully the reclaiming of each member who was struggling. If we neglect the members we have, who will want to join us? If we see wholeness in each member, others will beat a path to our door just to experience this in their lives. I bear witness that this is true. It was the testimony of those who were being helped and healed that drew many others to want to be a part of such a church. All the power of the cross, the Resurrection, and Pentecost are still available in the life of every church. And to live this way is an authentic witness to our Lord, to our message, and to our life together.

In the New Testament those who experienced financial loss found the rest of the members selling their goods and laying the proceeds at the apostles' feet so that no one in the church lacked anything (Acts

4:32–35). Literally, "all the believers were together [unity] and had everything in common" (Acts 2:44). This is what God purposed, and this is what the living Christ and the Holy Spirit developed in the churches in the New Testament. There were difficulties (see Acts 6), but the apostles and the members vigorously maintained the unity in the church family, and we must do the same. The name of our Lord is at stake, and the convincing of our lost world is in our hands.

Power in the Body

There is an old tale that teaches a great truth. It is a story of a captain who was valiant in battle. So dominant was the warrior in battle that his sword was greatly feared among the enemy. Word about his sword became legendary among the people. Soon the king himself had heard of the infamous sword, and he sent a messenger to find the sword and bring it back for him to examine.

If we neglect the members we have, who will want to join us?

When the messenger returned with the sword in hand, he presented it to the king. But the king was taken back; he didn't understand the stories he had heard. "Why are the people afraid of the sword? It appears very common, very ordinary." The messenger replied, "Sir, I brought you the sword, but nothing more. If I had brought you the hand that wields the sword, you would fully understand the fear."

Do you understand that the hand of God through the Holy Spirit wields a Christian's life? We may be common, ordinary in the eyes of men. But when a Christian is filled with the Holy Spirit, God can bring down strongholds through our lives. When a church is filled with the Holy Spirit, God can turn a world upside down. The key is never our abilities, but the power of the Holy Spirit working in and through us to accomplish the will of the Father.

A Story from Mel

As a pastor, I have the privilege of serving the Lord in many different capacities. Perhaps my favorite thing to do is visit those who are not yet Christians and share with them the good news of Christ. Over the years I have learned many things but none so important as knowing the absolute necessity of the Holy Spirit working through my life.

I remember the day I put to use my vast educational training to argue with a lost person about the existence of God. You need to understand that I not only completed a master of divinity degree from a large and well-respected seminary, but I was also at that time completing a Ph.D. with a major in theology. I was ready, I thought, to overwhelm this poor, unsuspecting lost person with an irrefutable argument that would leave them pleading with me to help them have a personal relationship with God. As you might imagine, the results were not what I had hoped. The best I could get out of him was a blank stare that equaled the stone faces on Mount Rushmore! I completely missed the mark; the poor fellow did not have a clue about what I was so eloquently telling him. As much as I value education, it will never be a substitute for the Holy Spirit working through my life.

That realization was proven true when I recently went to visit a young couple to share with them the gospel. I have become confident in sharing with people over the past few years, but this particular night I was out of sync. It was the end of a long day that had been filled with meetings. I was tired, and my brain was just not very sharp. As is my custom, I took another young man with me to "show him how it was done."

The visit didn't start well. We couldn't get anybody to answer the door. After ringing the bell and banging on the door for some time, we figured out that we were at the wrong house. We regrouped, found the right street, and approached the right house. We were let in, but the reception was less than warm. They were courteous, as most Canadians are, but we sensed a distance that was a bit awkward. We made it to the kitchen, sat down with a cup of coffee, and made small talk to break the ice. I was ready to move the conversation toward spiritual things when I realized that I had forgotten my Bible! I apologized and asked if they had a Bible I could borrow, and like most people they had one "somewhere in the house." They found it, and I began to inquire about their relationship to God.

The wife sounded a little guarded as she began to describe her religious experience. She had been baptized as an infant, but her family never took her back after that initial introduction into that particular church. She and her mother decided to try a Catholic church when she was a bit older, but it was confusing to her, and she didn't last long there either. She was later married, and the couple decided to try out a few evangelical churches but didn't like any of them. After she walked me through all the various religious experiences in her life, she said, "Religion is so confusing, and I have a lot of questions that I need answered."

I offered to talk with her about her concerns but decided to cut to the chase and ask her one simple question. I said, "With all the various religious experiences you have had, I understand why you have so many questions. But let me ask you a question first. In all your life has anybody ever told you how to become a Christian?"

She said, "No, nobody has told me that."

I asked her another simple question, "Do you want me to tell you right now how you can have a relationship with God and become a Christian?"

She said, "Yes."

As I began to share with her, the friend I had brought with me quietly bowed his head to say a silent prayer for this dear lady. When he lifted his head, he was astonished to find that tears were streaming down her cheeks. Her husband ran off to get a box of tissue for her. And as I stumbled through a gospel presentation, I heard the Holy Spirit say to me, "Just make this short and get to the point; if you talk too long, you may ruin the moment!" Knowing that my mind was not sharp, I readily obeyed the Holy Spirit, and within just a few minutes she prayed to receive Christ. The next Sunday she came forward in church professing her faith in Christ and requesting baptism. Her husband was at her side, rededicating his life to Christ and requesting church membership.

As my friend and I left the house that night, we remarked to each other, "God was determined to save that woman in spite of our incompetence!" It was completely the work of the Holy Spirit, and He did it through one of the worst presentations of the gospel ever told! But the real story of that evening was what preceded that visit. A man in our church had been prayer walking that neighborhood for months. Another member had met this couple through their children at school and was praying for them. And before I went out to witness that night, I had called one of our prayer warriors to intercede on behalf of the couple. In other words the Holy Spirit was at work in their lives and used an unworthy vessel like me to complete His work. The Scripture is true: we can do nothing without Him (see John 15:1–8).

The power in the body is the full presence of God, actively at work accomplishing His own will. He does not release His power for us to use as we will. He gives us His Spirit to accomplish His purposes in our lives and the church. In the Old Testament He sent His Spirit to enable His servants to accomplish His calling in their lives. He worked through them! Now He has poured out His Spirit on all flesh (not just selected individuals who led the people of God). This is an amazing truth! The Spirit of God is resident to perform *everything* the Lord wants to do. Paul's conclusion: "Now to Him who is able to do above and beyond all that we ask or think—according to the *power that works in you*—to Him be glory *in the church* and in Christ Jesus to all generations, forever and ever. Amen" (Eph. 3:20–21). This passage reminds us that God Himself *is* the power working in us.

The world is waiting to know our God, not by word, but by demonstrated power. Did not Paul say, "My speech and my proclamation were not with persuasive words of wisdom, but with a demonstration of the Spirit and power, so that your faith might not be based on men's wisdom but on God's power" (1 Cor. 2:4–5). I get the feeling that all the world gets from the Christian community is an avalanche of words but no demonstration of the Spirit's power.

Imagine, if you will, a bright sunny day as you prepare to launch out into the deep waters of the sea. You have a sailboat with all the trimmings. You and your crew have made all the necessary preparations. Your rations are all stocked up for the journey. The boat is up-to-date on its maintenance log. You have the finest of equipment and the most talented crew available. So you raise the anchor, loose the moorings, and raise the sails; you are ready to sail. But nothing happens. The sailboat remains motionless in the harbor. Why? Because there is no wind to power the boat.

The key is never our abilities, but the power of the Holy Spirit working in and through us to accomplish the will of the Father.

Your church may have all the "trimmings," but without the wind of the Spirit, there will be no power. You may have all the necessary equipment and have gone through a checklist of the necessary components for a healthy church. You may have built a beautiful building and attracted many talented people who are willing to work hard for God. But your church will not sail without the presence of the Holy Spirit. There will be no power to accomplish the purposes of God. Interestingly enough, the Greek word for *Spirit* can also be translated *wind*. We need the wind of the Spirit in our sails. I have found that when the wind is blowing and the sails are full, people are so busy at

---

"Unless someone is born of water and the Spirit, he cannot enter the kingdom of God. Whatever is born . . . of the Spirit is spirit. . . . The wind blows where it pleases, and you hear its sound, but you don't know where it comes from or where it is going. So it is with everyone born of the Spirit."

JOHN 3:5–6, 8

their job that nobody has time to argue or bicker with one another. But when the sails are drooping and no activity is happening, we tend to stare at one another and begin to complain. Oh that we would be used by the Spirit to touch our world.

Here are some principles to help you understand how God's power works in us. First, the Holy Spirit will never work contrary to the Father's will. Second, the Holy Spirit never works where sin and unbelief are present. Third, the Holy Spirit never works where God's name is not honored. Fourth, the Holy Spirit will always choose to work through the local churches. Fifth, the Holy Spirit's work in the church is always God-sized [beyond all we can ask or think]. And sixth, when the Holy Spirit works in the church, it always brings honor and glory to God.

A Functioning Body

The Holy Spirit empowers and enables a church to function as a living body of Christ. He brings a heart to care for one another and the ability to work together for a common purpose. The Holy Spirit impressed a significant Scripture upon our church. He used a verse where Jesus spoke of His own ministry. "This is the will of Him who sent Me: that I should lose none of those He has given Me" (John 6:39). We began to see that Jesus took seriously the watch care over those the Father gave Him. Each person is important in His eyes and has a significant role to play in the purposes of God.

I get the feeling that all the world gets from the Christian community is an avalanche of words but no demonstration of the Spirit's power.

Jesus also said, "Everyone the Father gives Me will come to Me, and the one who comes to Me I will never cast out" (John 6:37). That means that God is the One who sends people to us, and we must receive all He brings our way. Our church, therefore, made a conscious decision carefully to receive all we believed God sent to us. We listened to their testimony and publicly entered into a covenant with them, promising to watch over them and to teach them as Christ had commanded us. It was always a meaningful time in our church. We saw many different people, often with many different problems, whom God sent to us. And in the twelve years I pastored that church, we did not lose people. It was a choice we made to receive, care for, and hold on to those whom God gave us.

So how does a church function as God intended? The Holy Spirit's presence in the church is, in fact, the very life of the church. He, by manifesting Himself in every member, enables the church to function. Each member is joined to Christ! Each member is joined to the Spirit! Each member is joined to each other! Each functions *in* the body, and *with* the body. As each part functions where God put it, the whole body responds to Christ, and the Father's will is accomplished in the world through His people.

The apostle Paul said as much when he wrote to the Corinthian church. Paul said that He planted, Apollos watered, but God gave the increase. So he would say in evangelism today: one built a loving relationship, another spoke a witness, yet others welcomed and ushered when they came to worship, the pastor preached, the music shared, many prayed faithfully, then God gave the increase . . . and all rejoiced together. God had worked through the entire body, all functioning where God had put them, the Holy Spirit enabling each by working in them to bring a lost person to faith in Christ. This is the body funtioning in evangelism. The same could describe the church on mission—reaching youth; caring for seniors; encouraging business people; ministering to jails, hospitals, schools, or any other place God desires to work. The body functions together with one heart and one mind, responding to Christ who is guiding them to do the Father's will.

A Story from Mel

The Lord has given me a burden for the church to function as a living body with Christ as the Head. So I have sought to encourage members to be connected to Christ and to be involved in serving Him in the church. I have come to realize that the Lord's activity is much more important than our activity. We asked the Holy Spirit to show us the individuals in whom He was working, and we set about to join Him in His work.

I put together a list of people who needed to respond to Christ. I did not put people on the list who needed Christ but only those where there was evidence that Christ was working in their lives. I went to one member who obviously had been gifted as an intercessor, and I gave her a list of twenty-one people to pray for in the days ahead. She took that list and prayed through it every day, pleading for God to work in their lives. We enlisted many others to build relationships and discover how they might let God use them in bringing these individuals to Christ.

Six months later every person on the list had made a public decision for Christ. On one occasion, as an individual came forward, I asked the congregation, "If you have prayed for Rick to make the decision he has made today, would you please stand?" It seemed like three-quarters of the people stood and rejoiced together. Who brought that young man to salvation? The body did.

That is the way God does His work—through the body of His Son. The church has all the resources it needs to do all that God asks of them. Those resources are all made available through the Holy Spirit. In one of the greatest pictures of a church, in 1 Corinthians 12, Paul confirms the filling of the Holy Spirit within every member of the body. The Spirit "manifests" Himself to every member. Every member

---

Now there are different gifts, but the same Spirit. There are different ministries, but the same Lord. And there are different activities, but the same God is active in everyone and everything. A manifestation of the Spirit is given to each person to produce what is beneficial.

1 CORINTHIANS 12:4–7

of the church will experience the Holy Spirit's enabling presence and power. Every member must, therefore, be encouraged, taught, and assisted to live out the Spirit's life in them in the midst of their church. For a major purpose of the Holy Spirit, within every believer, is to help the rest of the body to grow into Christlikeness. Each member has a vital role to play in God's plan for the church and must be treated as significant.

This can be done at the time a person first becomes a believer or when they are first added by God to the body. Jesus saw this radical

---

Now you are the body of Christ, and individual members of it.

1 Corinthians 12:27

---

significance when He said to His disciples, "I assure you: The one who receives whomever I send receives Me, and the one who receives Me receives Him who sent Me" (John 13:20). Every church, therefore, must see its church growth as an act of God and treat new members as a gift from God. In other words the entire church must see each new member as though receiving both Jesus and the Father. How would we treat them? How we are treating each member He sends us is, in fact, how we are treating Him. And that ought to be with great joy, with great care, and with great anticipation of how their presence will bless the congregation. This is not just a suggestion, a convenience, or even a preference. This is a divine command! Many a church's spiritual health is greatly affected at the moment new members are received. It is here that a church will be functioning as a living body or merely as a religious organization. Each person being received is either related to Christ in His living body, or is merely added to the roll of the church. The new member is either alive in Christ or dead in the structure of man-centered activity. When God adds them to the church, He is adding them to the body of His Son. Each person, therefore, is a "member in particular" with a special relationship to Christ as the

> *As obedient children, do not be conformed to the desires of your former ignorance but, as the One who called you is holy, you also are to be holy in all your conduct; for it is written, "Be holy, because I am holy."*
>
> 1 PETER 1:14–16

Head. The Holy Spirit immediately enables every member to relate to the Head and to each member He is adding to the body. This is the enabling work of the Holy Spirit in each church.

The greatest priority of the Holy Spirit, therefore, is to enable each one to know Christ and to love Him with all his heart. As a result, each member will also desire to serve Him and obey Him, and to relate deeply to the members of His body. But the only way in which the Holy Spirit can enable us to grow in our relationship with Christ and each other is to speak to each member concerning the way of holiness. For without holiness we cannot relate to God as He intended. The Scripture says to "pursue peace with everyone, and holiness—without it no one will see the Lord" (Heb. 12:14). The Holy Spirit will therefore speak to each member by convicting him of sin and righteousness, in order that he might progress forward in his relationship with the Holy One. The Holy Spirit will convey to us what He hears from the Lord. The Lord desires that we become like Him as a body, so He can do the Father's will through our church.

The Holy Spirit also enables every member to edify and build up the body. For as we help each member to grow into maturity, Christ will then have a healthy body through whom He can accomplish the

> *So if one member suffers, all the members suffer with it; if one member is honored, all the members rejoice with it. Now you are the body of Christ, and individual members of it.*
>
> 1 CORINTHIANS 12:26–27

Father's will. The Holy Spirit, therefore, must make us sensitive to what is happening in the body. When one member hurts or is sick, the entire body marshals to his aid in order to maintain health in Christ's body, the local church. That is how our physical bodies function, and that is how God desires for our churches to function.

What happens in your life when another in the church is hurting? Do you feel the pain? Do you respond and seek to bring healing? Two important factors must be in place in order for this truth to be implemented into the life of a church. First, we must be free to share our hurts within the body. Often, we suffer in silence and refuse to let anybody help us grow to maturity. Unless we provide the forum for people to share their needs, our churches will be filled with hurting people who suffer in silence. Second, we must intentionally look out for one another. Paul urged the church in Philippi, "Do nothing out

---

But now God has placed the parts, each one of them, in the body just as He wanted. And if they were all the same part, where would the body be?

1 CORINTHIANS 12:18–19

---

of rivalry or conceit, but in humility consider others as more important than yourselves. Everyone should look out not only for his own interests, but also for the interests of others" (Phil. 2:3–4).

Can you see how important it is for each member to be involved in the life of the church, investing their life in the lives of other members in the body? As we are each filled with the Holy Spirit, we then begin to function where God has placed us. His assignment is to help us serve the Lord as we serve one another and maintain the health of the body. I have found that some churches struggle with helping the members find their place of service. Most have a nominating committee to help in the process. But they are not primarily trying to "fill positions" in the church organization. They are to see that every member is functioning in the body where God has placed them and where the Holy Spirit is enabling them. They must be sensitive to what the Holy Spirit is doing and help people recognize what He is doing in and through their lives.

For example, not all are able to edify through music. Yet some are gifted with an instrument or with vocal abilities and use them to bless God's people as they worship. A skilled musician, however, may *not* be spiritually able to edify. His pride and skill may actually detract and hinder what God is doing in the midst of the church. A soloist may have a good voice, but he may have "quenched the Spirit" by ungodly living. Such should never be enlisted to sing merely for his voice.

The Holy Spirit enables some to be leaders of others, and they could be asked to lead a committee. Yet others are just plain hard workers, faithful to serve where there is a need. Others have a Barnabas spirit as encouragers. Still others have a tremendous burden for missions. In any case, since the Spirit equips every member for the common good, a nominating committee must be alert to the Spirit's equipping of every member, and they must assure that every member is actively helping the body to grow in Christ. Our church would even encourage the children to do their part in welcoming people and assisting the elderly. We had some mentally challenged young adults who saw their place to make others happy in the church, and the church was greatly blessed by their simple life characterized by joy.

Because the Spirit enables every member, and all believers, there are several things that automatically must follow:

1. Members are to be honored.
2. Members are to have a useful place in the body.
3. Members should have an opportunity to be consulted on major issues and decisions.
4. Members are to be included in the work of the church, each functioning from the place God has put them in the body.

The older lady may not, within herself, feel she is worth much in the church, or feel she can contribute much. But she can be a prayer warrior in all decisions, all ministries, and all activities in the church. Her home may be used for a Bible study, even if she cannot teach it. She can open her home to visitors or provide a room for a college student. She can write cards or make phone calls. A thousand things she can do, intentionally, and make a significant contribution to the growth of the others in her church. All this won't "just happen." It has to be done intentionally, as the church is obedient to God through His Word.

Study Questions for Reflection and Response

1. How important is it for every member of the body to be filled with the Holy Spirit?
2. Is your church experiencing the necessary power of the Holy Spirit? What is the evidence?
3. Are you allowing the Holy Spirit to work in your life and through your life to build up the body and impact the lost community around you?
4. Have you relied more on your natural abilities than you have the Holy Spirit to work through you? What is the difference?

God's Salvation Through the Church

How Does a Church Touch the World with God's Great Salvation?

"These men who have turned the world upside down have come here too."

Acts 17:6

But Jesus responded to them, "My Father is still working, and I also am working. . . . I assure you: The Son is not able to do anything on His own, but only what He sees the Father doing. For whatever the Father does, these things the Son also does in the same way. For the Father loves the Son and shows Him everything He is doing, and He will show Him greater works than these so that you will be amazed."

JOHN 5:17, 19–20

SEVEN

God Speaks to the Church

Experiencing God Together in Life

A Story from Mel

The truth of God's Word has a way of pressing His people to see if we really believe it enough to stake our lives on it. We often ask God to teach us the truth, but we hesitate when we are challenged to live according to the truth He has revealed. Yet that is how God teaches us. He shows us the truth and then gives us an opportunity to practice it. We pray for faith, then we find ourselves in a position that requires faith if we are going to follow the Lord. The church I pastor is having to live out in practical terms what it means to follow Christ as the Head of the body and fulfill the purposes of God. It is not enough to believe the truth; we must put the truth into action.

153

As our church was growing, we tried everything possible to provide accommodation for the new people God was bringing to limited facilities. We had multiple services, children's church in another area to free up more seats for adults, Bible study classes meeting in homes around the building, and whatever it took to meet the needs. Every office but mine was being used for Bible study classes, and I was determined to keep the pastor's office off-limits. After all, I needed some place to go between our two services in order to have a place of quiet. But then it happened; there was a group of non-Christians who wanted to study the Bible during that time and had no place to go. I gave up my office!

It became obvious that if we were to continue reaching people, we needed more space. We faced a decision. We faced a crisis of belief! What should we do? What was God's will? We sensed God leading us to proceed with a building project, but it appeared impossible for us to do! But isn't that the way God works? He always asks us to do the impossible according to human reasoning. But with God nothing is impossible.

We all know God can do anything, but something in particular is much different. In our case the church was fairly new and still carried a significant mortgage on its current building. We had already begun a costly development of our basement area in order to create more education space. Furthermore, our church's operating budget had just been increased more than 40 percent over the previous year's budget. To consider another major project just seemed to be too much of a stretch. But as the church began to pray and study the Scriptures, God gave clear direction as to what He desired for us to do.

A special committee was formed to look at our options and bring a recommendation to the church for consideration. We had several opportunities. First, we could borrow the money and carry a long-term mortgage. The bank had already indicated their willingness to finance the project, and it would allow us to begin immediately. But this was not what God wanted. It was clear that we were not to acquire a big debt; we were to trust God to provide another way.

Second, we could pay cash as we go and build debt free. The benefit of this option was that we would not be saddled with the burden of debt or use God's money to pay on a great amount of interest. As we prayed for wisdom, we sensed that this would not require much faith either. After all, that meant we would not take a step forward until we had all the money in our hands. That could mean two years, five years, or even ten years of fund-raising and waiting for money to come. We sensed that God was not telling us to take that option. He was not going to provide any money for what we were not already committed to do.

God began to lead us to a greater understanding of faith. We all believed that God wanted us to proceed soon, yet He wanted us to be debt free as a church. That is where faith comes in. God wanted the best of both options: to build the building as soon as possible and to be completely debt free by the end of the next year. We decided that God wanted us to pay out our existing debt before we broke ground on the new building. We would then acquire a line of credit (after all, we were not asking the contractors to walk by faith!) and start building the sanctuary as soon as possible. As a church we then made the commitment to quickly pay off the building by the grace of God. The timing to start the project is where faith was required, and the short-term commitment to be completely debt free allowed all of our people to sacrifice and participate in the project through their gifts and pledges.

The purpose of being debt free, however, was not to be debt free. Our focus was not on money but on the Lord. Our desire was to be obedient to God so that He could demonstrate to His people what He

---

Now without faith it is impossible to please God, for the one who draws near to Him must believe that He exists and rewards those who seek Him.

HEBREWS 11:6

could do with any people who would simply believe Him and obey. It became clear that God was more interested in building the character of the church than He was the sanctuary of the church. God spoke, and the world came into being; a new sanctuary for our little church was not a difficult thing for Him to do. He is not interested in giving us buildings; He desires to build faith in His people. As we continued to pray, we realized that the building had little to do with what God was saying. He was going to use this project as an opportunity for us to experience Him and build our faith, so that He could tell us what He really wanted to do through the church to accomplish His purposes. But our faith was not sufficient enough to reveal His ultimate plan. He must build our faith through obedience so that we would be ready to follow Him in the greater step of faith that awaits us in the future.

As the church shared together, there was a growing sense among the entire congregation that God was up to something much bigger than we ever realized. When we came to the decision to proceed with the recommendation, I had the church vote by secret ballot. I didn't want any pressure to "go with the crowd." I know how difficult it is to hold the opposite view of the majority and appear "unspiritual." The body needed to be absolutely free to vote how they sensed God was leading them. We had three options: (1) Yes, I believe God is leading us in this direction. (2) No, I do not believe God is leading us in this direction. (3) ?, I do not know what God would have us do at this point. All three are valid responses to such an important decision. So after a time of silent prayer, we voted. The results: zero negative votes, four votes indicating they did not know God's will at this point, and all the rest were a resounding YES! Essentially, we had a unanimous vote to proceed with great confidence.

How did God bring such unity in such a difficult "financial" decision? He had prepared our people long before this moment. They had already been burdened to pray. They already had confidence that God's Word was a "light to their path." They had been taught the ways of God are different from the ways of the world. They understood *koinonia* and the dynamics of a church family sharing their heart together. They were already committed to following Christ as the Head of the church before He spoke. They were in a position for God to speak, and He did!

The next two months confirmed the Lord's leadership in the church. He led us to set a goal of $450,000 to pay off our existing debt and begin the project. The challenge: we had to raise it in two months. In those two months, we did not do any fund-raising. We simply asked the church members to go home and pray about what God wanted them to give. Then they were to bring their gift on September 30 during the morning service. We called it the Loaves and Fishes Offering, knowing that God would have to take our gifts and multiply them in order to meet the need. On that day, families came forward to lay their gift in a basket. Then they knelt at the altar to pray, asking God to receive their sacrifice, bless it, and multiply it. Many families made a tremendous sacrifice that day. Yet tears rolled down their cheeks as they thanked God for the privilege of participating in such a significant moment in His plan. Can you guess that happened? With a total church membership of only 227, God blessed us with an offering of almost exactly $450,000! When a church hears from God and responds in faith, God is faithful.

God has been guiding His people from the beginning of time. Go through the Old Testament and see the difference God's presence made at any time and in all circumstances. When His people remained in a clear relationship with Him, He spoke to them, guided them, protected them, and accomplished His purposes through them. We should not expect Him to be different in our churches today.

The Father Speaks to His Son, the Head

God has made each local church a living body for His Son. Just as clearly as "in Christ, God was reconciling a world to Himself" (2 Cor. 5:19), so He is in Christ's new body—the local church—reconciling our world to Himself. This relationship of the Father to His Son, and

therefore to each congregation of believers, is utterly crucial to understand and to live out in our world.

Throughout the life of Jesus, the Father spoke to His Son, as He
[the Father] completed His eternal plan to redeem a lost world. Even
as a young boy Jesus told His parents, "I must be involved in My
Father's interests" (Luke 2:49). At Jesus' baptism the Father affirmed
His will, which was being done through His Son (Luke 3:21–22).
Throughout Jesus' three and a half years of ministry, the Father guided
Jesus always to do His will and to please Him.

The Father worked in the Son's life from the beginning to the end.
Jesus' life became the exact expression of God's purposes as He
released His life into the Father's hands. The Father gave Jesus twelve
disciples, and then He convinced them that Jesus was the Christ. He
guided Jesus through His ministry and encouraged Him about His
coming death and departure so that His purpose would be accomplished in Jerusalem. In Gethsemane the Father guided His Son
through the plan to redeem a lost world. The Father was there as Jesus
lay down His life on the cross and gave over His spirit into the Father's
hands. In the resurrection, God's power was demonstrated as redemption was completed. And the ascension back to the Father's side was
so that the Holy Spirit could be sent upon all believers who received
the gift of salvation. The Father's will was the focus of Jesus' life; not
His will, but the Father's was done! In His new body, the local church,
it is still God's plan to speak through His Son whom He designated to

> *"I assure you: The Son is not able to do anything on His own, but
> only what He sees the Father doing. For whatever the Father does, these
> things the Son also does in the same way. For the Father loves the Son
> and shows Him everything He is doing, and He will show Him greater
> works than these so that you will be amazed."*
>
> JOHN 5:19–20

be the Head of His body, the church. "He put everything under His feet and appointed Him as head over everything for the church, which is His body, the fullness of the One who fills all things in every way" (Eph. 1:22–23).

It is crucial to understand the relationship between the Father and His Son. The Father made His Son Head over the local church, and now it is crucial that the members of the body understand their relationship to the Head and the other members of the body. The eternal purposes of God, continuing to unfold in our day, are at stake.

The Son Speaks to His Church, the Body

Once Jesus called the twelve disciples, He was constantly telling them what He was hearing from the Father. The significance of this cannot be overstated. In Jesus' great high priestly prayer in John 17, He affirmed this relationship to His disciples as being the Father's will: "I have revealed Your name to the men You gave Me from the world. They were Yours, You gave them to Me, and they have kept Your word. Now they know that all things You have given to Me are from You, because the words that You gave to Me, I have given to them. They have received them and have known for certain that I came from You. They have believed that You sent Me" (John 17:6–8).

God spoke to Jesus, and Jesus spoke the Father's will to His disciples. This continued throughout His life as He related to the disciples; this is what He continued to do in His relationship as Head of the churches. The Book of Revelation begins, "The revelation of Jesus Christ that God gave Him to show His slaves what must quickly take place. He sent it and signified it through His angel to His slave John, who testified to God's word and to the testimony about Jesus Christ, in all he saw" (Rev. 1:1–2). John faithfully delivered God's message, through the living Christ, to the seven churches in Asia. The churches then had a word from God, through Christ their Head; they were clearly instructed as to what they must now do. It was far more important to know what was on the heart of God for their church than what was on their heart to do for God. Their lives were at stake, and God's

> *"I have called you friends, because I have made known to you every-thing I have heard from My Father."*
>
> JOHN 15:15B

eternal purposes that He intended to accomplish through them were at stake. Only God could tell them what He was doing and what He was about to do. He communicated His purposes through His Son, whom He appointed as Head of the churches.

The Vital Role of Prayer

The Father constantly revealed His will to His Son in prayer. For example, when the Father was about to give His Son twelve disciples, He prepared Jesus through an entire night of prayer. Consistently throughout the Gospels, before every major event in Jesus' life, we find Him spending the night in prayer. In fact, one of the most notable characteristics of Jesus' life was the quantity and quality of His prayer life. It was in prayer that the Father spoke to Him and gave Him direction for life. According to Romans 8:28–30, God desires that we "be conformed to the image of His Son," and that will supremely include our prayer lives. That is why Jesus said to His people that God had purposed that "My house will be a house of prayer" (Luke 19:46). Only as His people pray, and pray together, will they know the Father's purposes for and activity in their life together.

A vital part of a living body of Christ is the prayer life of each member. Their personal relationship with Christ will keep them in His will for the body. Their relationship to one another in their church will keep the body united under the Head. Then Christ, the Head, can guide each member of the body, and the entire body will know the will of the Father being lived out uniquely through them.

The prayer meeting, therefore, becomes one of the most exciting gatherings of any church family. This was always true of every church we have pastored. More seemed to be confirmed in the life of our church when we prayed together than in almost anything we did.

We took time to ask each member to share what God was saying to him as a member of the body (i.e., the *eye* shared what it was seeing, the *ear* what it was hearing). I would ask, "What have you seen God doing this week? What have you heard God saying this week?" Then as we prayed together, we would know more clearly what the Head was saying to our church. We assumed that the Head was speaking to all parts of the body, and now we saw the big picture of God's design. As a result, the whole body was seeking to be obedient and let God complete His work and purposes through us.

For example, one would report about a request from a group in another town for a new Bible study. Together we responded to the request. One member had a relative in the town who had been praying for a church for many years. Others commented that they had felt a real burden for that town but didn't know why. As the body shared together, a consensus followed, and we set in motion the steps necessary to obey God. As we obeyed, we saw people for whom Christ died being saved and a church begun; this occurred many times over. Prayer was vital to us, just as it was to Jesus in the days of His flesh. It was not what *we* wanted to do *for* God; it was God making His will and activity known to us as a church so that *He* could accomplish it *through* us.

We have discovered that prayer is vital to the church, for God will often ask us to do things that don't make sense to human reasoning. Unless we hear from God, we will never know God's will for our lives or our church. Several Scriptures have guided us at this point. First, Isaiah 55:8–9 says, "'For My thoughts are not your thoughts, nor are your ways My ways,' declares the LORD. 'For as the heavens are higher than the earth, so are My ways higher than your ways, and My thoughts than your thoughts.'" Unless we thoroughly understand this Scripture, we will be completely out of step with God's will for our churches. There is no possible way for us to know the ways of God by human reasoning alone. The best minds cannot understand God. The best books on church growth will not tell us the way God desires to reach our communities. The latest sociological studies will not tell us the way in which God is working in our world. The futurists will never decipher the plans of God. We must begin with the understanding that a finite being cannot understand the infinite God of the universe. He is unknowable to mankind by human reasoning. With that thought in mind, let us look at the next Scripture.

Proverbs 3:5–6 says, "Trust in the LORD with all your heart, and do not lean on your own understanding. In all your ways acknowledge Him, and He will make your paths straight." Again the Scripture reinforces that we are not to lean on our own understanding. Instead, we must trust in the Lord with all our heart; faith is absolutely necessary. We must have confidence that God will guide us if we trust in Him and acknowledge His right to be Lord in our lives. Let me put the truth of these two Scriptures together. Acknowledging that we cannot know the ways of God without Him revealing them, we must step out in faith and trust Him to guide our lives in the way that is right. But the third Scripture is crucial.

We have discovered that prayer is vital to the church, for God will often ask us to do things that don't make sense to human reasoning.

Jeremiah 33:2–3 says, "Thus says the LORD who made the earth, the LORD who formed it to establish it, the LORD is His name, 'Call to Me and I will answer you, and I will tell you great and mighty things, which you do not know.'" What a promise God has given to His people! Just because we cannot figure out the ways of God does not mean that we cannot know the ways of God. If we call on Him and if we take time to pray, He will answer us and tell us things we do not know. Is there anything you do not know? Then call upon Him!

When properly understood, these verses are powerful. Our churches are not to function according to creative reasoning; they must function according to the revelation of God as we spend time in prayer. Our problem is that we function according to what makes sense, but God has already told us that He would not make sense to human reasoning. We use our common sense, and we act upon what we already know we can accomplish. We never attempt anything beyond our own abilities. After all, we don't want to bring dishonor to God's name. Listen, God can take care of His own reputation. The only thing that brings dishonor to God's name is when God's people live like the world around them, never knowing what God could have done if they had only believed Him. We will never know the will of God for our church unless our church asks God through prayer.

A Story from Mel

I was pastoring a small church in Canada. Actually, two churches were struggling to survive. They decided to merge and came to Gina and me to ask me to come as the pastor of the restart. Including my family, the total membership of the merged congregation was twenty-one. Many dynamics were working against its success, yet God chose to bless, and the church began to grow. By the time the church had grown to an attendance of seventy-five, we felt God leading us to take a step of faith and call another staff person. I wish you could have heard the discussion of that church as they sought God's will in the matter.

After much time in prayer and sharing what God had said to the body, the chairperson of the finance committee stood up and let us know the exact details of what we were deciding. She said, "We are currently in a financial condition in which we are just barely able to pay our pastor. Within two months we will no longer be receiving the thousand dollars per month pastoral supplement that he receives from the convention as a church planter. We have already decided to renovate our sanctuary to make more room for people, and we don't have the money to finish that project. If Kevin and Alicia are to move from South Carolina, it will require a minimum of five thousand U.S. dollars to move them, and we don't have that. Since they are American citizens, they cannot be bivocational, and we will have to guarantee the Canadian government that we will pay them a full salary. At this point we don't have any money to pay them, but we sense that God wants us to step out in faith. So as a finance committee, we recommend that we extend a call."

After more prayer and sharing Scriptures that God had given us, we proceeded to vote by secret ballot. The result was a unanimous vote to step out in faith and call them. The couple accepted the call in May of that year and put in motion the plans to come. One problem was the need to sell their home. Not knowing from where their salary would come, it didn't make sense to move to Canada and pay rent and at the same time cover their mortgage back in Spartanburg. As they prayed, God simply reminded them that He had spoken, and they needed to trust Him. To wait for the house to sell would be walking by sight, and He was requiring them to walk by faith. So they committed themselves to arrive on September 1. August came, and they had not received one offer on their home. Still confident of God's call, they were making plans to move when they received a call from their realtor. A couple came to see the house, offered the exact price they were asking, and gave one stipulation of the deal: they had to take possession by August 15. The deal closed; they packed up their belongings and said good-bye to family and friends. They arrived the first of September. Not only did God provide all the resources for the move, the immigration costs, and the salary of this dear couple, but He also provided for my salary as the pastor and the building renovations to make more space for the people He was reaching. Now several years later this same couple is planting a new church by faith in the One who has been faithful.

An interesting side note about the move displays the hand of God. One year after the move, they returned to visit friends in their old church. They decided to go back and drive past their old house, only to find that their name was still on the mailbox. After talking to their neighbors, they discovered that nobody had ever moved into the house, and the owners were paying a neighborhood boy to mow the lawn. And they *had* to take possession by August 15.

When all circumstances are telling us one thing, we must still hear a word from God. We are not to function according to our own understanding, but we are to trust in the One who is the Head of the church. He is able to reveal the Father's will and bring the body into harmony in order to accomplish His purposes, but we will only know what the Lord desires if we spend adequate time in prayer.

As a pastor, I had to teach our people how to hear a word from God and how the church needs to process what He is saying. Our deacons not only met regularly for prayer, but we prayed over every decision we would bring to the church. On some occasions, after prayer, we were unanimous that a particular matter should *not* come before the church at that time. It always proved to be a right decision—after prayer. Thus, they maintained the unity in the church, as was their mandate as a group of deacons. Some members commented, "The church just votes to accept everything the deacons and pastor propose." I assured them that the reason it seemed that way was because the deacons never brought before the congregation anything they knew would divide the fellowship. The unity of God's people was far more important than any issue we could bring. During these times of prayer the Lord helped us to know the direction we must go and how to share it with the rest of the body.

Throughout the life of the church, we prayed to know the will of God. I cannot stress enough the importance of prayer. Without a vital prayer life, your church will be absolutely disoriented to the will of God.

The Vital Role of Worship

Worship is the *lifeblood* of God's people. God has designed the corporate life of His people in such a way that they constantly stand before Him. Every time they come into His presence in worship, they are forever changed. The apostle Paul encouraged the Corinthian church to remember that "whenever a person turns to the Lord, the veil is removed. Now the Lord is the Spirit; and where the Spirit of the Lord is, there is freedom. We all, with unveiled faces, are reflecting the glory of the Lord and are being transformed into the same image from glory to glory" (2 Cor. 3:16–18).

Throughout the Bible, when God's people stood in God's presence to worship, they trembled with awe. At the moment God entered into a covenant with His people at Mount Sinai, His presence overwhelmed them. "Moses said to the people, 'Do not be afraid; for God has come in order to test you, and in order that the fear of Him may remain with you, so that you may not sin'" (Exod. 20:20). God's deep concern was that His people not sin and turn away from Him. If they did, His eternal purposes to save a world would be greatly affected. When they worshiped God together, His presence would cause them to see any sin in their lives, turn from their sin, and turn back to Him. He could then speak to them, guide them, and work through them as they responded to His awesome presence. A time of worship corrected Isaiah and revealed to him the purposes of God. God could then send Isaiah to His people with a specific message they needed to hear (Isa. 6). Worship helped the church at Antioch know that God was ready to separate Barnabas and Saul for the work He had called them to do (Acts 13:2). The work of redeeming the Gentiles and affecting the entire Roman Empire began out of this moment of worship by God's people.

Worship includes many elements, but essentially it is always an encounter with God so that He can direct His people. In the many years I pastored, more seemed to happen when we worshiped than at any other time in the life of the church. The invitation moment often climaxed our worship, as people came forward to express what God had done in their lives. As the church met together, they were blessed to see and hear what God was doing all around them.

As a result of our worship services, we began many new ministries. On another occasion we had a visiting couple come forward to let us know they had been praying for a church to begin in their town seventy miles away. When the church heard their burden, they set in motion the beginning of a mission church in that community. Another time a couple, engaged to be married, shared that they were not morally pure, and with great brokenness they came to repent. This caused the entire church to respond with forgiveness, but it also alerted them to their own need for cleansing. God faced all of us with our sin, and there was much weeping as the Lord desired to make us a clean vessel for Him to use. Most of the significant decisions we made as a church came out of our corporate times of worship.

God spoke to us week after week as we worshiped. As the pastor, I had to: (1) know God, (2) know God's ways in worship, (3) help the people recognize that God was literally speaking to us as His people, (4) help God's people know what to do as God encountered us, and (5) help the church to be obedient and implement what God had said in the days that followed. Because of our special times of worship, we were constantly being changed into a healthy body through which Christ, the Head, could do His work.

Worship is far more than coming to church for a time of singing, preaching, and fellowshiping with our friends. Worship is an opportunity to encounter God face-to-face. But for us to reach this kind of encounter with God, the people must be taught. This was my responsibility as the pastor. So I took the church through a study of the life of Christ. Throughout that study I taught God's people how to recognize the voice of God personally, as families, and as a church. I taught how to know when God was speaking to us through the Scriptures. I taught how God speaks to us through prayer. I taught how to recognize God's activity around us and within us. In short, our times of worship became an exciting experience with God as we met together each week. Together we all heard a word from God; we all responded to God together, and we helped one another live out what God had said to us when we worshiped.

A Story from Mel

As we were writing this book, I had Dad fly up to Cochrane so that we could put the finishing touches on the manuscript. During the time he was here, in one of our Sunday evening services, Dad spoke about revival. Actually, we had another service planned, but the man who was scheduled to speak had to fly home to be with his father who had just had a heart attack. So we quickly put a service together, anticipating an informal time of sharing. God had something much different on His heart.

Near the end of the service, we asked for any questions from the congregation. There were a few comments, but there seemed to be an uneasy hush among the crowd. Finally, one young woman stood up and cried out in tears, "I can't sit still; my heart is about to pound out of my chest. I must confess my sin to the church." After she shared, several women came around her to pray. Immediately, another stood with great brokenness and shared that she must also confess her sin and began to share what the Holy Spirit was doing in her life. As we gathered around her, the floodgates seemed to open, and the Holy Spirit was moving among all who were present. One confessed that she had left her husband that day; another was struggling with pornography, and many others were convicted of their pride and spirit of self-righteousness. It soon became evident that we were in the presence of a Holy God who was dealing with His people as they gathered together for worship. After several hours had passed, some went home but could not remain there. One began to tremble, and he told his wife that God was at the church, and he had to go back and "make things right." People remained before the Lord that night until 1:30 A.M.

God continued to work through the week, causing people to gather for spontaneous prayer meetings. In fact, several gathered an hour before the regular prayer meeting, just to pray for the prayer meeting! Many of the moms waited until their children were in bed and then met at the church on Thursday night to pray. Many things have spun out of that time of worship, and only time will tell all that God will do in the days ahead.

I would not categorize this moment as one of the classic examples of revival, yet God was reviving His people during their time of worship, just as He desires to do any time His people gather for worship. That is what worship is all about! Corporate worship has a dynamic that cannot be duplicated in any other setting. Everyone who was at the worship service that night was glad they had chosen to link their lives with the people of God. For God spoke to us clearly, and we all heard Him at the same time.

The Spirit Enables All Believers, the Members

You can probably imagine how important it is that all members of the body have a relationship with Christ and understand their interdependence within the body of Christ. But how does the Spirit enable a church to build that kind of relationship with the Head and the body? First, the church must be taught by the Spirit what is happening when a member is being added. They must know that God is doing something special and that God is providing a new dimension for the body to be more complete in Christ by this new person. For the Scripture says, "God has placed the parts, each one of them, in the body just as He wanted" (1 Cor. 12:18). If God "wanted" to bring them into the life of the church, you can count on it, He has something He wants to do in their life through the church, and He has something He wants to do in the church through their life.

The Spirit will then help the members know how to respond to what God is doing in the life of this new member. The church ought to make this moment a special time, giving each member an opportunity to greet and speak with the one God has added. I have found that the care given to each new member began to draw those who were visiting to want to be a part of that kind of church. New members were

---

But speaking the truth in love, let us grow in every way into Him who is the Head—Christ. From Him the whole body, fitted and knit together by every supporting ligament, promotes the growth of the body for building up itself in love by the proper working of each individual part.

EPHESIANS 4:15–16

also overwhelmed at the sensitivity to their moment of obedience to God in joining the church. Through it all, the Holy Spirit was actively working during this special moment, helping the body to hear the voice of God and see His activity in their midst.

A further way in which the Spirit speaks to members is to help them to function in the body where God has placed them. "A manifestation of the Spirit is given to each person to produce what is beneficial. . . . But one and the same Spirit is active in all these, distributing to each one as He wills" (1 Cor. 12:7, 11). The apostle Paul was anxious that the early churches understood all that God had done in them and all that He had provided for them. All God's provisions were to help every believer grow in Christ until "we all reach unity in the faith and in the knowledge of God's Son, growing into a mature man with a stature measured by Christ's fullness" (Eph. 4:13). It is the Spirit's assignment to implement the purposes of God into each member of the body.

The Spirit, however, will always be speaking to the members concerning the building up of the body. He will not give gifts to people so that they can fulfill their own personal ministry. He distributes gifts to each member in order that they may edify and build up the body so that Christ can accomplish the Father's will through them. Paul describes how God provided for the churches apostles, prophets, evangelists, pastors, and teachers. They were given by God "for the training of the saints in the work of ministry, to build up the body of Christ" (Eph. 4:12). It was for the ministry of edifying the church. You can count on it; the Spirit will never lead a member to do anything that would divide or hurt the church. Too many people think in terms of self rather than the purposes of God. They think that the gifts of the Spirit are for them; they are not! The gifts of the Spirit are for the church. This is why Paul urges each one in the proper use of all that God has given, for the building up of others in the body. It is an awesome description! It is not merely "doctrine"; it is a picture of the practical ways in which the body (the church) grows together with the Holy Spirit speaking to and enabling each member.

I recall one of our ordinary members in one of our churches. He was from Germany and spoke in broken English. He was small and hunched over in stature. He couldn't teach or speak plainly, but he loved his Lord, and he loved his church. He had an infectious smile and was obviously overflowing with joy. The Spirit directed him to stand in the parking lot, just outside the main door to our sanctuary, and greet all who entered. He would extend his hand, grasp the hand of a visitor, smile, and say in broken English as he bowed slightly, "Welcome! Welcome to our church." I soon noticed that about six out of ten who joined said they did so because of Emil's first greeting. He really was used of God to edify his church.

Others in the church were given to hospitality and serving. Others taught in the nursery and made young couples feel welcome and secure that their children were well cared for. Some God used in evangelism, and others were comforting the children of God in times of struggle. Though the Spirit distributed many gifts to the people, all were to demonstrate the fruit of the Spirit. Love bound us together in wonderful unity. As each let the Spirit guide and enable him, love filled our church. We found that people were driving from many different communities just to get to our church. They said, "We have never seen a church love one another as this one does." They would drive for miles out of their way to be a part of such a church.

A further way God speaks to the church, through the members, is during a business meeting. In my son's church they call it a "congregational meeting" in order to avoid any misunderstandings that come with the term *business* meeting. For the church is not really a business; it is a living body that is responding to Christ, the Head. This is, however, a time of decision making. It is not a time to find out what the majority desire, but it is a time to know what the Spirit is saying to the church. It is good to remember that "when the Spirit of truth comes, He will guide you into all the truth. For He will not speak on His own, but He will speak whatever He hears. He will also declare to you what is to come" (John 16:13). In other words, the Father's will is expressed to the Spirit, who in turn speaks to God's people. In a business meeting, therefore, several things should take place:

1. Members should come prepared in their relationship with God (i.e., clean hands and a pure heart).
2. Members should come prepared to share what the Spirit is saying to them. They know it is not for them but for the church.
3. Members must listen carefully to what each of the other members is saying. They know that no one member has the whole mind of the Spirit; it must come through the body.
4. Members must agree ahead of time that when the body speaks, the church will have the mind of God in their decision.
5. Members must be prepared to work hard to do what their church believes God has said to them.

As a pastor I was always aware that the business meeting ought to be one of the most exciting and positive moments in the life of the church. This is where the church comes to know the heart and mind of their Lord. But I had to teach our people what a business meeting was; how they must be prepared spiritually through a right relationship with God; and to be ready to deny self, take up their cross, and follow Christ, the Head of the body.

As the issues in our church were presented and discussed, I had to teach the ways of God throughout and help them understand what God was doing, especially when we asked for a decision. First, we agreed *not* to ask, "Who is for this motion; who is against this motion?" That would only create an opportunity for division and hard feelings. Instead, we always said: "After having prayed about this matter before us and having heard what the Spirit is saying through each of us, how many sense God is indeed guiding us to proceed?" Then I asked, "How many do not sense we should proceed?" If the result was 60 percent to proceed and 40 percent not to proceed,

I helped the church understand what was happening. It was clear that God was guiding us to proceed, but it was also obvious that the timing was not yet right. There were still 40 percent that did not yet have a clear word from the Lord. So we would wait a month and return to see what God had now done in the body. This way, we never lost members over a decision of the church. We were far more concerned about *unity* in the body than the vote. Most of the time God enabled us to be unanimous. Other times we had an overwhelming consensus. But as we prayed and asked God to make His will known, we assumed that He heard our prayer, and the voice of the body was the will of God speaking through each member.

Some may be asking, "How does this work in a large church?" Some maintain that a large church can't bring all decisions to a business meeting. Indeed, not all decisions need to come to the entire body, for the church has already affirmed God's call upon their leaders and trusts that they will make wise decisions as the Holy Spirit leads them. Larger churches may have many staff members guiding specific areas of ministry; they may have an elected board or other levels of leadership. But each of these, including the many working committees, has several things that make them accountable and reportable to the church body. First, the church adopts a budget. That budget is an expression of what God is saying to the church concerning what He wants to accomplish through them. The leadership then ministers within the parameters that the church has already agreed was the direction the Lord was leading. They ought to seek affirmation from the body if the Lord begins to guide them in areas that move beyond their assignment. Second, each ministry group ought to report on a regular basis to the church, allowing other members to understand what God is doing and be able to affirm it or hold each ministry accountable to the direction God has given the body. The leaders should not feel threatened; they should be encouraged at the participation of the entire body with them in the task they have undertaken. Third, each member must be open to the involvement of other members in the body. Some major decisions could be immediately shared throughout the church to summon tremendous resources that are readily available in the body. They can be shared in the Sunday school or Bible study classes for prayer, discussion, suggestions, and involvement by all the members.

A pastor of a megachurch asked, "How can a church our size bring decisions to the body? For instance, we were forced to buy our own TV cameras and equipment for our weekly broadcasts. The cost was $1.5 million. Our leadership teams, including the finance committee, met and decided we should get a short-term loan, and the church approved our decision." I suggested that they could have: (1) shared it in the small groups in Sunday school, (2) had them know the need and pray together, (3) let them discuss and share as the Spirit guided them, (4) and report what the Spirit said to the people back to the leadership so they could make a more informed decision as the Spirit through the body gave counsel. I suggested that there will often be times when the people hear the need and are allowed to be a part of the solution; they will be led to help in ways never imagined. Some may have had a death in the family and wanted to give toward a memorial in honor of their loved one. Another may have received an inheritance and wanted to give toward a worthy cause. A Sunday school class may have been looking for a ministry project that they could get behind and give toward. There may be some shut-ins who were greatly blessed by that particular ministry and would love to give to see it continue. Then I said, "Is it possible that God had all the funds needed to meet this need and wanted the people to become a vital part in it all? This would have given the body an opportunity to build itself up in love, sharing together in a common purpose. You did what a corporation in the world would do, and you had it approved. But a church is not a corporation; it is a living body of Christ. Allow Him to direct the body through the working of the Holy Spirit and watch to see what He will do."

We must guard against decision making for efficiency rather than for the edifying of the body in love. There are times when it seems that involving the entire church is burdensome or time-consuming, but when the body is involved, the outcomes are always much more profound. Again there are many day-to-day decisions that the entire body has no business being involved in; they have established leaders who will deal with them. But the major decisions that impact the body ought to include the counsel of the Holy Spirit through the body. You will always have a much clearer picture of what Christ, the Head, desires to accomplish. You will always have the strong support of a body in whom the Spirit is guiding.

Statistics reveal that 80 percent of the churches in North America have fewer than two hundred people in attendance, and 90 percent have fewer than four hundred. Only 1 percent would be classified as a megachurch. But no matter what size a church is, it still must function as a body with Christ as the Head. Christ is not just a figurehead; He *is* the Head of the church. The organizational structures will obviously change as the church grows, but Christ will always be the leader, and the Holy Spirit will always guide and enable the people. Each church may need to ask Christ how that will look in their particular situation. For although the church is not merely an organization, it will be organized to help it properly function and effectively accomplish the purposes of God. The structure is to facilitate the relationship between Christ and His body, allowing the body to respond in obedience to His will.

Study Questions for Reflection and Response

1. Is God clearly speaking to you? To your church? Are you listening?
2. How vital is prayer in the life of your church?
3. Is worship in your church more entertainment than a serious, life-changing encounter with God?
4. Has your church sought to help every member be filled with the Holy Spirit so that the body might function as God intended?

This grace was given to me—the least of all the saints!—to proclaim to the Gentiles the incalculable riches of the Messiah, and to shed light for all about the administration of the mystery hidden for ages in God who created all things. This is so that God's multi-faceted wisdom may now be made known through the church to the rulers and authorities in the heavens.

EPHESIANS 3:8–10

EIGHT

God Works through the Church

Experiencing God Together in Life

Can you imagine what God wants to do and therefore can do in and through a church that is yielded to Him? An ordinary, yet extraordinary moment happened in my life to illustrate to me that God works through the ordinary people and that God works through small churches.

Jack Conner, his wife Bonna, and two of their five children moved from southern California to Prince Albert, Saskatchewan, Canada. They had come to pastor our first mission church. We spent much time together, though Jack was ninety-five miles north of where I was. One day Jack and I went out into the woods to pray and seek God's purposes for reaching out to our province and the nation. While we walked and prayed that strange afternoon, God laid on our hearts that He would bring into being one thousand new churches and missions if we and others would be faithful. We were two small churches, and there were fewer than thirty congregations in all of Canada within our fellowship at that time. Was this possible? Wrong question. Would we believe God and set out to do all He laid on our hearts to do?

We have learned that it takes time to see God fulfill what He said He would do. Two pastors could not do an assignment of that nature by themselves. If this was truly God's vision, He would lay that on the hearts of others as well. As soon as we set our hearts to plant churches, young and middle-aged adults began to respond to God's call to ministry. So many responded from our churches and others in the area that we began what we called the Christian Training Center (later the Canadian Baptist Theological College). In total, more than four hundred students were trained in a few short years. Today the Canadian Convention of Southern Baptists has endorsed a goal of establishing one thousand new churches by the year 2020. Their vision is to see "a church for every person across Canada and around the world." They have a fully accredited theological seminary with many students training and preparing for church planting. The Lord has also been gracious to allow my oldest son to be the president of that seminary, giving leadership to the next generation of pastors and church planters.

God's strategy is to work through His churches to extend His kingdom. When He desires to reach a nation, He will lay it upon the heart of leaders to plant churches. This is an exciting time to be alive, for this is what God *is* doing in our day. Have you considered how God can use your church in kingdom work, far beyond the immediate community of which you are a part?

A World Mission Strategy Center

God's strategy to extend His kingdom on earth is through the local churches that He establishes. Immediately after Peter declared his understanding that Jesus was the Christ, Jesus said to Peter and the other disciples, "Blessed are you, Simon son of Jonah, because flesh and blood did not reveal this to you, but My Father in heaven. And I also say to you that you are Peter, and on this rock I will build My church, and the forces of Hades will not overpower it. I will give you the keys of the kingdom of heaven, and whatever you bind on earth will have been bound in heaven, and whatever you loose on earth will have been loosed in heaven" (Matt. 16:17–19). The truth of what Christ said in this passage is enormous. Every church must understand what He was saying and how it applies to them.

Jesus recognized that no person would ever understand who He was unless the Spirit of God revealed it to him. In other words, if a person's mind has been enlightened to know the things of God, God is actively working in his life. When God begins to draw people to Himself, He has a purpose in mind. Jesus understood that when He saw the Father drawing people to Himself and gathering them together into a church, nothing could stand in that church's way. For the God of the universe was the Author and Creator of that church, and He would accomplish His mighty purposes through them just as He desired. The gates of hell itself could not prevail against those people, called out and gathered together by God. So Jesus could say, "I will build My church on the

---

"No one can come to Me unless the Father who sent Me draws him, and I will raise him up on the last day. It is written in the Prophets: 'And they will all be taught by God.' Everyone who has listened to and learned from the Father comes to Me. . . . This is why I told you that no one can come to me unless it is granted to him by the Father."

JOHN 6:44–45, 65

---

activity of My Father working deeply in the lives His people. And I will give them the keys to the kingdom of heaven. For through them, the church, the kingdom will grow." Thus, the church becomes a world mission strategy center. God implements His strategy and activity through every church He establishes, empowers, and guides to go into the entire world. With the keys to the kingdom, the churches preach the gospel, and all heaven is open to those who hear, believe, and receive Jesus Christ as Lord.

In the eternal plan of God, the New Testament reveals that each church is to be a center for world missions. They are a fountainhead of God's activity that flows into every corner of the earth, giving the opportunity for all people to hear the good news of God's great salvation. God desires that all nations be included; every person is to hear the gospel.

> *"But you will receive power when the Holy Spirit has come upon you, and you will be My witnesses in Jerusalem, in all Judea and Samaria, and to the ends of the earth."*
>
> ACTS 1:8

Jesus told the disciples that He would build His church, that He would give them the keys to the kingdom of heaven, and then He commanded them to "go . . . and make disciples of all nations, baptizing them in the name of the Father and of the Son and of the Holy Spirit, teaching them to observe everything I have commanded you" (Matt. 28:19–20). He also told them how His plan would unfold. They would start in Jerusalem, move into Judea and Samaria, and on to the ends of the earth. "Beginning at Jerusalem" was obviously a reference to the church He established in that city. They would have their Lord to guide them as they took the gospel of the kingdom of heaven to all the nations of the earth.

The Book of Acts spells this out in detail. First, Peter preached in Jerusalem, and that entire city was shaken when the gospel was preached. Then the Holy Spirit led Philip to go down to Samaria to preach the gospel in that region. A revival broke out, and multitudes were saved and entered the kingdom of heaven. The church at Jerusalem sent Peter and John to see all this, and "they traveled back

to Jerusalem, evangelizing many villages of the Samaritans"
(Acts 8:25). Then Philip was again led by the angel of the Lord to go
down on the road that leads to Gaza, a desert town, and he preached
the good news to an Ethiopian eunuch who was returning to North
Africa. The kingdom of heaven was again opened by Philip's preaching, and the Ethiopian ruler was saved and "went on his way rejoic-
ing" (Acts 8:39). But Philip continued to preach in all the villages from
Azotus to Caesarea.

All this activity was "strategized" by God's Spirit from the center
of His activity in the church in Jerusalem. The Lord continued to
make the church in Jerusalem a mission strategy center by God granting Peter a vision to reach the Gentiles. An angel had spoken to

---

*"And repentance for forgiveness of sins would be proclaimed in His
name to all the nations, beginning at Jerusalem."*

LUKE 24:47

Cornelius and by divine providence brought the two together. Peter
obeyed God, went down to Cornelius's house, and began to preach the
gospel to them also. While preaching about God's great salvation, the
kingdom of heaven was opened to Cornelius, and all those who heard
the Word entered into the kingdom. Peter baptized them all, and the
Holy Spirit suddenly came upon each one. Peter quickly returned to
Jerusalem to tell what God had done, and the whole church rejoiced
saying, "So God has granted repentance resulting in life to even the
Gentiles" (Acts 11:18).

The remainder of the Book of Acts demonstrates that every local
church was designed by God to be a center for His activity to spread
to other parts of the world, just like the first church in Jerusalem. The
church in Antioch began to function with the same mission awareness,
as did the church in Jerusalem. Again God was the One who told them
how He would do this in them. The Holy Spirit instructed them: "Set

apart for Me Barnabas and Saul for the work that I have called them to" (Acts 13:2).

Thus began one of the greatest church-planting movements in all of history. As we study the progress of this mission effort, we see that each congregation seemed to multiply into other churches as their members went everywhere preaching the gospel. It seems as though in every place they went to preach the gospel, people were saved and churches were established. Everything was done by the churches and through the churches, encouraged by the apostle Paul. We read in Acts 16:5, "So the churches were strengthened in the faith and were increased in number daily." The new believers traveled as far as Phoenicia, Cyprus, and Antioch, preaching the Word. Every church God established had become a world mission strategy center.

> *In the eternal plan of God, the New Testament reveals*
> *that each church is to be a center for world missions.*

When I was pastoring in Canada, this divine strategy overwhelmed me too. Though our church was few in number, I believed God would inaugurate His strategy through our church as well. The week I arrived, God had sent five men from a city of thirty thousand people, ninety miles north of us. As in the New Testament, they had come to ask us to come to them and preach the gospel. I did, twice a week, and a church was born. Soon other communities were asking if we would come to them also. Still others came and asked our mission churches if they could help establish churches in their areas as well. This pattern of God making *every* church and mission a world mission strategy center continued for the twelve years I pastored in that area. When I left, we had about thirty-eight new churches and missions, plus several other towns and villages with new Bible studies that had the potential of becoming another church. We had believed God when He told us in His Word to take the gospel to every person. So we mapped out our province and asked God to let us begin a church in each area, teaching each one that they then had the responsibility of taking the gospel to every person.

Are You Ready?

Are you ready? What a question! And in God's kingdom this question is life and death. Are you ready, as a church and as an individual member of your church, to have God work through you to accomplish His saving purposes in your world? Others have faced this life-deciding moment. When God commands a church to do what it has never done before or go where it has never gone before, every church must be ready! Christ said He had come from heaven not to do His own will, but "the will of Him who sent Me" (John 6:38). This is still what He is doing as Head over each church. Are you ready for God to do His will through you as a church?

> *Multitudes, multitudes in the valley of decision!*
> *For the day of the LORD is near in the valley of decision.*
> JOEL 3:14

The church I pastored in Canada had been a traditional church, practicing faithfully since the late 1920s. They had been performing religious activities for many years, but now it was obvious that God would do so much more. As the pastor, I sought to prepare the members to obey and follow their Lord. Before long He was directing us to begin new mission churches. They had never done this before, but they were ready when God spoke and began to lead them. Through one little church God began many new churches during those years.

Then God led the church to do work on the University of Saskatchewan campus; neither they nor I had ever done this work before. Soon we were not only reaching students and professors, but many of them were sensing God's claim on their lives. As a result scores of young adults responded to God and pursued a lifelong call to ministry and missions. We baptized more than 180 students and saw more than 100 respond to God's call in their lives. This led the church to obey their Lord in an area they had never before attempted. We began a theological college to train many who were being called of God. This Christian Training Center held classes for ten years and trained several hundred students.

Our church was ready when God led them to attempt things they had never done before, requiring huge steps of faith in the process. From these experiences, born out of obedience to God, the people came to experience more of God than they had ever known. As a result the church steadily grew toward Christlikeness. During this time the church added staff, started ministries among the mentally challenged, began a ministry in the jails, and started several ethnic Bible studies. Readiness to obey is crucial to experiencing God doing His work through the church.

On the other hand, many churches are not ready. I led a series of meetings in a church in Atlanta, Georgia. The church could seat more than twenty-five hundred people, but they were having only about fifty in attendance. Several of us challenged them to look at their changing white community and to ask God to give them a heart of obedience to follow Him with any challenge He might put before them. At each challenge the church said no! Soon the challenges from God ceased; they sold their buildings to another church and disbanded. Interestingly enough, the new church was ready, and in a few months the church was packed with people God wanted to touch.

Readiness means the entire church is in a deep and real love relationship with the Head, Jesus Christ, and the members God brought together as a body for His Son. In Revelation 2, Jesus warns the church at Ephesus that they had many good qualities, but they had lost their "first love." They were no longer ready to be of use to God. He warns them to "remember then how far you have fallen; repent, and do the works you did at first. Otherwise, I will come to you and remove your lampstand from its place—unless you repent" (Rev. 2:5).

In everyday life readiness is vital. A lighthouse must be ready for the storms that arise and the floundering ships that seek a safe harbor. Firemen need to be ready to face many emergencies where their readiness will save lives. Policemen and doctors need to be ready, alert, awake, and prepared to carry out their assigned tasks.

How much more should churches be ready when the eternal destinies of multitudes are in the balance? God may be ready to bring revival to a church so that through it many could be reached with the gospel. Before the great revivals of history, God's people had a great burden for prayer, personal and corporate cleansing, and holiness. Once attention was given to the necessary prerequisites, revival came suddenly, swiftly, and with great effect. The Moravian Brethren were meeting in Hernhut, Moravia, in August 1727. For days, even weeks, the church had been praying and repenting of sin. Suddenly, during a Lord's Supper service, God was present with such power that the entire body of believers was changed and made ready for one of the greatest missionary movements in history.

Readiness to obey is crucial to experiencing God.

Individuals must be ready, for God may use them in their church to begin a great work. In Wales, young Evan Roberts was ready, and God began a revival through his life. It impacted his church first, then it spread over Wales, and then to the ends of the earth. In a six-month period, 100,000 persons were converted.

The early church was ready, just as Christ had commanded them. When Pentecost came, they were ready and obedient to the work of the Holy Spirit, and three thousand souls were added to them in one day. Spiritual readiness was a mark of God's people when God used them. This is true throughout the Bible. Abraham was ready when God called him to leave everything and go where God would show him. His ready obedience has affected all the rest of God's people from that time forward. Joseph was ready, in spite of hardships, and God was able to put him next to the Pharaoh and save his own family. The major advances in God's eternal purposes have come through individuals and churches that are ready.

Two further aspects of readiness must be shared. First, a church must be ready for the enemy's schemes and attacks. An unready church will let sin run unchecked, and Satan will win. A church can fail to teach its people sound doctrine, leaving them vulnerable to false teachers and leaders, leaving them in ruin. Jesus warned Peter and the disciples about the enemy's plans and said, "Satan has asked to sift you like wheat. But I have prayed for you, that your faith may not fail. And you, when you have turned back, strengthen your brothers" (Luke 22:31–32). They were tested, but Jesus had readied them. Although they stumbled, they did not utterly fall. Instead they remained faithful to God and were greatly used to touch a world.

One further readiness, much needed in our day, is the readiness for Christ's return. In this regard Jesus warned in the parable of ten virgins. Five were wise, and five were foolish and unprepared. Not being ready denied them entrance to the wedding feast. Then Jesus warned his disciples, "Therefore be alert, because you don't know either the day or the hour" (Matt. 25:13). Over and over again Jesus gave this solemn warning. How much more should we be ready for God's activity in our lives?

Can You Imagine?

Can you even imagine what God could do through your life and your church? While serving as a pastor, I was led by God's direction to begin work on a booklet entitled, *What the Spirit Is Saying to the Churches*. Almost at the same time God presented a mandate to begin writing *Experiencing God: Knowing and Doing the Will of God*. This was completed and printed in 1990. I have learned that anything God initiates cannot be measured. Today, ten years later, the adult workbook has sold more than three million copies and is in many other languages around the world. It has touched lives all over the world, from prison cells to the president's office. I am often asked, "Could you have imagined what God would do with your obedience?" Of course, the answer is no!

Every member in a church has God-sized possibilities in their lives and in their church. Our church touched a single young man at our university, resulting in his salvation. Since then he has served as a pastor of a Native American church, finished seminary, directed all our work in Quebec, and is now serving as national ministry leader for the entire work in Canada. Could we, as a church, have imagined this? No!

As we read in Jeremiah, a sequence of verses is overwhelming:

(1) Jeremiah said to God: "Ah, Lord GOD! Behold, You have made the heavens and the earth by Your great power and by Your outstretched arm! Nothing is too difficult for You" (Jer. 32:17). (2) Then later, God said to him: "Behold, I am the LORD, the God of all flesh; is anything too difficult for Me?" (Jer. 32:27). (3) Then, based on this, God invites His people to respond accordingly: "Call to Me, and I will answer you, and I will tell you great and mighty things, which you do not know" (Jer. 33:3).

God always comes to His people with this approach—*faith!* The mind may imagine what God could do through His people, but faith believes and appropriates. Faith takes action in real life, achieving the purposes of God. Jesus said to those in His day, "If you have faith the size of a mustard seed, . . . nothing will be impossible for you" (Matt. 17:20). If an individual has the power to move mountains through faith, can you imagine what God can and will do through an entire church that believes Him and is fully yielded to obey Him? The church at Jerusalem was such a church, and it is said that they had "turned the world upside down" (Acts 17:6).

Obeying God one day at a time will ultimately see God do that which would otherwise be impossible for people to do. The apostle Paul assured the church at Ephesus that they would be "filled with all the fullness of God" (Eph. 3:19). Then he added, "Now to Him who is able to do above and beyond all that we ask or think—according to the power that works in you—to Him be glory in the church and in

Christ Jesus to all generations, forever and ever. Amen" (Eph. 3:20–21). Can you imagine the implication of this truth for your church? If *you* have a vision for your church, you are not even close to what God can do and wants to do in your midst. *His* plans are beyond what you even have the capacity to think! Don't just set goals for your church, for you may reach them and never know what God wanted to do, if you had only believed Him. Remember, the Scripture says that "without faith it is impossible to please God" (Heb. 11:6).

The mind may imagine what God could do through His people, but faith believes and appropriates.

God has chosen to do the impossible through His churches, and He does it in a way that man cannot explain—except in terms of God and His impossibilities. An exciting example is that of a church in Woodstock, Georgia. A good friend of mine is the pastor, and they are seeing God use their church beyond what he could have imagined. In the area of missions, they have used the strategy found in Acts 1:8, "You will receive power when the Holy Spirit has come upon you, and you will be My witnesses in Jerusalem, in all Judea and Samaria, and to the ends of the earth." In the year 2001, they sent mission teams to do outreach in local mission churches, and local multihousing units (Jerusalem). They sent teams to Las Vegas and other U.S.-based mission churches (Judea). They have been in Argentina, Hungary, Ukraine, Paris, Benin, Romania, Russia, and Portugal (Samaria). They have also sent teams to remote regions of Indonesia, Algeria, China, Uzbekistan, Thailand, India, Turkey, and Uganda (uttermost parts of the earth). This church has sent out sixty-five career missionaries, and their total mission giving for the year was $1,925,180. Incredible! This is a local church that is on mission with God. They are seeing God touch a world through their local church, just as God desires for each of our churches. This is obviously a large church, but any church, no matter what the size, can have a global impact. The key is not their abilities and resources; the key is God in their midst.

No discussion of God's salvation through the local church would be complete without including Paul's letter to the church at Corinth. Here is an ultimate description of God's love through His churches and the fathomless magnitude of His love made known to each church. "What no eye has seen and no ear has heard, and what has never come into a man's heart, is what God has prepared for those who love Him. Now God has revealed them to us by the Spirit, for the Spirit searches everything, even the deep things of God. . . . Now we have not received the spirit of the world, but the Spirit who is from God, in order to know what has been freely given to us by God" (1 Cor. 2:9–10, 12).

Can you imagine what God *already* has in place for your church? Do you believe Him, as He expresses this truth through the Scriptures? It was written to the local church in Corinth. There seemed to be no limit to what God had in place and to what He had chosen for them to know through the Holy Spirit. We don't know too much of this historical record, but Paul's two letters—1 and 2 Corinthians— do give us an indication that Corinth, one of the most godless cities in all the Roman Empire at this time, was profoundly affected by the gospel that was shared through this church. God did such an amazing work in this pagan city that Paul and the church of Corinth saw the power of God move in ways they could never have imagined.

God has so much He would do through every church. How should a church live out its life with these truths in their understanding?

And many of the Corinthians, when they heard, believed and were baptized. Then the Lord said to Paul in a night vision, "Don't be afraid, but keep on speaking and don't be silent. For I am with you, and no one will lay a hand on you to hurt you, because I have many people in this city." And he stayed there a year and six months, teaching the word of God among them.

ACTS 18:8B–11

First, every member, beginning with the pastor, must believe Him. To have a thorough knowledge of the nature of the church, the church must be taught what the Scriptures say. The Book of Acts is the best church growth manual I know! Therein is the greatness of God in His people and the way in which God's salvation was spread through the early churches.

Second, they must believe God is the same today as He was in the first century. When He chose to place Christ as the Head of our churches, He fully intended to channel all the resources of heaven through Him into our lives. It may take time for the church to move from where they have been to where God wants them to be. We must, therefore, be patient with one another. God is not through with us yet! Teach one another and help the members of your church body. Where some doubt, help them toward real biblical faith in God. May history record of you what David said: "I [we] waited patiently for the LORD; and He inclined to me [us] and heard my [our] cry. . . . He put a new song in my [our] mouth, a song of praise to our God; many will see and fear and will trust in the LORD" (Ps. 40:1, 3).

There Is a Cost

Most Christians, especially in the western part of the world, do not understand the cost of discipleship. I have had the privilege of travelling around the world, ministering to both missionaries and the people to whom they have been sent. As a result, I have seen and heard about the tremendous suffering believers are enduring around the world. In fact, there are probably more Christian martyrs today than in any other time in human history.

I saw a letter from a young couple that had gone to minister in a difficult area of Africa, where Christians were being severely persecuted. The letter was coded so that the authorities would not understand its true meaning. Think of the persecution as you read about the Christians in terms of "potted plants."

Out of the six plants that had been given to us, two have died. The other four are not doing so well; the heat is increasing, and the water is little. We don't know yet whether they will survive. Two new plants have been given, and they have been planted well, but it is very hot over here, and we don't know whether they will survive.

I met the young couple who wrote this letter when they were home on furlough. They relayed some of the struggles in that country and how it had affected the mission of which they were a part. The stories of martyrdom were so grim that I cannot include them in such a book as this.

Yet in the midst of such a tremendous cost factor to be a Christian, the couple relayed how God was working in a powerful way to bring people to Christ. In fact, the night before they left to return home, a

---

Now great crowds were traveling with Him. So He turned and said to them: "If anyone comes to Me and does not hate his own father and mother, wife and children, brothers and sisters—yes, even his own life—he cannot be My disciple. Whoever does not bear his own cross and come after Me cannot be My disciple.

For which of you, wanting to build a tower, doesn't first sit down and calculate the cost, to see if he has enough to complete it? Otherwise, after he has laid the foundation and cannot finish it, all the onlookers will begin to make fun of him, saying, 'This man started to build and wasn't able to finish.'

Or what king, going to war against another king, will not first sit down and decide if he is able with ten thousand to oppose the one who comes against him with twenty thousand? If not, while the other is still far off, he sends a delegation and asks for terms of peace. In the same way, therefore, every one of you who does not say good-bye to all his possessions cannot be My disciple."

LUKE 14:25–33

small band of Christians made their way to the missionaries' house in the middle of the night. On the roof of the home, they had a little plastic pool where they held a baptismal service for eight new believers. I asked the couple, "Tell me about the kind of faith those new believers have." The missionaries described the people who responded to the gospel with sincere gratitude to God. When they heard about the life, death, and Resurrection of Christ, they felt they owed everything to the Lord who laid down His life for them. They never saw this as a sacrifice but as a privilege. The love of Christ had captured their hearts.

Jesus never hid the cost of being His disciple. He made clear that His disciples would have to deny self, take up their cross, and then follow Him. We must deal with this mark of a true disciple, for it is also the mark of a true church. Although individual believers endured suffering, the cost was experienced and shared in the context of the local church. There would be no spiritual orphans or mavericks among God's people. The cost of following Jesus would be real, personal, and at times deadly. The cost could only be carried faithfully in the context of God's people corporately. All God's people would share in the cost when any part of the body was suffering.

Unfortunately, I have found that today there is an intentional effort to avoid the cost of discipleship. And often, there is a deliberate abandoning of the people of God during times of cost, in order to go to another church where they can find times of blessing instead. What a cop-out! What a tragic misunderstanding of discipleship! What an affront to God's great salvation! Our generation can be so self-centered, forsaking God's will when the cost of discipleship gets hard. Church hopping is usually nothing more than a selfish desire to be happy, when the Lord desires that His disciples be holy. He desires for them to make a difference where He has put them and not simply go to the place where their needs are better met.

Too many people today look for shortcuts in their Christian life or substitutes for the hard, painful, and weary work of a disciple. They want instant gratification and pleasure but no cross. They look for ease and comfort in life, but they are unwilling to count the cost of following Jesus. If they do not receive honor, position, and recognition, they search out other churches that will grant recognition so they can be "satisfied" in their Christian life. The thought of scars or wounds, like their Master's, does not even enter their heads. They will accept no pain or sorrow even though their Savior suffered greatly. They want all the benefits of God's great salvation with no costs attached. This is too often characteristic of individual believers, yet more tragically it is also the same in the churches of which they are members.

> *"A disciple is not above his teacher, or a slave above his master."*
> MATTHEW 10:24

"Make us successful so my family and I can be happy!" "I can't afford to give financially to the ministry of the church; I have too many other obligations!" "Don't ask me to be a part of starting a mission church; it would *cost* our family too much!" On and on I hear "disciples" disqualifying themselves as disciples of Jesus.

Jesus made clear to all of His disciples that He was going to suffer in order to accomplish the Father's will for His life. In fact, one of the most powerful images that Jesus left the disciples concerning the cost of doing the Father's will is seen in the upper room after the Resurrection. The doors were locked when Jesus appeared to the disciples and simply said, "Peace be still." He then showed them His hands and side, revealing the cost of doing the Father's will. As the disciples gazed at the wounds in their Lord's body, they heard Him say these words: "Just as the Father has sent Me, I also send you" (John 20:21). Can you picture the scene? Do you feel the moment? The wounds of the Savior made a lasting impression on the disciples concerning the cost of following Jesus. For "just as" the Father sent Him, now they were being sent into the world to do the Father's will.

When was the last time you looked at the Savior's hands and side? The cross for Jesus was real; it meant great suffering on behalf of sinners. If we want to make an impact on sinners in our world, there is a cost. Are you willing to pick up your cross and follow Jesus?

I now want to deal with some specific costs that will be found in a church. It is not enough to talk in generalities at this point, for we have a hard time applying this aspect of God's great salvation. But in our desire to grow toward Christlikeness, in our pursuit of knowing and doing the will of God, there are some stumbling blocks along the way. I have found that they are nearly all connected to "the cost factor."

Church hopping is usually nothing more than a selfish desire to be happy, when the Lord desires that His disciples be holy.

First, there is the cost of giving. For the church to accomplish the purposes God has for them, sacrificial giving will always be involved. Every time I think of sacrificial giving, I think of dear old Iva Bates. She was a widowed farm lady, living on a meager pension and a modest savings account. When the Lord challenged our church to give toward a building project, she was led to participate as a member of that body. So she came and brought a check for five thousand dollars. Since I knew that she didn't have much money, I went to her only daughter and asked about Iva's situation. I discovered that she only had nine thousand dollars total in her account to live on for the rest of her life. I told her daughter that I couldn't let her mom do that; it wasn't right! Then she said something that has stayed with me ever since: "Would you deny my mother the privilege of sacrificing for her Lord?" It crushed me.

But the Lord's promises are true; He does care for the righteous. When I was about to leave that church to go to another place where the Lord was leading me to serve, I just had to go and see Iva's daughter again. I said, "You don't have to tell me if you prefer, but could I ask a personal question? How much money does your mother have in her savings?"

> *Sitting across from the temple treasury, He watched how the crowd dropped money into the treasury. Many rich people were putting in large sums. And a poor widow came and dropped in two tiny coins worth very little. Summoning His disciples, He said to them, "I assure you: This poor widow has put in more than all those giving to the temple treasury. For they all gave out of their surplus, but she out of her poverty has put in everything she possessed—all she had to live on."*
>
> MARK 12:41–44

Her daughter replied, "It is an amazing thing. I checked the other day and discovered that she had $11,000 in her account, and I have no idea where it came from."

There is a real financial cost to following Christ. Every believer will be challenged at this point. For Jesus to be Lord of our lives, He must take precedence over our material possessions. Unfortunately, many fail this test. That is why the Scripture says, "The love of money is a root of all kinds of evil, and by craving it, some have wandered away from the faith and pierced themselves with many pains" (1 Tim. 6:10).

Another cost might be God's call on a church to reach out to the youth of their community. Some will not be willing to change their church in order to reach the young people. There might be different music, more noise, higher costs for youth activities, or the hiring of a youth minister. Some are not willing to receive unsaved youth who look and act differently.

I was in my son Mel's church the other day and noticed a large hole in the wall of the Sunday school hallway. When I asked what happened, he simply said, "Growing pains. Our youth group is enjoying tremendous growth, and our building is taking a beating. We will teach them respect for God's house, but isn't it great to see God bringing many young people to salvation?"

He also mentioned that he has had to teach the church about the cost of reaching youth. He reminds the church that he was one of those youth wrestling in the hallways just a few short years ago. In fact, some adults in his church today used to baby-sit him as a child. Mel laughs as he warned the church, "Be nice to these rambunctious youth. Someday they may be your pastor!"

A tremendous cost will come when God wants to call out laborers. That may mean that He will lead the church to look toward the local college or university. A church must be ready to pay the price to reach the students. They tend to have vision, energy, and faith but little money. They will often want to be a part of extensive mission and outreach projects, use contemporary music equipment, and request funds to minister more effectively. But if a church is willing to count the cost and sacrifice, the rewards will far exceed the costs. However, the costs are real, and some will resist the changes needed to do the will of God.

God may also remind a church, during a time of home or foreign missions study, that He wants their church to become involved with Him in many new ways. Mission trips are costly, but they touch a world that needs to know Christ. The trips will also affect those who go. Some may sense God's call into ministry or missions. Parents will suddenly realize how real the cost is to them when they give their son or daughter over to God for the rest of their lives.

Starting a new mission church, close to home or in another region, may cost the loss of members and money in order to establish a strong foundation. It is costly to be obedient to God in starting new churches. It may take the pastor away for weeks at a time, and he may even feel called to move to the new mission or to a missionary career overseas.

In some ways there is always a costly risk to obeying God in touching a world. For example, a church may be given a burden from God to reach out to a large number of deaf people in the community. A church where I was interim pastor voted to do this, but they did not realize how this would change or interrupt their comfortable church life. Soon our basement was crowded with the deaf and their families. The noise level soared while we were in worship. Undisciplined children began to run throughout. Our supplies began to be used and not replaced. We began to receive calls to help counsel and help in ways we had not anticipated. Everything changed. Fortunately God enabled us to do what He called us to do. We adjusted, loved, and were patient and kind. As a result, we saw many deaf people saved and a growing church develop. Later, they found their own place to meet, but we had the joy of being on mission with God to the deaf community.

Reaching language groups, such as Chinese, Laotians, Cambodians, East Indians, or Spanish can make many costly demands in churches. When churches in the Vancouver area began to reach out to different ethnic groups, I remember little things like the lingering strong odor of oriental cooking that we were not used to smelling. We had to overcome the difficulties related to communication barriers and cultural differences. I understand the real-life costs to reaching people for Christ, but if a church can remember the incredible "adjustments" God made with His Son for us, we may be ashamed of our complaints. For just as Christ made sacrifices in order that we might come to know God, so He will ask us to make sacrifices so that others may come to know Him as well.

> *For you know the grace of our Lord Jesus Christ: although He was rich, for your sake He became poor, so that by His poverty you might become rich.*
>
> 2 CORINTHIANS 8:9

When we read passages like Philippians 2:5–11, we are forced to reconsider our reluctance not only to "count the cost" but also to "pay the price" to be involved with Him on mission in our world. Jesus chose to empty Himself as the Son of God so that He might humbly come to earth in the likeness of a man to be our Savior. He did not remain comfortable in the heavenly places, but He went straight to the difficult places and became a friend of sinners. We cannot remain comfortable and go with Christ at the same time. There will be a cost when He leads us to minister to the prisons, the abortion clinics, skid-row mission projects, English as second language classes, etc. Every individual, as well as the church corporately, should "count the cost" to follow Jesus. They must deny self and take up a real cross.

We cannot remain comfortable and go with Christ at the same time.

Jesus announced that some would not be willing to pay the price. What they don't realize is that the cost of not following Jesus is far more severe. Jesus said, "Whoever wants to save his life will lose it, but whoever loses his life because of Me and the gospel will save it" (Mark 8:35). If a church faces the cost in being used of God and chooses to turn back, they may never recover from the consequences of that decision. For when a church is more concerned with "saving their life" by trying to protect their lifestyle, their comfort, or their possessions, they *will* lose their life. They will lose the reason God chose to grant them salvation.

This may be a much-needed time in your church to face honestly your involvement with your Lord as He seeks to be on mission in our world. For Christ, the Head of your church, is seeking to do the will of His Father through you. When we refuse to do what He asks us to do, the Father's plan to touch the world is impaired.

In this regard, there is another area that may be costly—if you obey your Lord and pray for laborers. For if God should hear your prayer as a church, He may begin to call out many from your church. This can be demanding for the pastors who walk with the people during this time. The pastor and staff may need to spend time with parents who really need help understanding their role in the call of one or more of their children. The leadership of the church will need help to know how to walk alongside a church from which God is calling many into service. Time with each one called will be absolutely crucial. They will need help through their ongoing decisions now that they are called. They will need counsel in the courses they might take in school, the college or seminary they will attend, the spouse that they will marry, the financial demands they will endure, and the potential opposition in their own family.

I watched God call many from the churches I pastored, and God led me to spend countless hours with them in the process. Many of them came from another faith, and the parents were furious, even to the point of forcing them out of the home. It will take much time and sacrifice to help each one through these moments so that they will not become discouraged along the way. A church will pay a great price to stay around the *called* until they are trained and in the field of service God has chosen for them.

> *Then He said to His disciples, "The harvest is abundant, but the workers are few. Therefore, pray to the Lord of the harvest to send out workers into His harvest."*
>
> MATTHEW 9:37–38

Pastor, because you are seen as their father in the ministry, there will be demands on your life for the rest of your life. Recently I spent time in Canada and met with many who responded to God's call on their lives twenty-five to thirty years ago. They are now leaders in our Canadian Convention of churches and still seek me out for counsel and encouragement. Now, because we stayed alongside them, a number of their children have responded to God's call and are currently serving the Lord.

God Is Glorified in His Churches

A number of Scriptures reveal how God is "glorified" in His people. That is to say, God is revealed openly before a watching world as He really is. The apostle Paul understood that "the incalculable riches of the Messiah," which were a "mystery hidden for ages in God," were now to "be made known *through the church* to the rulers

> *Now to Him who is able to do above and beyond all that we ask or think—according to the power that works in you—to Him be glory in the church and in Christ Jesus to all generations, forever and ever. Amen.*
>
> Ephesians 3:20–21

and authorities in the heavens" (Eph. 3:8–10). Isn't that a powerful affirmation of the church? This is God's plan to show the world who He is in all His fullness. The manifold wisdom of God is openly displayed before a watching world through the life of His churches. Glory comes to God when His people live out in their lives what God has provided through His mercy and grace.

The world does not need to see good people doing good things for their God. They need to see God doing "above and beyond all that we ask or think" among His people. When the church allows God to fill them with His presence, the world will see and glorify Him because they have experienced Him in the life of His people. They will know His love because the church sincerely loves all people. They will know His power because the church steps out in faith and attempts what only God can accomplish. The world will stand in awe of God when His people let Him be God in them and through them. When God begins to heal marriages, return wayward children, heal alcoholics and drug addicts, provide for physical needs in times of crisis, and give wisdom to business people, the world comes to know the difference God makes in our world.

On the other hand, when a church does only what the world would do, the world never sees God, and He is denied the glory that is rightly His. For God to be glorified or honored as God in His churches, the churches must turn to Him just as He told them to do. The Scripture says, "Call upon Me in the day of trouble; I shall rescue you, and you will honor Me" (Ps. 50:15).

The world and God's people come to know what God is like when God's people let Him display His mighty work through them. In the Scriptures are many examples, but consider the way Daniel allowed God to work in and through his life. Such was the impact of his life before a watching world that the pagan King Darius made the following decree: "I make a decree that in all the dominion of my kingdom men are to fear and tremble before the God of Daniel; for He is the living God and enduring forever, and His kingdom is one which will not be destroyed, and His dominion will be forever. He delivers and rescues and performs signs and wonders in heaven and on earth, who has also delivered Daniel from the power of the lions" (Dan. 6:26–27). God was glorified through His servant Daniel!

Study Questions for Reflection and Response

1. Is your church a world missions strategy center?

2. Do you sense the presence of God guiding your church during times of congregational business meetings?

3. Is your church ready to pay the price to be obedient to Christ and touch the world?

4. How do you believe God is glorified in a church? Is He being glorified in your church? What adjustments need to be made?

Then Jesus came near and said to them, "All authority has been given to Me in heaven and on earth. Go, therefore, and make disciples of all nations, baptizing them in the name of the Father and of the Son and of the Holy Spirit, teaching them to observe everything I have commanded you. And remember, I am with you always, to the end of the age."

MATTHEW 28:18–20

NINE

The Church on Mission with Their Lord

Experiencing God Together in Life

A Story from Mel

Seminary life was winding down, and we knew God was preparing us for ministry in Canada. Gina and I had a wonderful time pastoring in Texas while in school, but we were ready to follow the Lord to the next assignment He had for us. Several churches began to contact us, but as we prayed about God's will, He directed us to a small, struggling church in British Columbia, Canada. In fact, it was in the worst condition of any church that had talked with us. But God is the Master, and we are the servants, so we pursued it.

The church was around forty years old and had dropped in attendance to about eight to ten people. They decided to merge with another struggling church plant so that they could call a new pastor together; that made a total of nineteen members. We flew up to meet with the people and confirm God's direction in our lives. When we arrived, the situation looked worse than we had first thought. We were the only pastoral candidates that would talk with them about coming. The financial situation was obviously pretty bleak, and it became apparent that even the money they promised for a salary was mostly "in faith" that God would provide it from somewhere. We walked through the building and saw that it was falling apart and infested with termites. I immediately thought of the beautiful renovations and education wing that we had just finished at our previous church. We looked at the congregation and saw only a couple of children and no youth or young adults. I thought about my five-month-old daughter and the growing children's program at the previous church. We realized that the church had no sound system, no computer, no photocopier, no equipment of any kind. I thought of the brand new sound system we had just bought, the new church van we had purchased, and all the equipment that we had in the previous church. We looked at the housing market and were disappointed that we would not be able to buy a home. I thought about the home we were leaving at the previous church. We discovered that the next closest church in our convention was two and a half hours away, and they were running about forty people. I thought of the many churches and pastors in our association of churches who were a great source of encouragement at the previous church. We would soon discover that many people in the community were convinced that our building was demon possessed and needed a cleansing. I thought of the reputation our previous church had gained for being a place where God was at work.

As I began to compare the place of service I was leaving to the situation I was considering, I thought of the many other churches that wanted us to come to their church as pastor. I thought of the pastoral experience I had gained and the Ph.D. I was completing. I quickly surmised that I deserved a larger church with better pay! Wrong! Nothing could be further from the truth! I didn't deserve anything from God.

Serving anywhere in the kingdom of God was far more than I deserved. It was an honor just to be called a child of God and a privilege to be called to serve as a pastor of any church.

My wife and I were alone one evening during the visit. As we talked about what we were walking away from and what we were about to get into, my wife began to weep. As she held our baby in her arms, she asked, "Mel, do we really want to do this?" It broke my heart. So we prayed and sought the face of God together.

As we did, the Lord seemed to guide our thinking. He said, "Mission work is hard! If you don't go, who will?" Then it seemed as though He was silent again. He left us with the realization that sacrifice is all right.

The Father's will is often hard work, but somebody must go. The Lord gave us no assurances that He would bless the work and cause the church to grow. He simply said, "Mission work is hard, but will you follow me anyway?" Then the Holy Spirit brought a passage to our minds that He has used many times. "If anyone wants to come with Me, he must deny himself, take up his cross, and follow Me. For whoever wants to save his life will lose it, but whoever loses his life because of Me will find it" (Matt. 16:24–25). That night we knelt and prayed to God, laying our lives before Him and committing our lives to follow Him whatever the cost.

As soon as we made the decision to follow the Lord to this difficult assignment, the Holy Spirit brought immediate peace and assurance of His presence. He helped us to understand that if we step out in faith, He will be faithful. That is indeed what happened. What we thought was a sacrifice turned out to be one of the greatest blessings of our lives. We saw many lives transformed and a church grow and help start other churches in the area. What an exciting adventure it is to be on mission with the Lord! For He desires to use His church to touch the world.

God Is Not Willing That Any Perish

To every Christian who is sensitive to the Lord at all, the words begin to ring through their souls that the Lord does not want "any to

---

The Lord does not delay His promise, as some understand delay, but is patient with you, not wanting any to perish, but all to come to repentance.

2 PETER 3:9

---

perish, but all to come to repentance." For "the day of the Lord will come like a thief; on that day the heavens will pass away with a loud noise, the elements will burn and be dissolved, and the earth and the works on it will be disclosed. Since all these things are to be destroyed in this way, it is clear what sort of people you should be in holy conduct and godliness" (2 Pet. 3:10–11). God is merciful and long-suffering toward His people. He does not want any person to perish. He wants every person to hear the gospel and have an opportunity to repent and be saved from his or her sin. But too often churches become self-centered and are not willing to look beyond themselves to the needs around them. When a church becomes selfish, it will inevitably begin to have quarrels within the body. As a result, the lost world around them suffers grievously because His people stop taking the gospel to others who need it so desperately.

God has no Plan B. He purposed that His churches take His good news to the world. If we are not doing it, He demonstrates his great mercy, not judging us immediately as He could. Instead, He is long-suffering and patient in working with His people to repent. Too much is at stake. Withholding judgment from His people, however, will not be delayed forever, and "the day of the Lord will come" (2 Pet. 3:10). The patience of God with His people is throughout the Bible.

"Therefore I will judge you, O house of Israel, each according to his conduct," declares the Lord GOD. "Repent and turn away from all your transgressions, so that iniquity may not become a stumbling block to you. Cast away from you all your transgressions which you have committed, and make yourselves a new heart and a new spirit! . . . For I have no pleasure in the death of anyone who dies," declares the Lord GOD. "Therefore, repent and live" (Ezek. 18:30–32).

The reason for His patience? He is not willing that any should perish. So He works with and warns His people as He does with the church at Ephesus in Revelation 2:1–7. When a church loses its "first love," it ultimately has lost its reason for being, and it is therefore of no use to God.

As a pastor, I was regularly alert to the spiritual condition of the church. I was particularly concerned if we were losing our first love and were in danger. I saw this dramatically in a deacons' meeting when one of our men said, "Pastor, you should assign us visitors and others to visit." What he was asking for was prodding or additional motivation to go out and do their job. I said, "I won't do that. If love does not compel you to visit, I won't use any other substitute for love." I then turned in God's Word to teach them from 1 Corinthians 13, 2 Corinthians 5, and Revelation 2. God was gracious and brought every heart to unity and love. I never had to assign them someone to love. They did it out of pure hearts before God. It would have been easy to make love assignments, but it would have had a disastrous effect upon our church.

For Christ's love compels us, since we have reached this conclusion: if One died for all, then all died. And He died for all so that those who live should no longer live for themselves, but for the One who died for them and was raised.

2 CORINTHIANS 5:14–15

If God is not willing that any perish, He will lay His heart on our hearts, and we will know that it is the love of Christ that compels us. We must always guard our hearts and the hearts of the people in our church. Our Lord said to the disciples, "Go into all the world and preach the gospel to the whole creation." Then He added, "Whoever believes and is baptized will be saved, but whoever does not believe will be condemned" (Mark 16:15–16).

A Story from Mel

Not long ago I walked with a young couple in whom God was working. They were a young family with two children, enjoying the life they were living. Yet God began to draw them to our church and stir their hearts toward spiritual things. I recall the wife well, for she had virtually no religious background at all. She was eager to know the truth and discover how to have a relationship with God. As the Holy Spirit opened her eyes, she soon prayed to receive Christ as her Lord and Savior.

She made an appointment to come in and talk with me about following the Lord in believer's baptism. But when she arrived, I noticed a strange look on her face that I didn't understand at first. As we talked, she made this statement: "If what I have heard is true, and I believe it is, then that means my mom and dad will not be with me in heaven." And she began to weep. I then knew that she understood both sides of the gospel. Those who believe in Christ will be saved, but those who do not believe will perish.

Perish! What an awful word! Separated from God eternally and suffering this as a consequence of sin without repentance. We must carry this same burden in our churches and never lose it! Sadly, as we watch Jesus' disciples, He was drawing individuals to Himself, and the disciples would send them away. Even as the crowds got larger, the disciples urged Jesus to send them home. But Jesus said, "You feed them!" For he desired to continue teaching and preaching that maybe one more might believe and be saved.

> *For God loved the world in this way: He gave His only Son, so that everyone who believes in Him will not perish but have eternal life.... Anyone who believes in Him is not judged, but anyone who does not believe is already judged, because he has not believed in the name of the only Son of God.*
>
> JOHN 3:16, 18

We must instruct our leaders and God's people to seek the heart of God. Each Sunday school teacher must not only teach a lesson but also know personally if every member of the class is saved. He or she must seek to enlist them to "go out into the highways and lanes and make them come in, so that my house may be filled" (Luke 14:23).

Soon after D. L. Moody, the great preacher and evangelist, was saved, he was under such conviction about the lostness of the poor children and youth that he started his own Bible class. Quickly it had hundreds in attendance, and many were being saved. Could you do this? Could your church do this? Would the heart of God have you do this, as you seek to be on mission with your Lord to touch a lost world?

God Builds His Churches for Mission

The Father adds to the body as it pleases Him (1 Cor. 12:18), and Jesus builds His church upon His Father's activity in the lives of people He is drawing (Matt. 16:18). God puts members in each church to accomplish His purposes for that church. In other words, He fashions a church for His specific purposes. It is like the constant picture throughout the Bible of the potter and the clay (Isa. 64:8; Jer. 18:1–11; and Rom. 9:21–24).

Because I knew this was God's way for Him to equip the church and ready us for His assignment, I watched carefully to see whom God was adding to our body. This became a clear indication of what God was preparing our church to do, simply because we could see a pattern to those whom He was adding to us. I noticed God added a young woman with a great burden for the physically and mentally challenged. We saw this as God's way of alerting us to His purpose for our church. As she began to teach us and equip us to care for this special group of people, we began a ministry to those who are often neglected but precious to God.

We had been praying about starting a ministry on some Native American reserves, when all of a sudden God added nurses and doctors to our congregation. Whereas before we had a hard time getting accepted on the reserves, now that we came offering medical help, the doors were wide open for us to minister. God began to lead us into many significant ministries, simply because we were watching to see who He added and made the adjustments to how He was shaping our body. We did not copy what was successful in other churches. We let God shape us uniquely for the assignment He had for us. If each church let God build and fashion its body, He would have somebody to take the gospel to every person. If we copy others' successes, we will try to reach the same people with the same methods, and many will go untouched as a result. That is why churches are often so different from one another. But when we all do our part, we find that God's strategy to reach every person in our community is realized.

A caution is necessary at this point. Paul stressed the sovereignty of God to touch everybody in His church. So he reminded the Galatian church in 3:26, 28, that "you are all sons of God through faith in Christ Jesus. . . . There is no Jew or Greek, slave or free, male or female; for you are all one in Christ Jesus." No one should be turned aside or neglected because you don't feel he or she fits into your church. God has the sovereign right to add to your church as it pleases Him, and He doesn't need to ask your permission! He knows what He is doing, and it is always linked directly to His purpose for your church.

In recent years I have discovered that many pastors and church leaders can be intimidated by some of the people whom God adds. For example, when God adds top CEOs or other executive leaders from the business world, they often feel estranged and have a hard time fitting in. Often people who come from a lower social, educational, or economic standing are shunned. Some churches will not receive ethnic people who are not like them, even though they are people for whom Christ died. This is totally unacceptable to God. He is not willing that *any* should perish, and He alone has the sovereign right to add to a church whom He wills.

Often members within the church are greatly underused, while only a few carry the load. Each member must be taught that God has a purpose in mind for every member in the body. Great effort should be made to see that each one is strategically integrated into the body so that the whole body may function to its greatest efficiency. This includes the children and youth, giving them an opportunity to grow as they contribute in whatever way God has gifted them. It has always been God's pattern to build up each member of the body, so that Christ may have a healthy and strong body through which He can touch the world.

The Leaders Equip

A crucial Scripture that every leader must pattern his or her life after is found in Ephesians 4:11–16. Every verse and every word is significant. God gave special leaders to the church that are absolutely essential if the church is going to be the church God intended. The leaders were given for a special purpose, the "equipping of the saints." That means they are to help each member function effectively in the body where God has placed them. When they function in this way, the whole body is built up. As a result, they will grow toward (1) unity in the faith, (2) the knowledge of the Son of God, (3) a perfect or complete person, (4) the measure of the stature of the fullness of Christ, (5) ensuring that no one should ever be tossed by the waves and blown around by every wind of teaching, (6) speaking the truth in love, (7) growing up into all things into Him who is the Head—even Christ, and (8) causing growth in the body for the edifying of itself in love.

Some churches see the leader's task as primarily evangelism or soul winning. But that is not true in the New Testament. Leaders, especially the apostles, taught, taught, and taught every believer. The apostles insisted that they devote themselves "to prayer and to the preaching ministry" (Acts 6:4). Leaders, however, must understand that you cannot teach the people what you don't know. You cannot lead the people where you haven't been. You cannot take the people beyond your own walk with God.

When we examine what the apostles said in the context of their situation, they set an example that we must follow. In our day the larger the church and the more ministries we have, the less time we seem to spend in prayer and the Word of God. The apostles saw that the church in Jerusalem was growing rapidly and the needs were increasing. But the apostles knew that the redemption of the world had an awful lot to do with their personal and corporate walk with God. They said, "If we are going to give ourselves to anything, it will be to prayer and the Word of God." Thousands of people depended on *their* walk with God. They could not understand the ways of God or the purposes of God unless they spent time with God. For *they* were not the leaders of God's people; God was the leader, and they needed a word from Him. They had come to know that God's ways are not man's ways. So they studied God's Word, and they spent much time in prayer asking for wisdom to guide the people of God. What they gave the people was simply the overflow of their walk with God.

I have come to appreciate the challenge that a man named Bishop Quayle gave to a group of preachers: "Preaching is the art of making a sermon and delivering it. Why no, that is not preaching. Preaching is the art of making a preacher and delivering that. Preaching is the outrush of a soul in speech. Therefore the elemental business in preaching is not with preaching but with the preacher. It is no trouble to preach, but a vast trouble to construct a preacher. What then, in the light of this, is the task of the preacher? Mainly this, the amassing of a great soul so as to have something worthwhile to give—the sermon is the preacher up to date." The same is true with any leader of God's people; he or she must have an up-to-date relationship with God.

When a leader understands that the work of the kingdom is not done by our abilities but by God's, he is on the right track. For that requires that he hears a word from Him and walks in His Spirit. Too often we make decisions the same way the world does. We look at our bank account and see if *we* have enough money. We look at the economy to predict our future actions. We look at one another and measure *our* abilities. We gather facts and set our long-range goals and set out to achieve them. But God continually says, "Call on Me!" He says, "Call to Me and I will answer you, and I will tell you great and mighty things, which you do not know" (Jer. 33:3). As a leader, you must either walk with God or vacate your position. Too much is at stake for the people of God who are following your lead.

When you look at Jesus' life, you see that He spent much time studying the Scriptures and in prayer. He then took the things of God and gave them to the disciples. He spent a great deal of effort equipping them. His prayer in John 17 makes clear that this was His intended purpose. Look at how He equipped them, as He described in that chapter:

Verse 6	"I have revealed Your name to the men You gave Me."
Verse 8	"The words that You gave to Me, I have given to them."
Verse 9	"I pray for them."
Verse 10	"I have been glorified in them."
Verse 12	"While I was with them I was protecting them."
Verse 13	"They may have My joy completed in them."
Verse 18	"Just as You sent Me into the world, I also have sent them into the world."
Verse 19	"I sanctify Myself for them, so they also may be sanctified by the truth."
Verse 21	"May they all be one, just as You, Father, are in Me and I am in You."
Verse 22	"I have given them the glory that You have given to Me."

Jesus fully equipped His disciples. Every leader's job is to equip fully the members of the church. Jesus' instruction is clear in this matter. "Teaching them to observe everything I have commanded you" (Matt. 28:20). If a leader takes this command seriously, he or she will equip the people by teaching them several things:

1. How to have a relationship with God through Jesus Christ.
2. How to be filled with the Holy Spirit.
3. How to love one another with the love of Christ.
4. How to express *koinonia* for one another in the body.
5. How to study God's Word and pray.
6. How to live according to God's will and strive for Christlikeness.

The health of the body depends on the health of every member of the body. The members are absolutely interdependent with one another. If one member hurts, the whole body hurts. If there is division in the body, the whole body suffers. But most importantly, each church has the capacity to touch the world as the body of Christ. The ability of Christ to do His work effectively is directly related to the health and unity of the body. The leaders are the ones who must equip the body for such health.

Who are the leaders we are talking about? Certainly the pastor and staff, if the church has some. The deacons are also crucial, for their primary role is to maintain the unity and health in the body. These leaders must give personal care for every member. Both staff and deacons can potentially drift into becoming administrators of the church organization rather than equippers of the church members. If that happens, the whole body will suffer and will miss out on much that God had wanted to do through them. There are of course many other leaders that help build up the body. Whether they are teachers, a committee chairperson, or whatever leaders God raises up, they have a tremendous impact on the work of the kingdom as they equip the people of God.

I cannot express strongly enough how important it is that leaders walk with God. The Lord wants you to come to Him more than you can imagine. Listen to Isaiah 65:1–3: "I permitted Myself to be sought by those who did not ask for Me; I permitted Myself to be found by those who did not seek Me. I said, 'Here am I, here am I,' to a nation which did not call on My name. I have spread out My hands all day long to a rebellious people, who walk in the way which is not good, following their own thoughts, a people who continually provoke Me to My face." I fear that this may describe many leaders in our churches today. May we choose to run into His arms and find wisdom for the task He has given us. And when we do, we can take courage in the Lord. For He said, "Do not fear, for I am with you; do not anxiously look about you, for I am your God. I will strengthen you, surely I will help you, surely I will uphold you with My righteous right hand" (Isa. 41:10).

The People Are on Mission

This heading may sound strange, but it is not. It is relevant in our day. Too many churches do not study or look carefully into the New Testament to understand how they fit into the strategy of God to touch a world. There is no question that the Book of Acts describes the church as a people who were on mission with God. It was not merely the apostles or "professional staff" who were doing the work of church planting. The people of God were all preaching the good news of the gospel everywhere they went. And the result: they were turning the world upside down.

Look at the progressive witness in Acts and apply this pattern to your church. Jesus had given the Great Commission to the apostles concerning world redemption, but it is obvious by what happened next that the entire church in Jerusalem was involved. Jesus said, "You will receive power when the Holy Spirit has come upon you, and you will be My witnesses in Jerusalem, in all Judea and Samaria, and to the ends of the earth" (Acts 1:8).

When the Holy Spirit came upon them, He came upon all believers who were present. "When the day of Pentecost had arrived, they were all together in one place. . . . Then they were all filled with the

Holy Spirit" (Acts 2:1, 4). By the time Acts 4 arrives, the believers numbered five thousand men plus their families. Then comes a powerful verse, "When they had prayed, the place where they were assembled was shaken, and they were all filled with the Holy Spirit and began to speak God's message with boldness" (Acts 4:31). What a tremendous moment as the church was set on fire to fulfill its purpose, sharing the gospel with a lost world. As persecution arose under Saul of Tarsus, the Scripture tells us that on the day Stephen was put to death, "severe persecution broke out against the church in Jerusalem, and all except the apostles were scattered throughout the land of Judea and Samaria. . . . So those who were scattered went on their way proclaiming the message of good news" (Acts 8:1, 4).

The ability of Christ to do His work effectively is
directly related to the health and unity of the body.

As the dynamic power of the Holy Spirit came upon all the believers, they became a channel through which God would bless all people. As long as we maintain that purpose and are engaged in communicating the gospel, the power of God will flow through us with consistency. We are to be conduits or channels, not reservoirs or holding tanks of God's blessings. Our lives become dull and empty if we simply receive the Word of God through preaching and teaching and have no outlet to apply the truth we have learned. The Holy Spirit's power is given to believers to enable them to do the work of the Lord and be a witness to the world around us.

Just as Jesus had commanded them to be on mission, the testimony continues in Acts 9:31, "So the church throughout all Judea, Galilee, and Samaria had peace, being built up and walking in the fear of the Lord and in the encouragement of the Holy Spirit, and it increased in numbers." All of a sudden the church began to spread from Jerusalem and multiplied itself in the surrounding regions. These churches, however, were not started by the apostles, but by the people on mission. This explosive witness by the people began to reach all over the known world. It is recorded in Acts 11:19 that "those who had been scattered as a result of the persecution that started because of Stephen made their way as far as Phoenicia, Cyprus, and Antioch, speaking the message."

When we study the way in which the early church functioned, a pattern becomes clear that can give instruction to us in our churches. The result is that God extends His kingdom and His glory in the world through His people in the churches. The leaders, especially the early apostles, did several things that are important to recognize:

1. They gathered the people together into a visible congregation.
2. They taught the people to practice everything Christ had commanded.
3. They released the people to the Holy Spirit, who equipped them and sent them out into the world.
4. They encouraged the people as they went.
5. They prayed for the people to have boldness.
6. They recognized the people as having been faithful.

More and more churches are following this pattern today. While seminary-trained missionaries are greatly increasing in number, there is also an explosion of mission volunteers. People from all walks of life are going into their neighborhoods and around the world sharing the gospel of Jesus Christ. Laymen and women, youth, and even children are being sent out by the Holy Spirit. Builders, teachers, doctors, nurses, engineers, and many other professionals are giving their time, talents, and resources to further the gospel in the most creative ways. Everywhere I go I talk with people who are sensing some call of God to go—just as Jesus commanded.

And this is not by any means limited to the Western world. Unprecedented numbers of mission volunteers are going from the other countries of the world, often accepting some of the most difficult and dangerous areas to serve. Many are being imprisoned and even put to death. In China, there is a surge of love for the world, and

Chinese Christians are committed to send thousands of missionaries across the world.

What about your church? Could you be described as a people on mission with your Lord, following with great joy the command of your Lord? Does the pattern seen in the Book of Acts challenge you to go and do likewise? The Lord will use those who are trained, but He also delights in using the untrained layperson who is ready to go and share the gospel. In fact, the professional businessperson often has many more opportunities to go into closed countries where traditional missionaries are forbidden to enter.

A Story from Mel

Many stories have been told about how our church in Saskatoon was instrumental in beginning many Bible studies and congregations in towns all around Saskatchewan. I remember Dad and others going out and meeting with people in their homes, telling them about the love of God. As a teenager in those days, I also remember the part our youth group played in reaching out.

We had a Bible study going in a town called Colonsay about thirty-two miles east of Saskatoon. The town was known as the Isle of the Prairies, and indeed, the small band of Christians felt isolated. The Lord quickly pulled together a group of adults who were being led in a Bible study by Len Koster, our minister of mission outreach. But there was also an unusually large number of youth who were interested in the Lord but had nobody to lead them. So our youth group took on the assignment, driving out once a week to lead a Bible study. I remember borrowing Dad's station wagon, piling in five or six of our youth, and heading out onto the highway. I was only sixteen at the

No one should despise your youth: instead, you should be an example to the believers in speech, in conduct, in love, in faith, in purity.

1 TIMOTHY 4:12

time, but we would take turns giving a devotional and reaching out to the teenagers in that community. I look back and think of how moments like that mission opportunity helped shape my life and many others who were challenged to be on mission with God.

Have you even considered that God would send you? Would you immediately go to the Lord and see what His Spirit will say to you and your church? I wonder where He would send you and your church to minister if He knew you were ready to obey? Your family, your Bible study class, your choir, your youth group—all ought to be on mission. I remember being in a meeting when an executive leader of our mission agency said to a large crowd, "God has commanded us to go! To avoid that command, we will have to get His permission to stay home!" In that meeting Marilynn and I released our lives to go, and we are still going today. No Christian is exempt from being on mission with God to touch a world. Being a Christian is not just about going to heaven when we die; it is about denying self, picking up our cross, and following Christ to the ends of the earth.

I want you to hear this clearly. *Recognizing God* is not coming to Him. *Hearing God* in your heart is not answering Him. *Working* for the kingdom of God does not necessarily mean that you are living in the kingdom of God. Let me put it another way. Do you believe there is a God? Do you believe that He sent His Son Jesus to die for you? That God raised Jesus from the dead after three days? That Christ is coming back to take His people home? Great! But Satan believes every one of those statements. What makes you different? You must come to Him, pursue Him, give your life to Him, and grow in your relationship with Him. For God is a person to be loved, not an idea to be accepted. And your love for Him will automatically cause you to be on mission with Him. Have you moved beyond accepting Christ as God's Son to making Him Lord of your life and following Him to do the Father's will?

The Church's Reason for Being

Someone has wisely observed that God had but one Son, and He sent Him to be on mission with Him into our world. Jesus confirmed this in His final great prayer in John 17:18. He stated the Father's purpose in His life: "You sent Me into the world." But then He added our reason for being, "I also have sent them into the world."

During one of His first appearances to His disciples after His Resurrection, He spoke passionately to His followers who were in the room together: "Peace to you! Just as the Father has sent Me, I also send you" (John 20:21). It was on the forefront of Jesus' mind. He came back to His disciples and immediately communicated to them the Father's will for their lives. In the same way that Jesus was sent, now the disciples were sent into the world.

> *"For the Holy Spirit will teach you at that*
> *very hour what must be said."*
>
> LUKE 12:12

Knowing the assignment for the disciples, Jesus said, "Receive the Holy Spirit. If you forgive the sins of any, they are forgiven them; if you retain the sins of any, they are retained" (John 20:22–23). After giving the disciples their marching orders, He then equipped them with the Holy Spirit and gave them their message: repentance of sin and turning to God. In Luke's Gospel, this same reason for being is stated clearly: "Repentance for forgiveness of sins would be proclaimed in His name to all the nations, beginning at Jerusalem. You are witnesses of these things" (Luke 24:47–48).

.The whole reason for being was that they would carry out His mission in the world, just as He commanded. The eternal destiny of a world rested with the church. God's great salvation was now in their hands. But they took courage, because the Holy Spirit was sent to equip them in this great task. What a privilege to be stewards of such an incredible message! This is the message given to the church, that they might go and share it with the world around them. The same Holy Spirit who taught the early churches is the same Spirit God has given to us to guide and direct us to accomplish what God has for us. In whatever situation we find ourselves, the Holy Spirit will be there to help us.

Each church must regularly stand before God and ask Him why He put them together in that place at this time. The danger is that we accept tradition, religious activity, and strong marketing techniques to tell us who we are and why we exist. But if God were to reveal His will for the church, we might find ourselves functioning together differently.

God is a person to be loved, not an idea to be accepted.

When I accepted the call to pastor a church in Canada, all I had to go on was tradition and what I was told in seminary or in other pastors' meetings. I can't tell you how many times I was told what a "pastor ought to do" and how a "church ought to function." We were to be a "five-star church"—that is, to organize the church around the five areas of worship, Sunday school, discipleship, music, and missions organizations. Our church, however, was so small that we did not have enough leaders to run the programs. I soon discovered that the "organization" should never run the church; the Lord guides the church and develops the organizational structure as a means to carry out its reason for being.

As we went to the Lord in worship, we faithfully opened the Scriptures and had wonderful times of prayer as a congregation. We soon realized that our reason for being was turning out differently than what we were told we were supposed to be doing. The work we did in starting churches, campus ministry, and training ministers was directly from God.

It seemed as though everywhere we were turning, God was leading us to do things that were uniquely designed for the assignment He had for us. We were not bound by tradition or what others thought we should be doing; we were committed to following Christ as the Head of our church. We had no experience in what we were doing, and we knew of no other church anywhere that was doing what God had given us to do. Our reason for being was to have a totally surrendered relationship to Jesus Christ, so that the Head of our church could take us on the Father's assignment. We were not called to be a traditional church but rather to let God reveal to us what our reason for being was and obey Him.

I am constantly amazed that churches try to model other churches. We are not called to follow another successful pastor or church; we are called to follow Christ as the Head of *our* church. How foolish it would be to seek direction from anyone else but Christ who is standing in our midst! Don't fit into the mold of others; be true to your purpose as God reveals it to you through His Spirit. Only you can fulfill God's purpose for your life and for your church. It is equally important to realize that only you can thwart the purposes of God for your life and for your church.

Let me illustrate. When God set the Israelites free from bondage in Egypt, what was His plan for them? Where did He plan for them to

---

Now I want you to know, brothers, that our fathers were all under the cloud, all passed through the sea, and all were baptized into Moses in the cloud and in the sea. They all ate the same spiritual food, and all drank the same spiritual drink. For they drank from the spiritual rock that followed them, and that rock was Christ. But God was not pleased with most of them, for they were struck down in the desert. Now these things became examples for us, so that we will not desire evil as they did. . . . Therefore, whoever thinks he stands must be careful not to fall!

1 CORINTHIANS 10:1–6, 12

be? The promised land of Canaan. He desired for them to live in a "land flowing with milk and honey" (Exod. 3:8). But where did most of them end up? They wandered in the wilderness for forty years until an entire generation was dead. This is an amazing turn of events! How is it that God purposed for them to live under His blessings in the promised land, yet most of them never made it? Could the mighty Egyptian army keep them from going to the promised land? No. Could the giants that lived in the land of Canaan stop them from entering? No. Could Satan himself prevent the people of God from following God? Again the answer is a resounding no! If nobody could thwart the plans of God for their lives, what happened? They were rebellious and would not follow God. They chose to follow their own plan and not God's plan.

How foolish it would be to seek direction from anyone else but Christ who is standing in our midst!

Who can keep you from enjoying the plan of God for your life? You! Where are you living? Are you in the center of God's will for you and your church, or are you wandering in the wilderness a long way from where God wants you to be? Understand that His plan for your life is found in His presence. Apart from Him there is no plan! If you are with Him, you are in His plan to touch a world. And as you walk together with Christ as your Lord, He will never lead you astray. He will always lead you to do the will of His Father who is in heaven. As you step forward and walk by faith, He promises never to leave or forsake you.

Many people are like the one who says he wants to swim but refuses to let go of the edge of the pool. He may dangle his foot in the water; he may even splash around for a while. It is fun, but he is quickly bored. He walks away and says, "Swimming is boring, I've got better things to do!" Well, he has never really been swimming. He has never enjoyed playing in the refreshing water on a hot day.

> *Taste and see that the LORD is good;*
> *How blessed is the man who takes refuge in Him!*
>
> PSALM 34:8

I wonder how many Christians have put their little toe in but have never let go of their lives? They have accepted Christ but have gone no further into the Christian life that God has prepared for them. Soon they get bored and lose interest in the things of God. They have never really known what it means to walk with the Lord; they have never really known the exciting adventure of being on mission with Him that touches and transforms the world around us. Go after it! Let go of the past and pursue God with all your heart!

Jesus made an interesting statement in Matthew 7:21–23 that we ought to consider.

> "Not everyone who says to Me, 'Lord, Lord!' will enter the kingdom of heaven, but the one who does the will of My Father in heaven. On that day many will say to Me, 'Lord, Lord, didn't we prophesy in Your name, drive out demons in Your name, and do many miracles in Your name?' Then I will announce to them, 'I never knew you! Depart from Me, you lawbreakers!'"

According to this passage, all that really matters to the Lord is that we do the Father's will. Those who follow Him in doing the purposes of God for their lives will be rewarded with eternal rest. But what is surprising to some is that those who had done many miraculous works "in Jesus' name" would be turned away. How could that be? How could it be that He would turn away those who were doing good things in His name? Simply this: they did not obey Him. They chose the activities that they wanted to do but never listened to what He was asking them to do. And He will always guide us to do the Father's will. His response to them will be, "I never knew you. You may say all you want that you know me, but I am telling you, I never knew you! The works you did, they were according to your plans, not mine. They fulfilled your own desires, not mine. They were according to the pleasure of men, not God."

Let me ask you, does He know you? Has He had any influence upon the decisions of your life? Are you involved in doing the Father's will, or are you setting out to accomplish your goals and dreams? When the Lord calls your name and desires to involve you in the Father's work, are you ready and responsive to His voice? Are you there when He needs you, or are you living your life with a false assurance that you will see Him in heaven some day? Oh that we would understand that God has a purpose for our lives and for our churches! His plans are always best. His plans will have an impact on eternity. We, therefore, ought to be known as a people on mission with their Lord.

> *"Why do you call Me 'Lord, Lord,'" and don't do the things I say?"*
> LUKE 6:46

There is no greater joy than serving the Lord and knowing His pleasure in our lives. There is no better place than to be in a church that is walking in such a relationship with Christ as the Head of its body. God is not willing that any should perish, just as He was not willing that you should perish. Let's be about our reason for being. Let's follow our Lord as He touches our world through His people in the churches.

Study Questions for Reflection and Response

1. How seriously have you taken the lost condition of non-Christians? Of your family? Of people in faraway places?
2. Is your church structured more for *self* or for *others*?
3. Could you say that each person in your church has an understanding of what it means to be on mission with God? Do the seniors? Do

the youth? Do the children? Do the business people? Do the home-makers?

4. Do you sense that the activity of God in your church and in your family has anything to do with your own personal walk with Him?

5. Do you understand your reason for being from God's perspective?

God's Salvation and the Kingdom

What is God's purpose for the church
in the kingdom of God?

Jesus went to Galilee, preaching the good news of God:
"The time is fulfilled, and the kingdom of God has come near.
Repent and believe in the good news!"

MARK 1:14–15

"Therefore, you should pray like this: Our Father in heaven, Your name be honored as holy. Your kingdom come. Your will be done on earth as it is in heaven."

MATTHEW 6:9–10

TEN

The Nature of the Church and Its Relationship to the Kingdom of God

Experiencing God Together in Life

Jesus taught His disciples to pray to their heavenly Father with something significant on their heart: "Your kingdom come. Your will be done on earth as it is in heaven" (Matt. 6:10). Later He assured them that they were to be involved in the fulfillment of that prayer. He said, "And on this rock I will build My church, and the forces of Hades [hell] will not overpower it. I will give you the keys of the kingdom of heaven" (Matt. 16:18–19).

Believers in China believed their Lord when the Communists took over their nation and all missionaries had to leave. From a human perspective the future of Christianity in China looked rather bleak. But circumstances, no matter how grim, cannot thwart the plans of God, and He had plans for Chinese Christians. At the time Communism attempted to crush Christianity in their country, there were probably one million believers. When the country opened up again just a few decades later, the estimates are that there were as many as one hundred million believers. More people are coming to Christ in China every day (around 20,000) than anywhere in the world. Nothing can stop the rule of God in the hearts of His people. God continued to extend the kingdom through "house churches," just as He did in the New Testament when the early Christians were also being persecuted. If God can do it in countries where "churches" are not allowed to meet, what could He do through our churches in countries that are free? How we need to learn about God's plan to extend His kingdom through His churches and to watch Him touch the world through them.

Thy Kingdom Come

The kingdom of God is of primary importance to the Heavenly Father. It was also at the heart of His Son's preaching. Jesus urged people to "seek first the kingdom of God" (Matt. 6:33). Mark 1:14–15 records that Jesus went to Galilee, preaching the good news of God: "The time is fulfilled, and the kingdom of God has come near. Repent and believe in the good news!" When Jesus taught the disciples to pray, the Lord's Prayer started this way: "Our Father in heaven, Your name be honored as holy. Your kingdom come. Your will be done on earth as it is in heaven" (Matt. 6:9–10). It may be interesting to note that Jesus never preached about the church. He preached solely on the kingdom of God and what it was like, as did the apostles after Him. In fact, Jesus mentions the kingdom 112 times, while He mentions the church only three times. The "good news" that Jesus proclaimed was that the kingdom had come with the coming of the King!

That same focus on the kingdom is found in the Book of Acts as the early church began to spread. Jesus instructed the disciples in everything they were to do before He returned to the Father. Listen to what the Scripture says He taught them in the time between the Resurrection and the ascension: "After He had suffered, He also presented Himself alive to them by many convincing proofs, appearing to them during 40 days and speaking about the kingdom of God" (Acts 1:3). The disciples were well versed in the ways of the kingdom. The apostle Paul, probably the greatest church planter in human history, went to Ephesus and preached the same message that Christ had preached in the days of his flesh. Acts 19:8 tells us that "he entered the synagogue and spoke boldly over a period of three months, engaging in discussions and trying to persuade them about the things related to the *kingdom of God.*" To the end of his life, Paul's message remained the same. In the last chapter of Acts, we find Paul under house arrest in Rome. "From dawn to dusk he expounded and witnessed about *the kingdom of God.* He persuaded them concerning Jesus from both the Law of Moses and the Prophets" (Acts 28:23).

We need a fresh understanding of the kingdom's centrality and its powerful influence on our lives and on the churches across the world today. Without such an understanding, we will live our lives outside the purpose of God's great salvation. We will not know where we belong in the scheme of God's strategy to touch a world. Remember, God is not trying to make you or your church successful. He desires that His kingdom come on earth as it is in heaven. Churches are not an end unto themselves; they are to build the kingdom of God. That was the purpose for which Christ established the church.

Let me take a moment to help you understand the nature of the kingdom. First of all, the kingdom is identified with the reign of Christ, who fulfilled the messianic promise of a coming King. The Scripture uses the phrases "kingdom of heaven," "kingdom of God," and "kingdom of Christ," all meaning essentially the same thing. Simply to describe the kingdom in terms of territory or even the subjects under the King does not do it justice. *Kingdom* is king dominion, kingly jurisdiction. The primary idea is kingly authority. Let me give an illustration from the first-century world so you can understand

what a contemporary of Jesus would think when he heard the word
kingdom.

One of the marks of a kingdom was the coinage used in that
region. The king or the ruler of the area had the right to mint coins in
his own name. In fact, when the caesars turned over one after the
other, one of the first things the new caesar did was to remint coinage
with his own image and inscription on it. Wherever the coins were,
that represented the reign of that king. In a sense those coins belonged
to him, and he had the right to ask for them back in taxes, in particular, the Roman poll tax. If you were in the kingdom of Caesar, you
gave back a silver denarius each year; a reminder that you were part
of that kingdom.

In Luke 20:20–26, the religious leaders were trying to trap Jesus by
asking one of the most crucial and emotional questions of the day, "Is
it lawful for us to pay taxes to Caesar or not?" (v. 22). The religious
leaders wanted Jesus to say, "No, good Jews should not pay taxes to
Caesar. We are slaves of no man, for we are the people of God." Most
of the Jews felt this way. But if Jesus answered as they expected, the
Roman guard was right there to take Him away to prison for rebelling
against the Roman Empire. Even if Jesus said they should pay taxes,
He would lose face in the eyes of His Jewish followers, and He would
lose His growing popularity. Either way the religious leaders thought
they were winners.

Jesus, however, turned the tables on them. He responded with a
question, "Show Me a denarius. Whose image and inscription does it
have?" (v. 24). Somebody reached into his money bag and drew out a
coin. They all saw the image of Caesar on it. Jesus then said, "Give
back to Caesar the things that are Caesar's" (v. 25). They lived within
the borders of the Roman Empire, they enjoyed protection from the
enemies, they walked along the roads that Rome had built, they
enjoyed the commerce that came from the safety of the sea, and they
ought to pay taxes back to Rome. After all, the coin has Caesar's
picture on it, so give back to Caesar the things that are his.

But that is not all Jesus said. He said give back "to God the things that are God's" (v. 25). Now the basis of Jesus' argument concerning money was "whose image" was on it. So if a coin bears the image of Caesar, it belongs to him. But that which bears the image of God belongs to God and should be given back to Him. When the Jews heard that, they heard something that we may not immediately grasp. For when they heard the word *image*, their minds raced back to the first chapter of Genesis, which says "God created man in His own *image*, in the *image* of God He created him; male and female He created them" (Gen. 1:27). Jesus was not just teaching that we should pay our taxes to Caesar and our tithe to the temple. The higher teaching of Jesus was that those who bear the image of God belong to Him and ought to give their lives back to Him. The people were amazed at Jesus' words and became silent.

Churches are not an end unto themselves; they are to build the kingdom of God.

The reign and rule of Jesus is wherever His image is found, and those who are born again bear the image of Christ. Paul said in Romans 8:29, "For those He foreknew He also predestined to be conformed to the *image* of His Son, so that He would be the firstborn among many brothers." He also said in Colossians 3:9–10, "You have put off the old man with his practices and have put on the new man, who is being renewed in knowledge according to the *image* of his Creator." Every person who has been born into the family of God and now bears His image and likeness belongs to the kingdom of God. For that is where Christ rules and reigns in their hearts. The kingdom of God, then, is found wherever Christ is reigning.

The words of Jesus in John 18:36 are an important statement concerning the nature of the kingdom: "'My kingdom is not of this world,' said Jesus. 'If My kingdom were of this world, My servants would fight, so that I wouldn't be handed over to the Jews. As it is, My kingdom does not have its origin here.'"

Jesus did not equate this world with His kingdom. The territory of His kingdom is not found in geography but in His spiritual reign that is far beyond mere physical boundaries. Jesus said to Nicodemus, "I assure you: Unless someone is born again, he cannot see the kingdom of God. . . . Whatever is born of the flesh is flesh, and whatever is born of the Spirit is spirit" (John 3:3, 6). To be born into the world is not equivalent to being born into the kingdom. The kingdom is not fleshly but spiritual. It is not determined by land and sea but by the wind of the Spirit. Only those who have been born again are in the kingdom; new birth is the gate that leads into the kingdom.

The apostle Paul said, "He has rescued us from the domain of darkness and transferred us into the kingdom of the Son He loves, in whom we have redemption, the forgiveness of sins" (Col. 1:13–14). In other words, salvation transfers the believer into the kingdom, for those who have not been given salvation in Christ are still living in darkness, outside the kingdom. Two people can stand side by side, one in the kingdom and one outside the kingdom. The kingdom had come with the coming of the King, yet Jesus was standing in front of people who were outside the kingdom. The kingdom was near; they could almost reach out and touch it, but they were not in it! After the Pharisees questioned Jesus about when the kingdom of God was coming, He replied: "The kingdom of God is not coming with something observable; no one will say, 'Look here!' or 'There!' For you see, the kingdom of God is among you" (Luke 17:20–21). The religious leaders were looking for a kingdom on earth, but they could not see the kingdom in their midst.

The message Jesus preached was "Repent, because the kingdom of heaven has come near" (Matt. 4:17). Other translations of this verse say that the kingdom of heaven is "at hand," "is near," or "is upon you." In some new sense, the kingdom of heaven had arrived on earth with the coming of Jesus. The kingdom had always been, for the King had always been. But Jesus made the statement, "If I drive out demons by the Spirit of God, then the kingdom of God has come to you"

(Matt. 12:28). So the kingdom now was present in a way it had not been before His coming.

To further understand the kingdom of God, one must have a thorough understanding of the King. For what made this kingdom different from all the other kingdoms of the world was the nature of the King. Jesus has been given all authority in heaven and on earth. Jesus was born, not only as the Savior, but also as the King. Matthew 2:2 records

> *Now to the King eternal, immortal, invisible, the only God,*
> *be honor and glory forever and ever. Amen.*
>
> 1 TIMOTHY 1:17

that the wise men came from the east asking, "Where is He who has been born King of the Jews?" They had been made aware of the prophecies concerning the coming Messiah who would rule over the kingdom. They knew that Jesus was the fulfillment of those prophecies, and they came to worship Him. Christ, as the Messiah, was the King of kings and Lord of lords. Christ was born King, simply because He was King before He was born. He was called the "Son of David," the "Son of man," and the "Son of God," all of which were names identifying the Messiah. In the Gospels, He was called "King of the Jews" and "King of Israel," indicating that the people had identified Him with the coming kingdom of God. But if His kingship was ever questioned, the vision of John in Revelation 19:16 unveils His position: "And on His robe and on His thigh He has a name written: KING OF KINGS AND LORD OF LORDS."

Jesus never applied to Himself the term *King*. Not only was it politically dangerous while living in the Roman Empire, but also His followers had an incorrect understanding of His kingship. This, however, does not detract from the fact that He is King and that He has a kingdom. He fulfilled all the prophecies of the coming King and was determined to teach the people what the kingdom was all about.

The kingdom will continue its growth until Christ returns at His Second Coming. At that time the King will return to judge once and for all those who refused to follow His rule in their lives, and the number of subjects in the kingdom will be complete. Until Christ returns, the number of true believers will grow as the church proclaims the gospel of the kingdom.

Christ was born King, simply because
He was King before He was born.

The kingdom's development appears to have three distinct stages: the preincarnate period before Christ came to earth; the period between the incarnation and the Second Coming of the Lord; and the period after Christ returns and establishes the kingdom in all its glory. The preexistent Lord came to earth to establish His kingdom and will someday return to bring it to completion.

Role of the Church in the Kingdom

Every generation of Christians must evaluate its role in God's great plan to bring salvation to the world and extend the kingdom of God. That plan is intimately related to the nature of the local church. The contemporary church, although relevant, is not to reflect the secular mind-set or be popular with the culture around us. The nature of the church and of its role in the kingdom of God has not changed since its inception. A proper understanding of the church is vitally important, for it is God's lifeline to a lost and dying world and the extension of His kingdom on earth.

Jesus urged people to "seek first the kingdom of God," not the church. But He also established the church as a divine institution for the proclamation and extension of the kingdom. Churches were created by God as a way to put feet to our calling and provide a means to take the gospel to the world. Churches are a visible demonstration that the kingdom *has* come, and the will of the King is being done on earth as it is in heaven. To emphasize the significance of the church is not to diminish the significance of the kingdom, for in the eternal plan of God, the work of the kingdom is to be accomplished through the churches.

The churches and the kingdom are naturally connected because of their relationship to Christ. For Christ is the King of the kingdom and the Head of the churches. He reigns over the kingdom and leads His people in the churches. The church has become Christ's new body in which He continues to do the work of extending the kingdom as He did while on earth. His message of "repent because the kingdom of heaven has come" is still to be preached through the churches to every generation. Each church, as the body of Christ, is the witness through the ages that He is still alive. It is the King's army sent out to defeat the enemy in the power of the Holy Spirit. Through the churches God eternally planned to make known to the principalities and powers in heavenly places all the manifold wisdom of God (Eph. 3:10). And as the sovereign King over all things, He gives to the church unlimited power in doing His will on earth. For the churches are the working arms of the kingdom, responsible for the practical implementation of the kingdom agenda.

A Story from Mel

I had just arrived in a new city, ready to pastor a small group of people who were trusting God to do a great work. As I sought to understand what God was doing in our city, I ran into many discouraged pastors. I knew that the city had a reputation as a hard place to grow a church. There were few churches and no large churches that were making a recognizable difference. Several people told me why they thought the churches were having such a hard time. They said, "There is a Native American reservation alongside the city that practices a lot of spiritualism in the hills around the area. The presence of evil spirits has made it so difficult for us Christians."

The first thing that crossed my mind was a sense of wonder. Why in the world would a Christian be worried about the teachings of a false religion when they know the one and only true God? I believe in the power of evil spirits, but I had the sense that many Christians did not believe in the power of the Holy Spirit of God. As powerful as the evil one is, how does he compare to the awesome power of God? Look at what happens when a person becomes a Christian, and notice the incredible power given to those who are a part of His church.

> He has rescued us from the domain of darkness and transferred us into the kingdom of the Son He loves, in whom we have redemption, the forgiveness of sins. He is the image of the invisible God, the firstborn over all creation; because by Him everything was created, in heaven and on earth, the visible and the invisible, whether thrones or dominions or rulers or authorities—all things have been created through Him and for Him. He is before all things, and by Him all things hold together. He is also the head of the body, the church (Col. 1:13–18).

We must never cower in fear against the enemy when we serve the King! We cannot be satisfied with serving a God who is smaller than He really is. Each church must boldly go forth in His name, "for in Him the entire fullness of God's nature dwells bodily, and you have been filled by Him, who is the head over every ruler and authority" (Col. 2:9–10).

When Jesus said, "Repent, for the kingdom of heaven is right next to you," what did He mean? What was He talking about? How is it right next to them? The kingdom was right in front of them because He was there. And they were about to see the rule of the King. They saw Him rule over sickness as He healed the lepers. They saw Him rule over nature as He calmed the storms. They saw Him rule over evil spirits as He cast them out of those who were trapped under their control. They saw Him rule over death as He raised the dead to life. They saw Him rule over all things, for there was nothing that the King could not do. When Jesus told them that the kingdom was near, He was indicating that the King had come to invite them to live under His rule.

Jesus made a powerful statement concerning the church and its participation in the kingdom. He said, "I also say to you that you are Peter, and on this rock I will build My church, and the forces of Hades will not overpower it. I will give you the keys of the kingdom of heaven, and whatever you bind on earth will have been bound in heaven, and whatever you loose on earth will have been loosed in heaven" (Matt. 16:18–19). Did you know that the keys of the kingdom of heaven have been given to His churches? It is an affront to a Holy God for Him to have given your church the keys to the kingdom of heaven and you not even know how to use them. Unfortunately, in many churches the keys are hanging on the key rack and are not being used. But when we enter the kingdom, we are participants in His work to extend the kingdom.

The church has become Christ's new body in which He continues to do the work of extending the kingdom.

Jesus then said, "Whatever you bind on earth will have been bound in heaven, and whatever you loose on earth will have been loosed in heaven" (Matt. 16:19). He is talking about the gospel. If we share the good news of the kingdom, He is present to bring the power of the kingdom to bear upon that situation. So if we come to a broken marriage, what do we say? I have confidently shared with many couples, "I understand the many problems you have are tearing you apart, but let me help you understand who is present to help your marriage. The King is here! Let me tell you what He can do that you cannot do without Him. All the resources of God are here to bring you to reconciliation." And I would work with them to bring the power of the kingdom into their lives and into their home.

The world's counseling has no power to bring healing to that which is broken by sin. Only God can do that. Does He know how to help your marriage? He created marriage. Does He know how to help your mind? He created your mind. Does He know how to heal a broken heart? He created your heart. But God is looking for a people and a church who understand that they have been given the keys of the kingdom and who are ready to use them to set people free.

The key to the kingdom is the Word of God being shared by the people of God. "For the word of God is living and effective and sharper than any two-edged sword, penetrating as far as to divide soul, spirit, joints, and marrow; it is a judge of the ideas and thoughts of the heart" (Heb. 4:12). And when God's Word is shared, the Holy Spirit takes that Word and sets people free with its truth. The apostle Paul said, "For to those who are perishing the message of the cross is foolishness, but to us who are being saved it is God's power" (1 Cor. 1:18).

In Matthew 13, Jesus told one of His kingdom parables, the sower and the seed. He said that the Word of God is like a seed. When the seed is put in good soil, it will produce a crop: "some a hundred, some sixty, some thirty times what was sown" (Matt. 13:8). When we plant the truth of God into a person's heart, that one truth can produce much fruit. That Word has its own life, for it will not return void (Isa. 55:11).

What happens when the Word of God is in your hand? A Christian who has been filled with the Holy Spirit now handles the Word of God with understanding, and in that Word is all the power of God to bring to pass what we need in this world. In fact, 2 Corinthians 1:20 says, "For every one of God's promises is 'Yes' in Him." That means that the moment God put you into a relationship with Christ, every promise God has ever given in His Word is now accessible to your life. That is why God gives to the church the keys to the kingdom of heaven. There is not a situation you will ever confront that He has not already made a promise of how He will deal with it redemptively. Christians can bring wholeness to any situation, for they handle the mighty Word of God. "Where sin multiplied, grace multiplied even more, so that, just as sin reigned in death, so also grace will reign through righteousness, resulting in eternal life through Jesus Christ our Lord" (Rom. 5:20–21). That means that God can deal with *any* situation!

So what promise of God will meet the situations you are in? Do you even know the promises of God, in order that you might appropriate them into your life? Do you know the Word of God, in order that you might help others who are in need of God's power to set them free? When Christ gave the church the keys of the kingdom, He made them the channel through which the promises of God would be available to the world. If we share God's Word with others, they will receive the blessings of God. If we do not share God's Word, we lock them out and keep them from knowing and therefore receiving the blessings of God.

How the Kingdom Grows

Jesus did not set out to reform society; He had something much greater in mind. He called men and women to enter His kingdom, not change the kingdoms of the world. For this world is passing away, and the kingdom of God will last forever. So although His presence will inevitably impact society, that was not His priority. His greatest desire is for everyone to enter into the kingdom of God and enjoy everlasting life. As God extends His rule in each generation and to the ends of the earth, it is His ultimate goal that "the kingdom of the world has become the kingdom of our Lord and of His Messiah, and He will reign forever and ever" (Rev. 11:15)!

I listened with wonder and awe as missionaries told what was happening among the Massai peoples in East Africa. For centuries it seemed to be impossible to make any inroads into this large tribal people. Many had tried to no avail. The missionaries turned to God in prayer and enlisted others to pray for this unreached people group with an even greater fervor. They literally prayed what Jesus told them to pray and inserted the Massai people in their prayer: "Father, may Your kingdom come among the Massai people." Soon, an opening came to speak to one of the tribal chieftains. With much prayer the missionaries shared, and the man became a Christian. Immediately he ordered all his people to hear God's good news that was for them too. Soon hundreds were being saved, then thousands, and now tens of thousands. Churches were immediately started, pastors were trained, and the Scriptures were taught. The heart for evangelism and missions gripped their hearts, and they sought to tell the good news to people all over the region. Much later a friend of mine was among them and spoke to a chief who was also their pastor. As my missionary friend tried to talk with them from the Book of Acts and the Great Commission, he challenged them to take the message of God's great salvation to other people also, until the whole world has heard the news. The tall, handsome leader smiled and pointed to the horizon. "Do you see that smoke rising? We have already taken this good news to them. And if you get there, you will see other smoke rising even farther away. We have been there, too. We have made a promise to God that we would take the news of His salvation as far as we see the smoke rising!"

My friend was overwhelmed but not really surprised. As people are saved and churches are established, they will extend God's rule, God's kingdom "as far as the smoke rises!" It is God's eternal plan; His kingdom will be extended and will grow until His rule fills the earth (Ps. 72:19). Surely this is the witness of the early Christians. They believed (Acts 2:40–41), God added to their number (Acts 2:47), the believers went everywhere preaching the Word (Acts 8:4–8), the churches were multiplied (Acts 9:31), and they spread the good news throughout the whole earth (Acts 11:19–21). This is how God's kingdom grows.

It was God's intention to build His church. The church would have the keys to the kingdom of heaven; and everywhere they went to proclaim the gospel, people who heard and believed would enter in and be saved. They would immediately be added by God to His people and gathered together into churches where they lived, and Christ would take that body of believers to extend the kingdom even further through their lives. This was God's plan in the first century, and it is His plan in our generation. But it is vital that every believer understands the kingdom of God and the place of the churches in God's plan.

There is no limit to what God can do through one church if they are willing to follow Christ and fulfill the purposes of God in extending the kingdom. In Matthew 13, Jesus talked about how the kingdom grows. He said that the kingdom of heaven is like yeast. It takes only a little bit of yeast to impact the entire amount of dough. Where does it start? Wherever it is placed. In the same way, what will happen if a church is placed into a community that does not know God? That church, if it is walking with the Lord, will begin to impact the entire community. Its influence will be felt because of the presence of Christ in the midst of that congregation.

Further, Jesus likened the kingdom to a mustard seed. When it was sown into the ground, it was the smallest of all the seeds. But given time, it would become a large tree in which the birds of the sky can nest in its branches (Matt. 13:31–32). As long as the seed has within itself the potential to grow, it will. Your church may be small, but it has all the potential of heaven to grow. For the King of the kingdom is resident and desires to impact the community in power. It may take time, but the steady and faithful service of a kingdom-oriented church will be rewarded with fruit that will last. That is the nature of the kingdom of God.

Could God take your church, like a mustard seed, and use it to bring glory to Him and extend His kingdom? There is not a doubt in my mind that He desires to do that with every church, for that is why He established churches in the first place. He wants to extend His rule into family after family, business after business, community after community, and nation after nation. But He needs a people who will believe Him and follow Him to the ends of the earth.

Confusion between the Church and the Kingdom of God

What is the relationship between the churches and the kingdom? I use *churches* in the plural because I find that many people confuse the church and the kingdom, making it sound like the two are identical. They are not. When you are born again, you are not born into the church; you are born into the kingdom of God. You enter into a relationship with God where He is Lord. And anybody who tells you that you accept Him as Savior and then later surrender to Him as Lord is speaking absolute foolishness. You could not enter into the kingdom of God unless you submitted to His rule. He is Lord by the nature of redemption. Salvation means that you enter a kingdom where there is a King who rules over His subjects.

One of the misunderstandings of the church is that it takes priority over the kingdom. Some people put all their emphasis on making sure we are in the church and give it greater significance than the kingdom. The proper question to ask is not, "Have you accepted Jesus and joined the church?" but, "Have you been born again by the Spirit of God, and what is the evidence that Christ is now Lord of your life?" It does not matter that your name is on a church membership role; it only matters that you have been transformed by the power of God and are living under the rule of Christ. And when that transaction has taken place, there is evidence of new life. Jesus said in Matthew 13:11, "To know the secrets of the kingdom of heaven has been granted to you." For those who are born again are now living *in* the kingdom and have spiritual eyes to see the activity of God, spiritual ears to hear the voice of God, and a new heart that is sensitive to know the will of God.

Now that God rules in the Christian's life, He begins to rule in every part of his or her life. His rule affects the home, the workplace, and every other part of his life. But when we think in terms of salvation and not the kingdom of God, we are disoriented to what God was doing when He chose to save us. For example, is there a difference between having a family that is "saved" and a family that is living under the rule of God? There shouldn't be, but I often hear people say something like this: "My children are not walking with the Lord, but at least they are saved." My mind immediately asks the question, "What is the evidence that they are saved, for salvation does not mean church membership but living under the rule of Christ." We may assume that going forward in a church and being baptized in a church is the essence of salvation, but that has little to do with being born again into the kingdom of God.

Is it important that we know our children are in the kingdom of God, regardless of their church membership? Should we look for the evidence? We cannot take that question lightly, for their eternal destiny is at stake. If we are careless on this one, we cannot recover. We must look to see whether the evidence that someone has entered the kingdom of God is clear in his or her life. How many times have I heard people say, "My children used to be active in the church, but they are not anymore." When I ask, "How long have they been inactive?" They say, "For the last twenty years they haven't had anything to do with the people of God." That would scare me half to death if it were my child! I told every one of our children, "If you ever move away from the Lord, I will be on your doorstep the next day." Because my children have left home does not mean that I have ceased to be their father. I will be their father to the end of my life.

My oldest son told his friends in seminary, "I can always get Dad to come visit me." They asked how he could do it with my busy schedule. He said, "I write Dad a letter and put just a little bit of heresy in it, and before the week is out, he is on my doorstep!" When I heard what my son said, I took it as a compliment. The eternal destiny of my children was important to me, and they knew it.

It is important that we know the difference between the church and the kingdom and understand that entering the kingdom is essential to salvation. As soon as we confuse the two, we are in trouble. But once we have the priority of the kingdom in place, we then must take seriously the role of the churches within the kingdom. For the church is the best place to grow as a Christian and fulfill our role within the kingdom.

The other major confusion of the church and kingdom is a de-emphasis of the local church. I am concerned that many in our day have misunderstood the purpose of the church in the kingdom. Too many people see local churches as merely denominational entities and actually blame the churches for the perceived failures in the kingdom. This is a tragic mistake that has weakened the effectiveness of the local church in carrying out the will of God. Each church is a sovereign creation of God, established for the purposes of bringing His great salvation to the world.

Churches who have linked their lives with a larger denomination are not merely following man-made institutions, which practice man's tradition and create divisions within God's kingdom. Yet this is an increasing perception by some. In fact, denominations in our world are the greatest picture of New Testament Christians, for they practice unity of heart and soul for the purpose of proclaiming the gospel together. They can accomplish more together than they ever could by themselves, and the kingdom of God is extended through them. I believe that a unified denomination with a clear word from God is the most powerful force in the world, but that is exactly why Satan has targeted them and is seeking to divide them.

The many self-appointed groups who choose to remain outside the churches and criticize everything they do are tools that Satan uses. God intended that the edifying be done from *inside* the body, not from the *outside*. Don't listen to those who cause division and strife, casting stones from afar. But invest your lives *in* the churches and seek to build them up into Christlikeness. When people insist on being a member of an "invisible universal church" and refuse to commit to a local church, they are following an unbiblical and harmful philosophy that is destroying the plan of God to extend the kingdom. There was a time when coming to Christ meant joining His body but not anymore. "I don't have to go to church to be a Christian" is a common response among those who prefer to be in the "invisible church" and thereby avoid accountability to the body of Christ. A depreciation of the local church has damaged its effectiveness to hold believers accountable to the Word of God and has left many Christians detached from the people of God. Don't be fooled; God loves each and every church, and He is using them to do His purposes on earth.

Our oneness with all Christians is found in the kingdom of heaven. This unity is real and runs deep, compelling us to walk together with all other believers. But it remains true that God extends the reign of His kingdom through His churches. The churches, therefore, are absolutely essential to the purposes of God. That is the focus of the

New Testament Scriptures, and that is the plan of God to touch the world.

The Power of the Kingdom Is Unleashed through Christ's Churches

A Story from Mel

I have become aware of the power of the kingdom to set people free as I have pastored God's people but never as clearly as the night I had a young lady come to my door just before midnight with a loaded gun in her possession. Her life, as far as she was concerned, was not worth living, and suicide appeared to be the best option. Tragically, she had gone to another Christian's home for help, but all she received was some alcohol to drown her sorrows. Yet, instead of easing her pain, it gave her the artificial courage she needed to take her life and leave behind her husband and five children. As her car passed our home, she thought she would stop and talk to the pastor as a last resort.

My father happened to be leading a revival in our church and was in the living room as I answered the door. The two of us began to minister to her by showing her the promises of God in the Scriptures. She began to argue with us and make excuses, but we kept pressing her to hear what God's Word said concerning her life. I will never forget the moment she not only heard the Word but also accepted it as true. Her body went completely limp as God lifted the burden from her life. We noticed an immediate difference in her life, and it continued in the days that followed. Whereas she had been depressed and deeply troubled, now she was full of joy and at peace. Whereas she had been wearing dark and gloomy clothes, now she came to church in bright and cheerful dresses. But more than anything, the look on her face testified to the power of God to set her free.

As a young pastor at the time, I was struck by the privilege I had to be a part of seeing God do a miracle in her life. I became moved at the thought that God had placed our church as a channel of His mighty power in our community. I thought of the apostle Paul who said, "My speech and my proclamation were not with persuasive words of wisdom, but with a demonstration of the Spirit and power, so that your faith might not be based on men's wisdom but on God's power" (1 Cor. 2:4–5).

God has chosen to transform lives and extend His kingdom through His people. This is true biblically and historically. For example, God placed His hand on John and Charles Wesley, using their lives in a tremendous way to encourage the people of God and extend the kingdom of God. In 1729, during their studies at Oxford, they began The Holy Club. As God began to work in the lives of those who were drawn to the meetings, the power of the Holy Spirit was unleashed upon them. All over England, wherever these men—including George Whitfield—went and preached, multitudes were saved. Thousands of people met the Savior through the lives of these men, who were wholly yielded to God. But even more dramatic, the new-found faith in Christ began to find New Testament expression in the newly formed churches. In the churches every believer was thoroughly discipled, and the impact of these "Methodists" literally changed the face of England. As God's power was unleashed through these churches, child labor laws were established, freeing thousands of children from a form of slavery in the mines. For the first time laws were passed outlawing slavery, and the beginning of a labor movement was established, bringing much-needed rights to the working-class people.

The social change was an expression of the rule of God, the kingdom of God. But nowhere was the unleashing of the power more dramatic than in times of revival and spiritual awakening, which were nearly always accompanied by an explosion of world missions. God's people began to express the heart of God that "the earth will be filled with the knowledge of the glory of the LORD" (Hab. 2:14).

I could use many illustrations to demonstrate the amazing power of the kingdom that is unleashed through His people. But let me turn to the great revivals of 1857–60. As a result of what God accomplished in those days, the Student Volunteer organization began in Australia and New Zealand. J. Edwin Orr states, "The Student Volunteers sought to enlist every Christian in the objective of evangelizing the world. Their watchword was 'the evangelization of the world in this generation.' In their main objective, they were hugely successful, for in half a century, more than 20,000 students reached the foreign mission fields of the church, an astounding and heartening achievement."[1]

If you want to be a part of turning the world upside down, seek first the kingdom of God and understand your role in the purposes of God. This will always lead you to link your life with the people of God, and you will experience God together as you follow Christ the Lord. For Christ will lead you to know and do the will of the Father in the world in which you live. Let me leave you with this powerful passage that demonstrates the incredible power that God desires to unleash into our world through the churches:

> I pray that the eyes of your heart may be enlightened so you may know what is the hope of His calling, what are the glorious riches of His inheritance among the saints, and what is the immeasurable greatness of His power to us who believe, according to the working of His vast strength.
>
> He demonstrated this power in the Messiah by raising Him from the dead and seating Him at His right hand in the heavens— far above every ruler and authority, power and dominion, and every title given, not only in this age but also in the one to come. And "He put everything under His feet" and appointed Him as head over everything *for the church*, which is His body, the fullness of the One who fills all things in every way (Eph. 1:18–23).

Study Questions for Reflection and Response

1. Does the average church member understand what the kingdom of God is?

2. Are you seeking the kingdom of God as your number one priority?

3. Does your church fully expect that God's power will be released through them?

4. Is your church diligently praying for God's mighty power to be demonstrated in their midst?

5. Have you neglected the role of the local church as the primary means of extending the kingdom?

1. J. Edwin Orr, *Campus Aflame*, ed. Richard Owen Roberts (Wheaton, Ill.: International Awakening Press, 1994), 106.

*"Therefore, you should pray like this: Our Father in heaven, Your name be
honored as holy. Your kingdom come. Your will be done
on earth as it is in heaven."*

ELEVEN

Wider Interdependence

Experiencing God Together in Life

The kingdom of God involves all believers. If anyone has a true and saving relationship with Jesus Christ, he or she is in "the family." He is my brother, she is my sister, and God expects me to treat them that way. There is no other option for the person who has been born again into the family of God. We felt the weight of this extended relationship with God's kingdom when the World's Fair came to Vancouver, British Columbia, in 1986. I was the director of missions at that time, giving leadership to the churches in the area.

The first thing God led us to do was establish a comprehensive prayer ministry that bonded all of our work together. God began to work among us in a significant way. As a result, we felt that we must also build meaningful relationships with the four other Baptist groups, which had not worked together for many years. As much as we desired to reach the lost, we had a greater sense of urgency to reach out to our brothers and sisters in the Lord. God enabled us to bring the groups together and gave us the privilege of leading worship services for all Baptist groups on the Expo site. God greatly blessed those times of worship and gave us strengthened relationships with one another.

We also were given many opportunities to share our common faith in the Lord. Through the Pavilion of Promise (the only Christian pavilion at the World's Fair), we had daily opportunities to witness to the throngs of people that came from all over the world. When we compared our statistics with the other believers we were working alongside, together we saw more than twenty thousand professions of faith in six months. We had the privilege of being a part of kingdom work, and God blessed the nations of the world that had come to Vancouver to celebrate the World's Fair. But God also blessed us locally, for we saw three new congregations begin during this time, and we built lasting relationships with other believers. There is no way to know what God will do through your life and your church when you move outside of your particular group and serve alongside other believers to do kingdom work.

> *I, therefore, the prisoner of the Lord, urge you to walk worthy of the calling you have received, with all humility and gentleness, with patience, accepting one another in love, diligently keeping the unity of the Spirit with the peace that binds us.*
>
> EPHESIANS 4:1–3

In the greatest prayer ever recorded, Jesus prayed, "I pray not only for these, but also for those who believe in Me through their message. May they all be one, just as You, Father, are in Me and I am in You. May they also be one in Us, so that the world may believe You sent Me" (John 17:20–21). Jesus was referring to everyone who would believe the gospel, starting from the disciples' testimony all the way down through the ages until He returns again someday. Just as He and the Father are one, so all believers in Christ will be one with one another. There would be a wider interdependence and unity among His people and His churches. Because of their common relationship in the Father and in the Son, they would be forever linked together. They are all kingdom citizens united under one King.

The twelve tribes of Israel all entered a covenant with God; each was different in size, significance, and nature. Yet all were included among the covenant people of God. God expected them to bond together, especially when they stood against common enemies. As Christianity spread, there would be unique and noticeable differences among the believers. Yet they still remained "one body and one Spirit, . . . one hope . . . one Lord, one faith, one baptism, one God and Father of all, who is above all and through all and in all" (Eph. 4:4–6). Each believer is profoundly "connected" with every other believer. Each church, therefore, has the same connectedness with God's people whom He has placed in other churches. Let's look at this *koinonia* relationship in its relationship with other believers within the kingdom of God.

God's Kingdom Includes All Believers

Everyone who is born again by the Holy Spirit enters into the kingdom of God. This makes them a child of God and an heir to the kingdom of God. Because they are children of God, they automatically are my spiritual brothers and sisters, and God expects me to treat them as such. This is by God's design from the beginning of time. His purposes to touch a world include the intentional and meaningful relationships of all His children. We are now serving under the same King—Jesus! Paul made this clear in Galatians 3:26–29. "For you are all sons of God through faith in Christ Jesus. For as many of you as have been baptized into Christ have put on Christ. There is no Jew or Greek, slave or free, male or female; for you are all one in Christ Jesus. And if you are Christ's, then you are Abraham's seed, heirs according to the promise."

One of the greatest blessings God can ever give a person is a genuine and meaningful relationship with other believers. You can go anywhere in the world and be with your spiritual family. In that relationship you will find comfort and security. You will find tremendous joy and exhilaration when you find another believer on the other side of the world. You will find strength and encouragement as you work together. You will accomplish far more in the Lord's work as you work side by side with other believers around the world.

Let me explain what I mean with a simple illustration. War draws neighbors into a common battle. The two world wars compelled many nations to fight side by side for the same cause. The Gulf War drove many armies together as a united front against a common enemy. Although each nation had many capable leaders, one general was in charge to coordinate the efforts. They did not form one massive army; they fought side by side. The kingdom of God is at war with the forces of Satan. Each church is to fight side by side, taking orders from Christ the King who coordinates the combined efforts. Everyone is needed in this eternally significant battle. No church can fight in isolation, for Christ desires a united front within the kingdom. Those who are following Christ as their leader will ultimately link their lives with God's people around the world.

The strength of God's army, however, is found in the strength of the local churches. As the visible body of Christ on earth, it is equipped to fulfill its ministry and mission. Empowered by the Spirit of God, the local church engages in kingdom work. The work will be complete when Christ returns at the great Second Coming to establish the kingdom in its fullness and turn it over to His Father. But until then each church has its role to fulfill in God's plan to touch a world—not in isolation but in a united effort with all other believers around the world.

The potential of each church is enormous, far greater still when they work together. When Christ is present, the fullness of the godhead is available to meet every need the churches encounter. As each church follows Christ, it will take its place among all churches around the world in doing kingdom work. He brings great unity amid diversity when churches understand their role in working together for a common goal. There is no room for competition. There is no room for "civil war." There is a place for everyone in kingdom work. This is the strategy of God to touch a world with the gospel of Jesus Christ.

Why is it then that some churches isolate themselves and do their own thing? If they choose to do their own thing, I guarantee you that they *are* doing their own thing and not the purposes of God. The Christian cannot love God with all his or her heart and not seek to build relationships with others in the family of God. It is spiritually impossible. And when God desires to impact a community, He will always bring His people to work together for the greater cause of extending the kingdom. This does not mean that churches or denominations ought to compromise their convictions; rather they must do their part in kingdom work and pray for the others whom God is using. I have never done anything to go against my convictions, yet God has allowed my life to be involved with every Christian group imaginable. Both at home and around the world, I have found that I have some dear brothers and sisters in the Lord in denominations other than my own. In fact, I am regularly asked to be a part of other groups to encourage them as they fulfill the assignments God has given them. As a result, my life has been greatly enriched, and God's people have been encouraged.

The potential of each church is enormous,
far greater still when they work together.

One of the ways you can assess the quality of your love for other believers is to observe what happens when you see positive or negative situations in other churches. How do you react when you see the church down the street reaching people and growing by leaps and bounds? Do you rejoice that the kingdom is being extended, or do you see them as competition? Does a spirit of jealousy creep into your heart? Let me put it another way: What goes through your heart when you see others who are hurting? Do you feel the pain when you see another church in trouble? Does it bother you to see a church in your area disband? Or do you rejoice over the people who transferred into your church as a result? How you respond to the blessings or the misfortunes of God's people is a direct reflection of your relationship to the God of those people.

A Story from Mel

I remember calling a fellow pastor who lived in a city five hours to the north. I immediately sensed that his heart was troubled. He was known to be one of the most positive and upbeat pastors around but not on this day. As I probed, I discovered that the church had not paid him the previous month, and he was getting hungry. He could not pay all his bills, and he was concerned about his witness to the community. The church was small and obviously struggling, and this young, single pastor was lonely and in great need of encouragement. As I listened to him, my heart broke. I could not just sit there and let him hurt.

I went to our church and shared the need. Just as I thought, they immediately responded by taking a love offering, and they made a commitment to pray for him regularly. We formed an impromptu mission team to go up to encourage him and the church during an upcoming weekend. We sent a group that led in music for the worship service, the preaching, the Sunday school classes, and met with some of the leaders in the church. But our primary desire was to love a brother who was hurting. We sent a follow-up team to the church a month later, just to keep the relationship fresh and do what we could to help another church get on its feet.

I believe our team had a positive impact on that pastor and his church, but I know our people were blessed in the going. The fellowship on the trip up and the new relationships gained in another city were invaluable. This is what loving your brother is all about. This is what kingdom work looks like.

The Uniqueness of the Assignments

When God saw that the churches—His people—were neglecting the poor, the down-and-out, the broken, and the skid-row alcoholics, He raised up a people through whom He could save these who were being overlooked. In 1878, this group of God's people officially called themselves The Salvation Army. Under the direction of William Booth, they were faithful to minister in a difficult "assignment" from God. When nobody else was willing to go and be a "friend of sinners" and reach out to people with great need, this group of God's people took their assignment and wholeheartedly followed the Lord. As a result, God granted salvation to multitudes, restored homes, and affected societies around the world. God has also used this group to quicken the hearts of His churches for the broken people in our communities.

God also stirred in the hearts of His people to meet another need within the kingdom. When "holiness" was neglected in the churches, God once again raised up a people with an "assignment" to bring His people back to a proper understanding of holiness. Coming out of a Methodist background, the Church of the Nazarene was born in 1919 and began to have an effect on all God's people. They were given a unique assignment, and they fulfilled it admirably—bringing holiness back to the forefront in the Christian community.

"For I was hungry and you gave Me something to eat; I was thirsty and you gave Me something to drink; I was a stranger and you took Me in; I was naked and you clothed Me; I was sick and you took care of Me; I was in prison and you visited Me." . . . And the King will answer them, "I assure you: Whatever you did for one of the least of these brothers of Mine, you did for Me."

MATTHEW 25:35–36, 40

God also saw that the churches were losing their heart for world missions. So in 1897, He raised up a people called the Christian and Missionary Alliance, giving them an unquenchable thirst for missions. Under the leadership of A. B. Simpson, a Presbyterian minister from New York City, they immediately carried out their assignment from

God to take the gospel to the entire world. Thousands responded to God's call to the mission fields of the world and continue their assignment to this day. As they began to fulfill their assignment, God, once again, quickened the heart of His people to evangelize the world. I am bold enough to say that these children of God, with their unique assignment, have played a large role in sparking what we are seeing today across the Christian community—the largest force of mission volunteers in all of Christian history.

> *As the One who called you is holy, you also are to be holy in all your conduct; for it is written, "Be holy, because I am holy."*
> 1 PETER 1:15–16

As God raises up His people, granting unique assignments to each, He is not creating disunity, but diversity. That strategy has always been characteristic of God's activity. Whereas some believe that denominations are man-made or even a work of the devil, I see it differently. The rise of denominations is not a divisive and fracturing influence among God's people. Rather, I sense the eternal purposes of God unfolding in diversity, which has been the mark of God throughout the Bible and Christian history. More is being done to reach out into our diverse cultures than ever before. God, in His great wisdom, has "specialized" forces that are penetrating our world and finding ways to reach people that seem unreachable. We ought to be careful not to criticize or work against what other believers are doing, for we may be going against the purposes of God.

> *"You will be My witnesses in Jerusalem, in all Judea and Samaria, and to the ends of the earth."*
> ACTS 1:8

John said to Him, "Teacher, we saw someone driving out demons in
Your name, and we tried to stop him because he wasn't following us."
"Don't stop him," said Jesus, "because there is no one who will perform
a miracle in My name who can soon afterward speak evil of Me. For
whoever is not against us is for us. And whoever gives you a cup of water
to drink because of My name, since you belong to the Messiah—I
assure you: He will never lose his reward."

MARK 9:38–41

I have seen new leaders, however, arise who "did not know the
LORD, nor yet the work which He had done for Israel" (Judg. 2:10).
They can promote a negative interpretation on the activity of God,
attributing it all to either the sinful work of men or the activity of
Satan. As a result they criticize and cast judgments over groups that
are working together on a common goal. Watch out for those who
always seem to create divisions and separate the people of God. For
God hates "one who spreads strife among brothers" (Prov. 6:19).

When we consider the work of various denominations, we must be
careful not to attribute to Satan what is obviously a timely and purposeful work of God. It would be foolish to call the work of denominations a divisive force in the Christian community. For the purpose
of denominations is not to segregate Christians from one another, but
it is to reach every person within a community. Denominations allow
churches of like mind to work closely together, enabling them to do

To the weak I became weak, in order to win the weak. I have become
all things to all people, so that I may by all means save some. Now I
do all this because of the gospel, that I may become a partner in its
benefits.

1 CORINTHIANS 9:22–23

great work in the kingdom. A Pentecostal church will reach a particular group, while the Baptists will reach another, and the Methodists
will reach still others. One church cannot meet the particular needs of
every person in a given community. Just as there is a variety of different people on earth, there is a variety of churches that can reach every
last one of them. Let's not put down others in the family of God; let's
bless them and encourage them in the assignment God has given them.
We have been far too concerned about people following *us* than about
people following Christ and the assignment that God has given them
to accomplish for the sake of the kingdom.

In our day, can God raise up those who are deeply sensitive to the
Holy Spirit, to quicken all His people to the absolute necessity of the
workings of the Holy Spirit? He can! Can God give an assignment to
another group to raise up an army of men, challenging them to be
spiritual leaders again? He can and He has! Can He establish a people
who champion the cause of unborn children, raising the concern
among all His people? He must! But this is not to give people their
own self-centered "ministry." Instead, they are to be used of God to
quicken the churches to their responsibilities. I believe He is giving
unique assignments to His people in the churches, with the desire to
bring to life *all* the churches and *all* the people of God. Evangelism,
discipleship, family life, prayer, volunteerism, and much more are
unique assignments granted to churches to encourage the entire
family of God to be involved in doing the work of God.

With such diversity, can there still be God-honoring unity?
Absolutely! Some seek out and press for "uniformity." They ask each
group to give up their unique assignment in order to have unity with
others. This would be tragic! Uniformity is not the same thing as unity,
just as diversity is not disunity! Unity comes, as Jesus indicates in John
17, from the same relationship with the Father and the Son. Unity is
of the heart, not in the externals of religion! Make sure that you do
not degrade a brother because he is not doing what you are doing; he
may be called to another assignment that looks different. But be

assured that God is working through him in His plan to touch an entire world.

Creative Cooperation

Cooperation! *Koinonia*! This is basic and foundational in the life of God's people and therefore in the churches and among the churches. In our day one of the most significant examples of cooperation among churches is found in the life of a denomination. Churches, and groups of churches, voluntarily choose to cooperate together to fulfill the commands of Christ. They can do together what they could not do alone. Historically, God's people have seen a common need, which none could adequately meet alone, and they have chosen to cooperate together for its accomplishment. This was not just good strategy, but it was under the direction of the Holy Spirit. As a result, God's people have developed hospitals and health care, education through colleges and universities, training of those called into ministry and missions, missionary efforts to take the gospel to every nation, evangelistic meetings that touch an entire city, and many renewal movements that encourage all churches. God is mandating these to His people in the churches. And, fortunately, they are responding to the Holy Spirit's directives.

I remember how God used my life and our church to be an encouragement to those who worshiped in churches of a different denomination. A Nazarene pastor was going through a brokenness in his church and in his family. I "just so happened" to visit him at his office on a Friday morning. It had been my custom to take most Fridays as a time when I would make my way to pastors in other denominations. The Lord had encouraged me to pray with them and learn of their ministry, in order that I might help carry the load. This particular day, the Nazarene pastor met me at the door of his office and, with eyes red from weeping, fell on my shoulder and cried out, "God has sent you to me!" His ministry was in crisis, and his family was suffering greatly. Because of our time together that morning, I encouraged our deacons to help his deacons and to encourage them. Our sons tried to reach out to his son who was going through a struggle. As a result, a man's ministry was saved, his own son was restored, and fellowship returned to his church. God showed us how to reach beyond our own circle and cooperate with His people in the kingdom.

In the early days that I pastored in Saskatoon, I am convinced that we could not have accomplished all that we saw if God had not brought alongside of us churches that would partner in the work. We had so little to work with, so God brought some of the finest people in the family of God to help us. But that is what happens in kingdom work. We can accomplish much more together than we can ever accomplish by ourselves. Every year we had mission teams coming from various parts of the world to walk with us. In fact, First Baptist Church of Denton, Texas, brought a large group of young adults every year in an ongoing partnership that was a mutual blessing. Since we had many mission churches, we would share the groups that would come, having concerts or outreach Bible clubs in towns and villages all around us. It was a wonderful time to work together in the kingdom. Those who are strong ought to help those who are weak, and when the weaker or smaller churches gain strength, they will in turn be an encouragement to others.

A Story from Mel

I, too, came to know the joy of partnering with others in doing mission work. Our little church had many people come a long distance to encourage us and help us accomplish what God called us to do. Our building was old and run-down; some parts were unusable, for all practical purposes. So we set out to renovate the building, trusting that God would help us as we worked. A group from Knoxville, Tennessee, brought a group of twenty-one people to work on the renovation. We tore down every wall and ceiling in the building, ran all new wiring, pulled up all the flooring, and began rebuilding. Some of the people on the team took their only week of vacation to come and help us. They spent their own money for plane fare and expenses on the trip. And as they were leaving, I can still see a picture in my mind of tears coming down their cheeks as they said, "Thank you for letting us come!" It was overwhelming for our people to see such love.

But the work was not done in the week they were with us. We continued to build, paying for materials as we went along. We got near the end of the restoration and were a little short of money. The structure was pretty well together, but we needed to have insulation put in the attic of two buildings. Some of our Sunday school classes had been meeting outside during the construction, but winter was coming and snow was on its way. We didn't know what to do but to pray and ask God to provide. I remember the Monday morning that my secretary, who was also a Mission Service Corps volunteer from Texas, and I prayed to begin the week. I was feeling especially burdened about getting the building finished and getting the people out of the elements. So we prayed, trusting God to care for us now as He had so many other times. After prayer, my secretary brought the mail. I noticed a letter from a church in Bartlesville, Oklahoma. The pastor simply said, "We felt the Lord leading us to partner with you as you share the gospel in Canada." Enclosed was a check for $5,000, the exact amount we needed to finish the work.

As I read the letter to the church that week during our Wednesday night prayer meeting, I watched a rough old guy in our church begin to weep. He asked, "Why are people so kind when they don't even know us?" The answer is simple. We are all serving the same King, and He chose to bring in reinforcements to help us in the battle. As we prayed to God for help, He heard our cry and encouraged another church to be the channel of His blessing. The church in Bartlesville was obedient to God, and we received the blessing that left a lasting impression on our people. As a result, we began to look for churches we could bless.

In the years that I pastored, our church helped other churches know how to start mission churches, how to begin ethnic or language work, and how to do a variety of ministries. It was a wonderful experience as we walked together as churches to do kingdom work. But the cooperative efforts must reach outside of our existing relationships.

I have already mentioned the World's Fair that came to Vancouver, British Columbia. We knew there would be approximately 24 million visitors to our city of 1.5 million. No one church, or even one group of churches, could make the kind of impact needed at this moment in history. The five Baptist groups in the city had broken relationships going back to the late 1920s. God lay on our hearts to be the catalysts for reconciliation and cooperation during this time of reaching people during the World's Fair.

There are many stories of how God brought down walls and built up a new relationship between those groups. When I left Vancouver to move to Atlanta, the five Baptist groups had a farewell gift for us. Using the five rings in the Olympic symbol, they intertwined the insignia of the five groups. It was presented with the saying, "For the first time in sixty years, there are no barriers between our groups. We are one in Christ, and you have helped us to stand before the Lord together." Creative cooperation is the work of the Holy Spirit and is at the heart of God for His people. Our cooperation became a pattern for other groups, and *koinonia* prevailed in ever-increasing ways across the city and the province.

The apostle Paul did not accept cooperation as an option but as a command to the churches. When the church at Jerusalem went through difficult times, Paul freely wrote to the churches urging them to take up an offering and let him and his companions deliver it to the saints in Jerusalem. This they did! Paul's writing in 2 Corinthians 8:16–9:15 describes his heart that churches cooperate in kingdom work. The cooperation between churches became a source of great joy to the people and brought glory to the Father. The people gave freely and cheerfully to help the other churches in need. This ought to be a model for us today, helping one another in the name of Christ.

God's Kingdom on Earth

The disciples had noticed the huge differences between the prayers of Jesus and their own prayers. The Father was always responsive when Jesus prayed, but there was little response from heaven when they prayed. So one day, as He was praying, the disciples asked Him to teach them to pray like He prayed. I sense the whole universe stood still to hear His answer. What would He tell them? How would He teach others to pray to His Father? His answer, if followed, would change the course of history!

Surprising to some, He taught us to pray with an interdependent spirit. Prayer should begin corporately, "*Our* Father." He reminds us that we are a covenant people with God. We must work together. But even more, we must pray together! At Pentecost, when God did a mighty work, they were together—praying.

Next Jesus said to be concerned about God's name and His reputation among the peoples of the world. Pray: "Father, Your name be honored as holy." That intrinsically meant that His people would live in a way that would bring honor to Him; God would do such an obvious work among His people, the world would marvel at what He had done.

He was praying in a certain place, and when He finished, one of His disciples said to Him, "Lord, teach us to pray."

LUKE 11:1

Once He prayed to their common Father, and once He had asked for God to be honored among all His people, Jesus then prayed that the Father's kingdom "come on earth as it is in heaven" and that His "will be done." As the disciples prayed together and sought to do His will, God would guide them to know how His kingdom—His rule—would come on earth as it is in heaven.

The disciples came to realize that there is no possible way God's kingdom can "come on earth" without radical and thorough interdependence among God's people. Listen to the things that would be written in the New Testament, giving evidence to the convictions of the early apostles:

> Now the one who plants and the one who waters are equal, and each will receive his own reward according to his own labor. For we are God's co-workers. You are God's field, God's building (1 Cor. 3:8–9).
>
> I testify that, on their own, according to their ability and beyond their ability, they begged us insistently for the privilege of sharing in the ministry to the saints, and not just as we had hoped. Instead, they gave themselves especially to the Lord, then to us by God's will (2 Cor. 8:3–5).
>
> Whether I come and see you or am absent, I will hear about you that you are standing firm in one spirit, with one mind, working side by side for the faith of the gospel (Phil. 1:27).
>
> If then there is any encouragement in Christ, if any consolation of love, if any fellowship with the Spirit, if any affection and mercy, fulfill my joy by thinking the same way, having the same love, sharing the same feelings, focusing on one goal (Phil. 2:1–2).
>
> Since I heard about your faith in the Lord Jesus and your love for all the saints, I never stop giving thanks for you (Eph. 1:15).

My wife and I have traveled to more than eighty countries of the world. We have spoken to and worked with our missionaries and their families. We have driven through many of the densely populated cities of the world and felt overwhelmed by the masses of people. "How can each of these be reached with the gospel?" we cried out in pain. As we shared together, God unfolded the hundreds, if not thousands, of ways He is touching them—not through just one group but through all of His people. He is touching them through missionaries and nationals alike, through personal witnessing and radio, through Bible correspondence courses and the *Jesus* film, through moments of crisis like earthquakes and violent storms, to compassion shown in hospitals. The message of the gospel is being spread by means of boat, bicycle, airplane, and Land Rover. His kingdom continues to be extended to the boat people and the high mountain people, to the megacities and the remote villages, to the tribal chiefs and national leaders. I have personally given my study *Experiencing God* to national presidents and recently saw a copy being given to a very powerful president of a radically militant country.

More and more international mission boards and agencies are working together with mutual interdependence to ensure that every unreached people group has an opportunity to hear the gospel and come under the rule of God's kingdom. Many broadcasting groups and thousands of independent radio stations around the world are telling the good news. People are using tape recorders and hand-cranked miniature recorders to tell the message to the illiterate millions of people. Some group of God's people is targeting almost every group in the world today.

Christians in business are telling the good news in a powerful movement among the business community. Some are targeting princes and kings, while others are reaching out to the street beggars of major cities. Publishers are extending their efforts to touch the people of the earth by every possible means at their disposal. Christian musicians are travelling the world to add their voice to the witness. Youth are going as volunteers; retired older adults are living their retirement for the Lord, and families are taking vacation mission trips. God is marshalling His people in a cooperative interdependence that is unprecedented in history.

As God extends the kingdom, many who cannot physically go are doing what they can to help others do their work. Countless prayer warriors are on their knees supporting the progress. God's people are giving financially in order that they may participate in that which has eternal significance. They have realized what is really important in life and what will leave a lasting impact. According to the Scripture, we have one life to live, and people want to make it count. Jesus said,

"What will it benefit a man if he gains the whole world yet loses his life? Or what will a man give in exchange for his life? For the Son of Man is going to come with His angels in the glory of His Father, and then He will reward each according to what he has done" (Matt. 16:26–27). Jesus also said, "Don't collect for yourselves treasures on earth, where moth and rust destroy and where thieves break in and steal. But collect for yourselves treasures in heaven, where neither moth nor rust destroys, and where thieves don't break in and steal. For where your treasure is, there your heart will be also" (Matt. 6:19–21). What a powerful statement: "Where your treasure is, there your heart will be also." God is turning many hearts toward His kingdom, which will last forever.

Revival and Awakening

The history of God's people demonstrates that God extends salvation to all people. There are no movements where God's salvation does not extend beyond one group of people. When God begins to impact the land in a mighty move of His Spirit, many unusual things begin to occur that stretch God's people. He will force them out of their comfort zones. Genuine revival and spiritual awakening impact all of God's people, producing incredible unity among the family of God. They pray together, labor for souls together, worship together, and sing praises to God together for the wonders of His mighty work among them.

The 1960s, however, brought a major cultural shift in the way people think. It had begun earlier in the century, but this period seemed to spread its influence like no other time. This shift unfortunately had a radical effect on the local church with extreme self-centeredness, isolation, and independence. Churches began to pull away and function as independent groups, intentionally isolating themselves from the rest of the Christian community. This led to a despising of what some call "tradition." Nothing was sacred, and *self* was supreme. This has led to an explosion of divorce, homosexual arrogance, abortion, crime, drugs, and political turmoil. The damage done within the churches is almost beyond belief and demonstrates how far some have drifted from God's ideal.

The impact on the church was devastating. No greater harm could come to the church than to lose the sense of interdependence or to devalue our life together. The self-centered spirit has caused an amazing amount of turbulence in family life, in ministry, and in staff relations and has destroyed true fellowship (*koinonia*) within many churches and among churches.

A Story from Mel

In one of the churches I pastored, a youth minister on staff had a heart to cooperate with other churches in the city to reach the teenagers and encourage one another in their work. The youth leaders would get together on a regular basis and pray for one another. They would plan evangelistic activities together. They would meet for "youth worship" together. They loved to be together and sought to reach out and include as many as possible.

Unfortunately, not all groups wanted to participate. When one church was asked to join them in a city-wide youth worship service, they declined. Their response was, "We have Spirit-filled worship at our church." I don't know what that meant, but I assumed that he thought we had "Spirit-emptied" worship or in some way were inferior to them. How sad that they would not join with other Christians and encourage one another. They have missed out on a great blessing, for God is moving among the other churches in a great way.

This self-centered spirit has crossed all denominational lines, and I believe it is the cause of many independent ministries and parachurch groups being formed without being connected to the rest of God's people. In fact, many have been formed because they could not get along with God's people. They wanted to do their own thing and not be held accountable to anybody or any group. They do nothing more than produce an abundance of maverick groups who bring dishonor to God. The result is spiritual anarchy, each group doing what is right in their own eyes and being unconcerned about what is happening to their brothers and sisters in the Lord.

But even more devastating to me is its effect on revival and awakening. The century of 1900–2000 was the only century in a long time that did not experience a national revival and awakening. No amount of national or global failure drew God's people together in revival. Two world wars, global recession, many regional wars, the rise of Communism, and devastating spiritual decline have not shaken us from self-centeredness. The Christian community has not yet been drawn to a sense of spiritual desperation to seek God together. We have not yet sought His intervention in *revival and spiritual awakening* that would touch an entire nation and affect our world.

Revival and spiritual awakening depend emphatically on the interdependence of God's people. Revivals are kingdom experiences and require a wider interdependence among God's people, especially on the level of the local churches. James Stewart in his little book, *Come O Breath*, states that "many people are looking for revival in the wrong place. . . . God's revivals can only take place in the body of Christ . . . in the assemblies of the Lord's people." This is biblically and historically true. Therefore, a believer who is thoroughly taught by the Scripture always prays, "O God, send a revival to your people, the body of Christ!" All the revivals in the Old Testament were in the midst of the gathered people of God. In the New Testament the outpouring of the Holy Spirit at Pentecost was as the believers were gathered together. History continues to bear witness to the fact that revival and times of refreshing come among God's people corporately.

Let me describe the wider interdependence that is present in revival. First, a few people are suddenly saturated with the presence of God. Their hearts are set on fire by God's presence. God immediately moves on a wider circle of believers, usually the church where these belong. The entire church is saturated with God, bringing great conviction of sin, repentance, cleansing, and overwhelming joy into the life of the entire church. Instantly, the presence of God fills the entire community, especially among the people of God in the other churches.

As a result, their lives are deeply affected and gloriously changed. At the same time the community of lost people has an immediate conviction of sin and seeks the Lord for salvation, often crying out in great agony of soul over their sin. None of this is orchestrated by men through advertising, marketing, or organizing. It is simply the presence of God among His people, bringing them to a renewed relationship with Him through Jesus Christ and the work of the Holy Spirit.

Churches spontaneously work earnestly together for the glory of God. Nobody wants to keep it to himself or herself but freely helps anyone or any group that seeks a fresh touch from God. If you want to know if a revival is counterfeit, see if the people try to keep it to themselves or if it spreads through the community to other churches. The word of such a moving of God has the potential to spread across an entire region, a nation, and across the world. The saving, cleansing work of God is so real that church leaders are often given opportunities to respond in national dialogue with the world around them. No segment of God's kingdom remains unaffected. As a result, the interdependence of God's people in extending the kingdom brings much glory to God, and the world sees Him as He really is.

Any local church can be a part of this experience with God. People, however, do not work it up; it is a sovereign work of God in its timing, in its nature, and in its place. God always works through a people who are sensitively responsive to Him. Never does He work through a people who are indifferent, casual, or careless in their relationship with Him. He will not bring His blessings upon a people who quickly come and go from His presence. He desires that we linger before Him, crying out with a keen awareness that we need His presence in our lives. He will often wait to see if His people are serious about their prayer for revival, simply by how they persist in their asking.

What then can a local church do to be a people prepared for their Lord? John the Baptist, who prepared God's people for the coming of the Son of God, preached to God's people:

He went into all the vicinity of the Jordan, preaching a baptism of repentance for the forgiveness of sins, as it is written in the book of the words of the prophet Isaiah: "A voice of one crying out in the wilderness: "Prepare the way for the Lord; make His paths straight! Every valley will be filled, and every mountain and hill will be made low; the crooked will become straight, the rough ways smooth, and everyone will see the salvation of God" (Luke 3:3–6).

Given the deplorable state of the churches spiritually today, what are some cautions and what sincere preparations can be made in any local church?[1] I suggest the following cautions be considered in any size church:

1. We may be living as a church in isolation from other believers. This may be within the church itself or in relations with other churches.

2. Megachurches are especially vulnerable to living within their isolation, being self-reliant in their own eyes.

3. The culture has affected the churches' movement toward self-reliance and toward the world's definition of *success*. This makes their participation in spiritual revival unlikely with God unless they make adjustments to Him.

4. There may be a desire for control that will keep us from realizing our deep interdependence with others that is required by God in times of revival.

5. Revival cannot be "worked up" or deserved because of our activity. Revival is a sovereign work of God in its timing, its place, its manifestation, and in the leaders He chooses.

With those cautions in mind, let me also give some thoughts on how a church can "prepare the way of the Lord" and be positioned for God to use them:

1. Understand that God's name is at stake in our day. He is a jealous God who desires to manifest Himself and His glory among the people. He must be the number one priority.

2. His glory is affected by our lives before a watching world, and He will be at work in His people. Often there are a few people who become grieved over the condition of His people in the world.

3. God still requires that we "deny self, take up our cross, and follow Him." There must be a passion to follow God at all costs.

4. Prayer always precedes and accompanies true revival of God's people.

5. A return to serious worship, rather than happy entertainment, will always prepare for revival.

6. A deliberate involvement with other believers and other churches is a step toward revival.

7. A passionate preaching of God's Word, sharing the great truths of the gospel, is necessary to bring the people of God up to the standards of God.

8. A return to a meaningful encounter with God at the Lord's Supper, or Communion, will be evident in times of revival. The impact of the love of Christ demonstrated on the cross has done more to spark revival than almost any other thing.

A church that will release itself wholly to God will know what it means to be saturated with God and experience revival and awakening. But it is costly. It requires time with God, cleansing by God, and

> *"For whoever wants to save his life will lose it, but whoever loses his life because of Me will find it."*
>
> MATTHEW 16:25

availability to God on His terms. Those who are unwilling to pay the price will not know the power of God and will not experience revival! Revival has often been God's primary means of advancing the kingdom of God on earth. And He has chosen to do it through His people who have gathered together to do His will across the world.

Wider interdependence opens up a world that some have never known. How can you become a part of the larger family of God and enjoy the blessings of such a relationship? You begin to reach out to others. As you give yourself away, you will receive more than you ever imagined. You cannot reach out to others and not have others reach out to you. It is a law of the kingdom. If you truly deny self and seek the good of others, the Lord will always bless you in return far beyond what you have ever known. And because of your obedience to "love your brother," the Lord will touch many through your church.

Study Questions for Reflection and Response

1. Do you personally have close relations with believers outside of your local church?

2. Is your church actively cooperating with other churches in your denomination? Outside of your particular affiliation? Across your city?

3. Are you and your church praying alongside other churches in order that God might bring revival and spiritual awakening?

4. Have you been critical of others who are not like you? Have you hindered the work of others by not praying for them as you ought?

5. Does your church sense its need to be involved with others in order to fulfill its mission to touch the world?

1. Several books can assist a pastor, the staff, and leaders in the church concerning revival. Brian H. Edwards, *Revival! A People Saturated with God* (Darlington, England: Evangelical Press, 1990); Henry T. Blackaby and Claude King, *Fresh Encounter! God's Pattern for Revival and Spiritual Awakening* (Nashville: Broadman & Holman, 1993); James A. Stewart, *Come O Breath!* (Ashville, N.C.: Revival Literature, 1958); Richard O. Roberts, *Revival* (Wheaton, Ill.: Tyndale House, 1986).

Therefore I testify to you this day that I am innocent of everyone's blood, for I did not shrink back from declaring to you the whole plan of God. Be on guard for yourselves and for all the flock, among whom the Holy Spirit has appointed you as overseers, to shepherd the church of God, which He purchased with His own blood. I know that after my departure savage wolves will come in among you, not sparing the flock. And men from among yourselves will rise up with deviant doctrines to lure the disciples into following them. Therefore be on the alert, remembering that night and day for three years I did not stop warning each one of you with tears. And now I commit you to God and to the message of His grace, which is able to build you up and to give you an inheritance among all who are sanctified.

ACTS 20:26–32

TWELVE

The Church: God's Perspective

Experiencing God Together in Life

All Christians are servants. We are servants of Christ and therefore servants of the heavenly Father. Each believer and each church must seek to know what is on the heart of God at all times. We must choose to know God's perspective and work together to accomplish His will for our lives. When we look at the early church in Jerusalem, it is obvious that the Lord had changed their hearts to obey God as He showed them what was on His heart. For they had been a people who

> *For Christ's love compels us, since we have reached this conclusion: if One died for all, then all died. And He died for all so that those who live should no longer live for themselves, but for the One who died for them and was raised.*
>
> 2 CORINTHIANS 5:14–15

were close to the rest of the world, but they soon became a people on mission with God to impact the rest of the world. The early believers released their lives to God, and He used them to turn "the world upside down" (Acts 17:6).

As mentioned in chapter 3, on August 13, 1727, God found another little church that He eventually used to turn the world upside down. On that day He deeply touched a group of Moravian brethren in Hernnhut, Moravia. So profound was the encounter they had during a Communion service (Lord's Supper) that they offered their lives unreservedly to be used by God. The deep love of Christ, demonstrated on the cross, compelled them to give their lives in service to Him. Their response literally shook the world in its impact. They committed themselves to pray twenty-four hours a day, and it lasted continuously for one hundred years. More missionaries went out into the world from this church in those one hundred years than all the combined missionaries of all other groups of that day. Their missionaries were found in almost every corner of the earth. Anywhere you went, it seemed as though a Moravian missionary had already been there. One of their missionaries significantly touched the life of John Wesley, whom God later used to spark probably the greatest nation-changing revival in English history.

That is a taste of what God can do with any church that is released to Him. God can demonstrate His mighty power through each and every church that will let Him. And that is what He wants to do in our churches today. Each church, it seems, has a unique assignment that comes directly from the heart of God. Too often, however, we tell God our limited plans and ask Him to bless them. Oh how we need to come into His presence and ask Him His plans and then adjust our lives so that He can accomplish them through us.

From Genesis to Revelation we have the record of the nature of God, the ways of God, the heart of God, and the eternal purposes of God. His heart is expressed in an infinite number of ways. Any serious Christian or church could not miss His heart. And no serious Christian or church could possibly miss all He has done to accomplish His will, especially through His people. And in our generation we must seek to know how we fit into His plan to touch a world.

We forever need to be reminded that we are God's people. We ought to know what is in the heart and mind of God. We ought to work out our salvation in all its fullness, seeking to accomplish God's purposes for our lives. "For it is God who is working among you both the willing and the working for His good purpose" (Phil. 2:13). "His good purpose" then, is what we strive to know and do.

We already know how God's purposes began; we read about it in the Book of Genesis. He created man according to His own image and likeness. He gave him dominion over the fish of the sea, the birds of the air, the cattle, and every animal that roamed the earth. He created man and woman, telling them to be fruitful and multiply. Finally, after God's creation was complete, the Scriptures say, "God saw all that He had made, and behold, it was very good" (Gen. 1:31).

Although man was made in the image of God for the purpose of fellowship with Him, sin disrupted and destroyed the relationship. Sin always does! But God's love found a way to restore that fellowship through the life, death, resurrection, and ascension of His Son Jesus Christ. The initial fellowship could now be restored. The final fulfillment of God's eternal purpose is unfolded in the Book of Revelation.

Then I saw a new heaven and a new earth, for the first heaven and the first earth had passed away, and the sea existed no longer. I also saw the Holy City, new Jerusalem, coming down out of heaven from God, prepared like a bride adorned for her husband.

Then I heard a loud voice from the throne: Look! God's dwelling is with men, and He will live with them. They will be His people, and God Himself will be with them and be their God. He will wipe away every tear from their eyes. Death will exist no longer; grief, crying, and pain will exist no longer, because the previous things have passed away.
Then the One seated on the throne said, "Look! I am making everything new." He also said, "Write, because these words are faithful and true." And He said to me, "It is done! I am the Alpha and the Omega, the Beginning and the End. I will give to the thirsty from the spring of living water as a gift. The victor will inherit these things, and I will be his God, and he will be My son" (Rev. 21:1–7).

This is God's perspective! This is the big picture as God sees it! But what about in the meantime? Now that we have a glimpse of what is on the heart of God, how then shall we live? Or, as Peter solemnly states, "But the day of the Lord will come like a thief; on that day the heavens will pass away with a loud noise, the elements will burn and be dissolved, and the earth and the works on it will be disclosed. Since all these things are to be destroyed in this way, it is clear what sort of people you should be in holy conduct and godliness as you wait for and earnestly desire the coming of the day of God" (2 Pet. 3:10–12).

We are God's people. We ought to know what is in the heart and mind of God. And we ought to live out to the farthest limits the salvation God has wrought within us as His covenant people, "for it is God who is working among you both the willing and the working for His good purpose" (Phil. 2:13). But some may be asking, "God's ideal: is it realistic?"

God's Ideal: Is It Realistic?

The record is before us. The Scriptures reveal God's ideal plan for His people. Remember, at the beginning of this study, we agreed to have a God-centered approach to the Scriptures. We must keep God's position before us at all times. Is all this realistic from His perspective? As far as He is concerned, the answer is a resounding yes! Let me quote for you, and italicize for emphasis, the Amplified Bible's version of Paul's encouragement to the church in Philippi:

> Therefore, my dear ones, as you have *always obeyed* [my suggestions], so now, not only [with enthusiasm you would show] in my presence but much more because I am absent, work out (cultivate, carry out to the goal, and *fully complete*) your own salvation with reverence and awe and trembling (self-distrust, with serious caution, tenderness of conscience, watchfulness against temptation, timidly shrinking from whatever might offend God and discredit the name of Christ). [*Not in your own strength*] for it is *God Who is all the while effectively at work in you* [energizing and creating in you the power and desire], both to will and to work *for His good pleasure* and satisfaction and delight (Phil. 2:12–13).

This is Paul's letter to a local church. God was at work in the church, enabling them to do His will. God's ideal, from His perspective, is indeed realistic. God again gave this same assurance to the church in Ephesus. "Now to Him who is able to do above and beyond all that we ask or think—according to the power that works in you— to Him be glory in the church and in Christ Jesus to all generations, forever and ever. Amen" (Eph. 3:20–21).

The promises of God to work in every church include our generation. It includes your church, right now, where you are! All of God [Father, Son, and Holy Spirit] is with every church and in every church. He is our life! And all His purposes are therefore realistic and possible and honor Him when implemented in our church. The key is the nature of the relationship! If only our churches could understand that their potential rests solely in their relationship to God through Jesus Christ and in their ability to trust Him completely. Jesus described this vital relationship in John 15, as like a vine and its branches. Here is the Lord's promise for your church: "I am the vine; you are the branches. The one who remains in Me and I in him produces much fruit, because you can do nothing without Me" (John 15:5). Jesus went on to add an assurance to this incredible promise, guaranteeing that God's ideal is realistic. He said, "if you remain in Me and My words remain in you, ask whatever you want and it will be done for you" (John 15:7).

It is God's eternal purpose, God's ideal, that His people "abide in Him." This is true of an individual, and it is true of a church. Any church that chooses to abide, hear, and obey His Word as He guided them would "bear much fruit." If for any reason, they ran into any difficulty in living out God's idea, they only have to ask whatever they desired, and it would be done for them. God's ideal is absolutely realistic, given the presence of God in His people and the promises of God to His people.

Less than Obedient: Will God Bless?

What a crucial question to face. What a necessary question to answer, especially at this time in the study of experiencing God together as His people. Will God bless His people when they are less than obedient? This question can only be answered adequately from God's perspective.

With God, partial obedience is disobedience. And disobedience to God is a grievous sin; sin withholds the blessings of God as He intends to share with His people. Let me illustrate carefully, sensitively, and yet graphically. The picture is found in 1 Samuel 15. Saul had been anointed king over God's people. He had clearly been commanded to "listen to the words of the LORD" (1 Sam. 15:1). The Word of the Lord came clearly to Saul, and he knew exactly what he was to do. So Saul *began* to obey the Lord, but his human reasoning became a fatal substitute for obedience. "Then the word of the LORD came to Samuel, saying, 'I regret that I have made Saul king, for he has turned back from following Me, and has not carried out My commands.' And Samuel was distressed and cried out to the LORD all night" (1 Sam. 15:10–11).

Just like many churches that are confronted by God, Saul then begins to reason away and give excuses for his disobedience. Samuel asked him, "Why then did you not obey the voice of the LORD . . . and did what was evil in the sight of the LORD?" (1 Sam. 15:19). Saul's pathetic response demonstrates that he did not understand his radical accountability before God. He said, "I did obey the voice of the LORD" (1 Sam. 15:20). He then began to explain how the people put pressure on him, convincing him of a better way. So he partially obeyed what God had specifically commanded. From God's perspective partial obedience is disobedience, and the consequences for Saul's disobedience were fatal.

When Saul was finished explaining to God, God then explained to Saul how He looks on disobedience. "Has the LORD as much delight in burnt offerings and sacrifices as in obeying the voice of the LORD? Behold, to obey is better than sacrifice, and to heed than the fat of rams. For rebellion is as the sin of divination [supernatural fortune-telling], and insubordination is as iniquity and idolatry. Because you have rejected the word of the LORD, He has also rejected you from being king" (1 Sam. 15:22–23).

With God, partial obedience is disobedience.

As far as God is concerned, any form of disobedience is serious. When He gives a command to His people, He expects them to carry it out to the letter. When we disobey, He sees our hearts as rebellious and stubborn. He considers it as serious as the sin of witchcraft and idolatry. For when we choose not to follow the Lord, we are giving allegiance to substitutes for Him and His Word. We have allowed our limited human reasoning to take precedence over the expressed Word of God.

Should we in our churches then take it seriously when Jesus commanded us to teach "them to observe everything I have commanded you" (Matt. 28:20)? This means to help God's people keep the commands of God, practice them, and live them out in every area of their lives. A disciple is one who does what his or her Master and Teacher commands. The standard is nothing less than observing "all that Jesus commanded." This is not to say that perfection is our goal but complete obedience. Knowing that God will take us from where we are to where we ought to be, we strive to implement into our lives all that our Lord asks of us. To see what God desires of our lives and then intentionally "lower the bar" and settle for less than what was asked would be disastrous.

Let me give an example. Did not the Lord command us to go and make disciples of all nations? To insist that we have indeed obeyed, then reason away why we have not been a part of world missions, in one way or another, would bring upon us the displeasure of God. That is why the subtitle of this book is *God's Plan to Touch Your World*, not *God's Plan to Touch a Neighborhood*. That is also why the interdependent relationships with other believers are so important. For not every person will pick up and move to a foreign country to share the gospel, but every person can be involved in missions through his or her relationship to the rest of the body. Some will literally go and invest their lives in mission work, but everyone can pray, give financially, send materials, or be involved in short-term mission projects.

Only in obedience will God's name be glorified. And if His name is being profaned by our disobedience, He cannot and will not bless! His name is at stake before a watching world. I have known churches that began well. They walked in a love relationship with God and one another. I am thinking of a specific mission church that started out well, and then sin crept in. Relationships became strained. The pastor, the deacons, and other leaders in the church refused to deal with it. They covered it over, often by increasing their efforts in soul winning and mission projects. In their zeal to do *part* of what Christ commanded, they remained disobedient to a crucial matter on the heart of their Lord.

Let me say it again: partial obedience is disobedience. In the case I mentioned, the blessings of God were withdrawn. Sin continued, and the church began a downward spiral. They would have disbanded had not the church realized their sin, repented, and returned to obedience before God. The blessings of God immediately returned, and the church began to grow. Nothing is more serious than persistent disobedience in the lives of God's people. This is especially true when the church tries to cover it up with partial or selective obedience. God will not bless a church that does not obey Him. Yet to those who fear Him and walk in obedience, there is no way to measure His blessings.

It may be helpful to remember David's words and apply them to each individual and, therefore, the church in which they have aligned their lives. "Who may ascend into the hill of the LORD? And who may stand in His holy place? He who has clean hands and a pure heart, who has not lifted up his soul to falsehood [partial disobedience?], and has not sworn deceitfully. He shall receive a blessing from the LORD and righteousness from the God of his salvation" (Ps. 24:3–5). As we come before the Lord in worship each Sunday, we must find cleansing from sin and present an obedient heart before Him.

Another major failure of the churches today, affecting their relationship with God, is mixing the ways of the world with their obedience to God. God commanded that His people be separated from the world so that they could be exclusively His. When the people of God were set free from Egyptian captivity and were about to enter the promised land, He warned them not to mix the culture of those in the land with the commandments He had given them. They were to be

Then watch yourself, lest you forget the LORD who brought you from the land of Egypt, out of the house of slavery. You shall fear only the LORD your God; and you shall worship Him and swear by His name. You shall not follow other gods, any of the gods of the peoples who surround you, for the LORD your God in the midst of you is a jealous God; otherwise the anger of the LORD your God will be kindled against you, and He will wipe you off the face of the earth.

DEUTERONOMY 6:12–15

different; they were to be a people belonging to God. They were to be distinctly different from the people around them, so that the world might see the difference God makes among His people.

The New Testament is equally strong at this point. The difference between the ways of God and the ways of the world are as different as light and darkness. It is impossible for a holy people to act like the sinful world. Unfortunately, there is incredible compromise with the

---

Do you not know that friendship with the world is hostility toward God? So whoever wants to be the world's friend becomes God's enemy. Or do you think it's without reason the scripture says that the Spirit He has caused to live in us yearns jealously?

JAMES 4:4B–5 (SEE ALSO 1 JOHN 2:15–17)

---

commands of God in many churches today. Some will leave the impression that it is legitimate to use the ways of the world, for the ends justifies the use of any means. In other words, use any means as long as a soul is saved. But God's goals are not ours. He is interested in revealing Himself and His ways by *how* He does something. God desires to "strongly support those whose heart is completely His" (2 Chron. 16:9). Our world does not need to see good people doing good things for their God. The world needs to see God doing what only He can do through His people. Is the world encountering God in the *way* we serve Him? Or do we use the ways of the world and conceal Him before the world?

Jesus cried out to the Father in His high priestly prayer, just before He went to the cross: "Sanctify them by the truth; Your word is truth." Then He added a significant fact: "Just as You sent Me into the world, I also have sent them into the world" (John 17:17–18). The Father revealed Himself completely through His Son. His Son did not compromise. God worked exclusively through His Son. This is what God desires to do through His Son's new body, the church. He must be given the exclusive right to reveal Himself through each church, your church. Don't mix the ways of the world with the ways of God.

Jesus added one more significant factor in this matter when He prayed, "I sanctify Myself for them, so they also may be sanctified by the truth" (John 17:19). Oh that we would see more and more churches concerned with revealing God fully by their uncompromising obedience to the truth. Only then will God reveal Himself to them. May you be the example that draws many other churches to be set apart for God.

Returning to God's Ideal

At this point your hearts may be beating faster after God. The desire to return to this relationship with God may have arisen in your heart. You look at your church and see its potential from God's perspective, and you long to be a part of such an experience—not just for your own survival but for God's glory and for God's name. But you are looking at one another and asking, "But how do we return to God's ideal?" From God's perspective His ideal is realistic. You now sense it is the only way to please Him and the only way to honor Him. But how do we return to God's ideal?

> *Now without faith it is impossible to please God.*
> HEBREWS 11:6

The constant heart cry of God to His people is, "Return to me and live" (see Ezek. 18:30–32). This was what God said to the church at Ephesus in Revelation 2:5, "Remember then how far you have fallen; repent, and do the works you did at first. Otherwise, I will come to you and remove your lampstand from its place—unless you repent."

When God calls His people to repent, He desires for us to turn around and return to our first love relationship with Him. He did not

leave the relationship; we did! When you look carefully at Revelation
2–3, God calls for four of the seven churches to repent and return. The
cry of God sounds throughout the Bible. You must hear the Scripture
at this point to understand how much God desires for His people to
return to Him:

> Remember these things, O Jacob, and Israel, for you are My
> servant; I have formed you, you are My servant, O Israel, you will
> not be forgotten by Me. I have wiped out your transgressions like
> a thick cloud and your sins like a heavy mist. *Return to Me,* for
> I have redeemed you (Isa. 44:21–22).
>
> Therefore, thus says the LORD, "If you *return,* then I will
> restore you" (Jer. 15:19a).
>
> I will give them a heart to know Me, for I am the LORD; and
> they will be My people, and I will be their God, for they will
> *return to Me* with their whole heart (Jer. 24:7).
>
> Come, let us *return to the LORD.* For He has torn us, but He
> will heal us; He has wounded us, but He will bandage us
> (Hos. 6:1).
>
> "Yet even now," declares the LORD, *"return to Me* with all
> your heart, and with fasting, weeping, and mourning; and rend
> your heart and not your garments." Now *return* to the LORD your
> God, for He is gracious and compassionate, slow to anger,
> abounding in lovingkindness, and relenting of evil (Joel 2:12–13).
>
> "From the days of your fathers you have turned aside from My
> statutes and have not kept them. *Return to Me,* and I will return
> to you," says the LORD of hosts. "But you say, 'How shall we
> return?'" (Mal. 3:7).

I could take you to many more Scriptures just like these we have
read. But I want to stop at this last verse because it ends with an
important question: "How shall we return?" The Ephesian church
was called to return to their first love. They were commended for right
doctrine, zealous works, and their orthodoxy. Yet their church was in
a fatal condition because it lacked the *love* it once knew. They did not

love God as they used to, so their love for one another was flawed. They were practicing "the letter of the law," and it was bringing death. What they lacked was the spirit of the law.

---

*Our world does not need to see good people doing good things
for their God. The world needs to see God doing
what only He can do through His people.*

The different churches mentioned in Revelation, however, had different issues. The church at Ephesus left their first love, so they needed to return to the love relationship. The church at Pergamum had compromised the truth of God. They were called upon to return to the truth. The church at Thyatira was not dealing with sexual immorality in their church, and the church had become sick. They were to return to holiness or face the severe judgment of God upon the entire church, for His name was being profaned. The church at Sardis had a name for being "alive," but from God's perspective they were "dead," and their works were grossly incomplete. They were not living as the body of Christ doing His work, and they needed to return to Him before God moved in and brought judgment. The church at Laodicea was lukewarm; they had become complacent. They said to themselves that they were a rich church and needed nothing from others. From God's perspective they were an utter abomination, and He was about to cast them out of His sight. They were urged to return to God's standards for spiritual wealth and holiness.

He has made us competent to be ministers of a new covenant, not of the letter; but of the Spirit; for the letter kills, but the Spirit produces life.

2 CORINTHIANS 3:6

What strikes me as significant is that the Lord was giving each church, no matter how bad they had become, an opportunity to return. The opportunity would not be forever, but they all had the chance to repent and return to God's ideal. I don't know about you, but that brings me great encouragement! As long as you hear God's call to return, He is there to receive you with open arms. The key is bringing the church together and allowing the Holy Spirit to search

---

"Return to Me, and I will return to you," says the Lord of hosts.

MALACHI 3:7

---

our hearts. Only the Holy Spirit can show us what the Lord sees as He walks through our church. This will happen most often as God's people gather to worship, but true worship must focus on Him and not on self. He must be the center of every life.

I have been in many meetings where God brought cleansing to a church. If I had time, I could tell countless stories of God manifesting His presence in a way that brought the entire church to its knees. Weeping and crying out to God are spontaneous in the presence of a holy God. But when they rise to their feet again, they do it with renewed strength and joy beyond measure. The focus of their lives takes on a new direction. The fruit of their lives from that point forward cannot be measured. For when they returned to God, God returned to them in all His majesty and glory. And now He has a church through which He can touch the world.

In all this there is the Lord standing at the door of each church. He is knocking, but He is on the outside. He is begging for someone to hear Him, open the door, and welcome Him to the spiritual table in the church. It seems that He is looking for one. Could you be that one for your church? Or better yet, could the whole church stand together and seek to live out God's ideal for their church? Out of a renewed relationship comes a fresh love for God that draws people to hear His voice and obey His words. It brings a renewed *koinonia* that changes the dynamics of the entire church family. You will discover that joy returns, love returns, fruitfulness returns, hunger for the Word of God returns, prayer returns with a fresh awareness of the presence of God, and a freedom to be on mission with God returns. To return to God's ideal to an intimate love relationship produces a renewed life in the Spirit.

Maintaining God's Ideal

I had the privilege of watching my son baptize his daughter. Mel has made it a part of every person's baptism for the new believer to give a public testimony. Christa was seven. She was excited about being baptized, so she rehearsed what she had planned to say and had her mother type it out for her to read from the baptistry. After reading her testimony, she said, "I also want to sing a song of how I am going to serve Jesus." And she did! This was a first for me. As this took place during a Sunday morning worship service, I watched the reaction of her church family. All were extremely happy! Some were weeping, and others were rethinking their own relationship with the Lord. The whole church, including the visitors, was deeply touched. They were experiencing God's ideal for a church. And this moment of baptism was one way to maintain it.

Baptism can either become a casual, even dead, religious ritual or a significant time of renewal. It allows the church to rejoice together over one who has responded to Christ as Lord, and it challenges all who are present to review their own walk with Christ. Another significant time in the life of the church is Communion, or the Lord's Supper. We mentioned these ordinances when we considered the new covenant, but we want to emphasize their importance again at this point.

The apostle Paul wrote to the church in Corinth about the Lord's Supper. Look carefully at how he described this moment in the life of believers.

For I received from the Lord what I also passed on to you: on the night when He was betrayed, the Lord Jesus took bread, gave thanks, broke it, and said, "This is My body, which is for you. Do this in remembrance of Me."

In the same way He also took the cup, after supper, and said, "This cup is the new covenant in My blood. Do this, as often as you drink it, in remembrance of Me." For as often as you eat this bread and drink the cup, you proclaim the Lord's death until He comes (1 Cor. 11:23–26).

According to this passage, the Lord's Supper is a significant moment where Jesus commanded the church to be "in remembrance of Me." In remembering Jesus and His death on the cross, the church would have the opportunity to renew their covenant of love with the Lord and would in this way maintain God's ideal as the living body of Christ. Paul warns, however, that those who are careless or casual about the body and blood of their Lord would put the entire church in grave danger. He goes so far as to say that carelessness in this matter would be the cause of some actually dying and others getting sick.

But those who take the Lord's Supper seriously, examining themselves before partaking, have found it to be a great moment of renewal and even revival. It has been a significant instrument in maintaining God's ideal. Because of its significance, the Lord's Supper should not be tacked onto a service, merely to save time. This is a serious affront to God and His Son and will rob the people of a deep and meaningful encounter with their Lord.

Of course, the supreme opportunity to maintain God's ideal is found in the regular times of worship. Worship was designed as an opportunity for God's people to encounter Him. Here they are to stand before God, hear from God, and adjust their lives to Him and His will for their lives. I can truthfully say that as I pastored, more happened to us as we worshiped than at any other time. Carefully planned and led, the people are solemnly and joyfully led into God's presence. With hearts and minds prepared and ready, God encounters His people corporately like at no other time.

The day of Pentecost is a visible example of what happens when people worship. In that encounter they were gathered together with one heart; they experienced the presence of God together; fear came upon every soul; they continued with gladness, and the Lord added to the church daily those who were being saved. Here was God's ideal experienced, enhanced, and maintained in worship.

Worship is not merely for spiritual entertainment or to promote self; it is for God. It is a time to honor God and give Him opportunity to speak to us. Guard times of worship carefully; it is the heart of the church. Do not regularly turn the worship of God's people into an evangelistic service. If you do, God's people will wither and die spiritually. They cannot survive in God's ideal without true worship.

The worship services have many opportunities for God to keep His people practicing His ideal. He speaks through times of prayer, the careful reading of His Word, the music, times of quiet meditation, the faithful exposition of Scripture, and certainly during the invitation to respond at the end of the service. As the pastor guides the people through their encounter with God, He will share what God is doing. He will interpret how the body must respond to what God is doing. He will also teach the people specific truth about God and His ways.

I worked diligently to prepare God's people and myself for each time of worship. We all, therefore, had great expectation when we came into His presence. We knew that the Father, Son, and Holy Spirit were all present and active. Each person was challenged to respond to God as He spoke to his or her heart and brought conviction concerning what was on His heart. As each person had the freedom to respond, the entire body was edified and built up as we experienced God together. For if one member of the body was touched, all of us were touched.

When someone came forward to pray, I encouraged people to come alongside and pray for him or her. Many times someone came under great conviction of sin and responded to God with a heart of repentance. I would often listen to them, pray with them, and then ask them to share with the church so that we could walk with them in a redemptive manner to bring full restoration into their lives. The apostle Paul said that in the body, a redemptive community, when one member hurts, they all hurt (1 Cor. 12:26). Too often, however, the body is never given the opportunity to know when a person is hurting, and therefore cannot respond to bring healing. As a church, we

> *We proclaim Him, warning and teaching everyone with all wisdom, so that we may present everyone mature in Christ. I labor for this, striving with His strength that works powerfully in me.*
>
> Colossians 1:28–29

sought to share with one another and care for one another as God intended for us to do. As a result, the whole body was edified, "growing into a mature man with a stature measured by Christ's fullness" (Eph. 4:13). The invitation time at the end of our services was not only a wonderful time for maintaining God's ideal for the church, but the unbelievers and visitors were often deeply moved of God themselves, desiring to become part of such a fellowship.

Another significant ingredient of maintaining God's ideal is the faithful preaching and teaching of God's Word. This is done during the worship service, but it is also done in many other places as well. It must be done week after week, year after year, if a church is to maintain its spiritual health. It is not pop psychology that God's people need but regular feeding on God's Word. This takes planned, careful exposition of God's Word. To give people the great truths of God's Word will do more to maintain God's ideal for His church than any other single thing.

One more crucial element that must be a part of the church is prayer. If a church wants to maintain God's ideal, it will become a house of prayer. Jesus said that it was God's eternal purpose for His churches to be houses of prayer. But a church must be taught and guided so that prayer is a way of life for every member, every family, and the church body as it meets together. Though every believer has a built-in desire to pray, they must be taught. They are taught pre-eminently by example, but also by practical teaching. The leaders must strive to create an atmosphere of prayer, and the people will follow the leaders whose hearts are truly bent toward prayer.

A Story from Mel

I had a pastor visit me while he was on vacation one summer. He could see in our service that God was mightily at work, and he longed to see the same thing in his congregation. He began to share the trouble he was having and how discouraged he and his wife were becoming. After listening for a while, I asked one question: "Tell me about the prayer in your church." He dropped his head and said, "I tried to have a prayer meeting, but nobody came but my wife and me. So we cancelled that program and don't have it anymore." It wasn't long before I received word that he had resigned as pastor, the church sold their property, and the people disbanded.

My heart broke. Prayer is not a program; it is our life! A church cannot survive without it. If my wife and I were the only ones praying, I would maintain a regular time of prayer and invite others to join us. Prayer is a key factor in maintaining God's ideal for a church. The early church practiced prayer constantly. Jesus prayed as a way of life. No church can maintain God's ideal without genuine and faithful prayer.

One last word about maintaining God's ideal. There is nothing like intentionally being on mission with God to fuel the fire for God. I am not talking about just doing missions, though that is obviously involved. Rather, I refer to creating a heart for God and His desire that none should perish but all should come to repentance (2 Pet. 3:9). His heart is for every nation to hear, for every person to have an opportunity to hear of His great salvation in Christ. A church, with the heart of God, following Christ as the Head, will be on mission with God in their world. The process of going with God will do great things to help any church maintain God's ideal.

When the life of the body is fully functioning, it is a dynamic experience. And as the pastor, I helped the church recognize what God was doing and helped them know how to respond to Him and one another. I sought to keep our eyes on Christ, the Head of the church. Whether through observing the ordinances of baptism and the Lord's Supper, gathering for worship, preaching and teaching, times of prayer, or mission endeavors, the Lord was always before us. He is the great motivator, compelling us by His love.

A Church before a Watching World

It is too easy to become self-centered, caring only for that which we think directly involves our lives. We forget that being a Christian is more than going to church on Sunday and loving the family of God. We not only gather on Sundays; we are also scattered throughout the week in many different places for the world to see. In case you didn't know, the world is watching you. If you claim to be a Christian, you must live in a way that is honoring God throughout the week.

The world watches as you drive to church on Sunday morning. They watch you drive to work Monday through Friday. They observe what you do on Saturdays and see how you live at home with your children. They watch to see if you have people over to your house and if you invite them to your house and to your church. They may see you

---

"You are the light of the world. A city situated on a hill cannot be hidden. No one lights a lamp and puts it under a basket, but rather on a lampstand, and it gives light for all who are in the house. In the same way, let your light shine before men, so that they may see your good works and give glory to your Father in heaven."

MATTHEW 5:14–16

at the service station, grocery store, or shopping in a mall. They may be with you at a school meeting, a sporting event with your children, a community meeting at city hall, or casting your vote at the school gym. Each member of your church is living out his or her life in Christ before a watching world.

I recall a time when we lived in a neighborhood where trouble arose. It was in part racially motivated, and tempers were high. A vigilante group of men, some of whom were carrying guns, had come together and called a neighborhood meeting in a certain house. They were going to discuss how to "get rid of the problem."

At the time our family was on vacation. Some people tracked us down, and I heard on the other end of the phone, "You must come back and attend the meeting. I know if you were here it would make a tremendous difference, and we would avoid a potential tragedy." We did go to the meeting, and I spoke as a Christian. The Lord was gracious to turn things around, and we were able to diffuse the situation. But long before this particular situation arose, we had "let our light shine before men." We had already gained a reputation of integrity. Because of the way God resolved the problem, some of our neighbors were drawn closer to the Lord.

God desires for us to be involved in the lives of our neighbors, for churches to have a positive impact upon the world around them. What does the world see when they look at your church? Your church is the body of Christ, walking in your community. They must see the difference He can make today, just as He made a difference in the world when He came in the flesh.

Jesus let His light shine before men, and they glorified the Father in heaven. Over and over again the Father performed miracles through Jesus' life. Matthew 15:31 records the impact Jesus had on His community: "So the crowd was amazed when they saw those unable to speak talking, the deformed restored, the lame walking, and the blind seeing. And they gave glory to the God of Israel." Luke also describes a similar reaction when Jesus healed the paralytic man in Luke 5:25–26: "Immediately he got up before them, picked up what he had been lying on, and went home glorifying God. Then everyone was astounded, and they were giving glory to God. And they were filled with awe and said, 'We have seen incredible things today!'"

This is what Jesus desires to do through us, through every church. We must live our lives in the midst of a watching world so that they may see Him in us. We cannot hide ourselves behind the walls of our church buildings; we must live out our faith in the real world where people live. When we do, the world will be drawn to Him.

I want to focus for a moment on a powerful passage of Scripture concerning the church before a watching world. Let's look again at Ephesians 3:8–12. Paul was given the privilege of proclaiming to the Gentiles the unfathomable riches of Christ. He was "to shed light for all about the administration of the mystery hidden for ages in God who created all things. This is so that God's multi-faceted wisdom may now be made known through the church to the rulers and authorities in the heavens" (vv. 9–10). Incredible! Every phrase in that passage is packed full of meaning for the church. We are to "shed light" in our communities so that people might see God for the first time. To the natural man, God is a mystery; He is hidden from their eyes because of sin. But His eternal purposes for the church were to show the world the wisdom of God. Let me try to outline the progression in God's plan to touch a world.

1. From eternity God purposes to use the church to reveal His wisdom.

2. All that God purposes was accomplished in Christ Jesus.

3. The church will demonstrate before a watching world the wisdom of God by the difference that Christ makes in their lives.

4. God reveals Himself by working among His people through the Holy Spirit, drawing a world to Himself.

5. God touches a world through the churches and brings glory to Himself.

To the extent that a church reflects the fullness of God in them, the watching world gives glory to God. The more they see of God, the more they will be drawn to Him. Let me illustrate on several levels. A church I was pastoring sought to live out the life of Christ in their lives. As best they knew, they wanted to live their Christian life unashamedly before others. Soon, there were some college students who heard how God was changing lives. Still others, who heard and saw the difference in these students, began to attend meetings as the church gathered together. Over the next few years, many students were saved and began to experience the powerful presence of the Holy Spirit in their midst.

This began to happen also as we obeyed the Lord in taking the gospel to the towns and villages across the province. In each place we encouraged the people to live out their faith before their friends and neighbors. As the communities began to see the Christians living their lives with joy, they began to take notice of the changes in their lives. When the "town drunk" was saved, the people acknowledged that only God could have done such a thing. As a result, people were drawn to God, and a church was born. In fact, when people in neighboring towns heard about what God was doing, they would call and ask if we could come help them as well. Transformed lives make a difference! When people look at your life or your church, do they see the difference God makes?

If you are willing, God will take your church and touch the world. He will invite you to come alongside Him and be a demonstration before the world of what He is like. He is not asking us to work hard and try to evangelize the world; He is asking us to deny self, pick up our cross, and follow Him into the world. Living out our faith as we go, God will touch the world through us. It is amazing the places He will lead your church if you are willing to follow.

This year alone our own church in Jonesboro, Georgia, is ministering to people in Alaska, Utah, Idaho, Wyoming, and New York. They are going to Guadeloupe, Venezuela, Liberia, Romania, and Cambodia. The mission teams include children, youth, young adults, and older adults. They are sending work crews, creative arts teams, and choirs. All is being done before a watching world. In every place there are those who encounter God working through His people. As a result, many are coming to God and finding salvation in Jesus Christ.

God is not asking us to work hard and try to evangelize the world;
He is asking us to deny self, pick up our cross,
and follow Him into the world.

Study Questions for Reflection and Response

1. Does your church have an understanding of God's ideal? Is it concerned about knowing and doing God's will?

2. Do you have an understanding of the nature of the church in the plan of God?

3. Do you believe that God could use your church to fulfill His purposes? Are you praying and working toward that end?

4. How do you believe the watching world sees your church? Are they attracted or turned off by what they see? What adjustments do you need to make?

5. How can you and your church maintain God's ideal, building up the body?

6. Review the Scriptures given and review what God is saying to you and your church. Make a covenant with one another to be a people, a church, on mission with God before a watching world.

7. Talk with your church about what God is doing through you, and let God have all the glory!

"You are from below," He [Jesus] told them, "I am from above.
You are of this world; I am not of this world. . . .
If you continue in My word, you really are My disciples.
You will know the truth, and the truth will set you free."

JOHN 8:23, 31–32

Conclusion

One of the greatest doctrinal needs in our day is a biblical under-standing of the place of the local church in God's great salvation. Cultural pressures have brought this need to the forefront as the world tries to shape the people of God into its mold. But God's ways are not our ways, and they never will be. The church that turns to the world for its methods to reach people instead of turning to God will be com-pletely out of step with Him and His plan to touch the world. But to understand the purpose of our salvation and the place of the church in the kingdom of God will greatly encourage the people of God and is a catalyst for evangelism and world missions.

Great revivals and awakenings have come when God brings His people back to a basic truth that has been neglected, discarded, or even rejected. This seemed to be true during the great Reformation, when the doctrine of "the just shall live by faith" was brought to light. As a result, we have come to understand that salvation is by grace alone, through faith alone. This truth struck Martin Luther, changed his life, and revolutionized the known world of his day. But that is the way God works among His people. Jesus said, "You will know the truth, and the truth will set you free" (John 8:32). When truth is reestablished in the life of God's people, incredible freedom comes to them, and God performs a mighty work through them.

Today, the essential place of the local church in the eternal plan of God has been sadly neglected, if not rejected. Because of this neglect, and even opposition, the work of God to extend His kingdom has been gravely affected. For it is in the local church that He affirms His presence in the midst of His people, who have gathered together to do His will. In the local church the lordship of Christ is supremely expressed as He directs His people as the head of the body. In the local church the Holy Spirit's indwelling and enabling is given for the building up of one another in the body. And as God works in His people, He builds a healthy body through whom He will work to touch the ends of the earth.

The church is supreme among God's purposes for every believer. *There* God's people are to experience a holy fear of God as they encounter Him in the Word. *There* God's people are drawn into a loving relationship with Him and one another as they experience *koinonia*. *There* God's people enter a covenant that produces blessing beyond measure. *There* the call of God is heard and received to reach out and touch a lost world. *There* His people accept the cost to be on mission with their Lord in extending the kingdom of God.

We are convinced that God is reviving His people to live together under Christ as the Head of their churches. We sense that Christ's return is near, the time is short, the hour is urgent, and the spiritual battle is on in our world today. It is therefore imperative that the strategic place of the local church in the eternal purpose of God become a priority among God's people. But that is what God is saying to His people all over the world today. And those who heed the call and return to the essential lordship of Christ in their lives will do more to touch our world than any other factor.

Our prayer for all who read, study, and apply the truth of God's Word concerning the church is that they and the communities in which they live will be blessed. As God begins to reveal His will for your life and for your church, may He also show you how to move toward His purposes and be an encouragement to the rest of God's people. May it be said of our generation that we saw the fulfillment of Jesus' prayer: "Your kingdom come. Your will be done on earth as it is in heaven" (Matt. 6:10).

About the Authors

Henry Blackaby (B.A., M.Div., Th.M., D.D.) has extensive leadership experience. He has been a senior pastor for almost thirty years as well as a director of missions in Vancouver, Canada, and a special consultant to the presidents of the North American Mission Board, International Mission Board, and LifeWay Christian Resources of the Southern Baptist Convention. Henry regularly consults with CEOs concerning leadership issues. Currently Henry resides in Atlanta with his wife Marilynn. He leads Henry Blackaby Ministries, which provides ministries to leaders in Christian as well as secular organizations. Henry travels frequently with national and international speaking engagements and has written books such as *Experiencing God: Knowing and Doing the Will of God, Experiencing God Day-by-Day, The Man God Uses, Created to Be God's Friend, The Ways of God, Spiritual Leadership,* and *On Mission with God.*

Melvin Blackaby (B.A., M.Div., Ph.D.) is the third son of Henry and Marilynn Blackaby. He has served as senior pastor in the United States and Canada and is currently pastor of Bow Valley Baptist Church in Cochrane, Canada, where he lives with his wife Gina and their three children, Christa, Stephen, and Sarah.